Pushed Out of the Closet

Without A Parachute

By Gunther Allen

Pushed Out of the Closet Without A Parachute

Copyright © 2024 Gunther Allen

All Rights Reserved. No part of this publication may be reproduced, distributed, or transmitted in any form or by any means—electronic, mechanical, photocopy, recording, or any other—except for brief quotations of the authors or editor.

Although the authors and editor have made every effort to ensure that the information in this book was correct at press time, the authors and editor do not assume and hereby disclaim any liability to any party for any loss, damage, or disruption caused by errors or omissions, whether such errors or omissions result from negligence, accident, or any other cause.

Table of Contents

Chapter 1: The Night We Met 1
Chapter 2: My Debut 24
Chapter 3: Rusty Pelican 47
Chapter 4: The Kiss 60
Chapter 5: Dean's Oscar Party 76
Chapter 6: Brown Betty 94
Chapter 7: Revelations 113
Chapter 8: Off to Hilo 139
Chapter 9: Big Island Easter 180
Chapter 10: Father's Day 205
Chapter 11: 4th of July, Olympics, & The Ritz 218
Chapter 12: Birthday and New Year 246
Chapter 13: Rock's Last Visit 260
Chapter 14: Losing All Hope 274
Chapter 15: The Memorial 293
Chapter 16: Deception and Betrayal 307
Chapter 17: Without a Parachute 323
Epilogue 354

Chapter 1: The Night We Met

It's intriguing how people often reminisce about the past with the proclamation, "Those were the best years of my life," when the truth remains that our memories are woven with both struggles and moments of happiness, intricately combined. The years between 1981 and 1989 marked a profound turning point in my life. I transitioned from a state of near pennilessness to embarking on a captivating tour across the enchanting landscapes of Australia and New Zealand, where I shared my musical talents and taught aerobics to a widespread audience. This era encompassed co-writing, co-producing, and co-starring in a mesmerizing musical endeavor, all while forging deep and meaningful connections with extraordinary individuals, among them the unforgettable Rock Hudson. These were the pivotal years that not only shaped my life but set the course for my career in the decades to follow.

Yes, you heard it correctly—I formed an unexpected bond with none other than Rock Hudson himself. This connection consequently stands out as one of the most poignant and impactful episodes of that time period, as well as my entire lifetime. However, before delving deeper into this remarkable encounter, it's important to address how my path serendipitously crossed with Rock Hudson, or rather, Roy Sherer, during the final two years of his life.

These were times marked by a swirl of conflicting emotions, combining moments of exhilarating excitement with heart-wrenching

Pushed Out of the Closet Without A Parachute

sorrow. All of this unfolded against the backdrop of the AIDS epidemic, casting a looming shadow that claimed countless lives while the world's leaders hesitated to confront its devastating impact. But let's not stray too far ahead; let's venture back to the beginning and uncover the tale of how fate orchestrated my introduction to the enigmatic and secretive man behind the radiant star, Rock Hudson.

As the 1984 Olympics approached, the indoor Volleyball Competition was scheduled to grace the renowned Long Beach Arena, affectionately known to locals as the Tuna Can, owing to its distinctive shape. Curiously, fate had a brush with art when, in 1992, eco-artist Wyland adorned the arena's exterior with his 33rd masterpiece from the "Whaling Wall" series. Yet, my involvement in this captivating tale centered on a different aspect: preparing the arena's interior in late 1983 for the highly anticipated world event.

Each day, we embarked on the arduous task of painting, working tirelessly to ensure every inch of the inside surface was flawlessly coated. The challenge was heightened by the fact that the arena's circular shape presented a unique obstacle. It was humorous to be instructed to paint a corner in a round building, but such is irony.

We knew that our efforts would contribute to creating a visually stunning arena that would be showcased around the globe during the 1984 Olympic Games. As the world's most skilled volleyball players prepared to compete on that grand stage, we took pride in knowing that our work, in some small way, would help shape people's perceptions of the event.

Pushed Out of the Closet Without A Parachute

One particular day stands out vividly in my memory. I was perched high above the arena floor on a scaffold, tasked with reaching an upper corner that seemed inaccessible to others. The height and reach required for this job were considerable, but having gone through lifeguard training as a young teenager, I had also conquered my fear of heights.

During my lifeguard training, I was pushed to my limits, both physically and mentally. One of the techniques we were taught was climbing up a towering thirty-foot rope ladder and then plunging into a mere five feet of water. Now, I won't lieit was no piece of cake; it felt like I had signed up for some extreme aquatic challenge, yet I was determined to make a splash—quite literally.

As I clumsily ascended that lofty ladder, I imagined the lifeguarding deities looking down on me, taking bets on whether I'd nail the dismount or perform an epic belly flop. The welts on my back were like badges of honor, evidence of my unwavering dedication to perfecting the technique, even if it meant a temporary discomfort of water shooting up in places where it shouldn't.

I persevered, day after day, until my entry into the water was smoother than a swan's glide. But to be honest, I learned a valuable lesson along the way—avoid heavy meals before attempting water acrobatics, especially when salt water is involved. Let's just say, my constitution had some serious complaints about the whole endeavor. Nevertheless, those experiences instilled a sense of fearlessness when it came to heights, which undoubtedly served me well in my lifeguarding career and now while I was climbing a ladder over seventy feet off the ground.

However, they also taught me the wisdom of reserving my high-flying skills for situations where lives hung in the balance—including my own.

As I precariously ascended the ladder to the highest point on the scaffolding, reaching for that elusive upper corner, fate seemed to have a different plan in mind. Suddenly, one side of the ladder's leg decided it was done with its earthly duties and took flight, while the other half had an intense love affair with the ceiling's infamous corner, resulting in a chaotic collision. It was like witnessing a surrealist masterpiece unfolding before my eyes—a true work of abstract art in action. Move over, Jackson Pollock—I had just unleashed my inner Picasso!

In an unexpected burst of artistic genius, a pale of paint transformed into an airborne explosion of colors, cascading down like confetti on New Year's Eve. The floor below became my unwitting canvas, and I, the unwitting artist, left my mark—quite literally. They say every artist must be willing to make a mess before creating a masterpiece, and at that moment, I embraced my newly anointed status as a Picassoesque daredevil.

Despite the danger unfolding around me, my grip on the ladder remained unyielding. Like a gecko on a windowpane, I clung for dear life, willing my hands to sprout suction cups. Move over, Spider-Man—there was a new hero in town armed with a ladder and a bucket of paint. As my heart raced and my adrenaline surged, I couldn't help but wonder if this was my true calling. No, not as a lifeguard or a painter, but as the world's first artistic superhero, equipped with a paintbrush and a can-do attitude.

With my feet back on solid ground, I couldn't help but thank my heroic co-workers profusely for their timely intervention. They were the true saviors of the day, and I owed them more than just a debt of gratitude. Perhaps I could repay them with tickets to the Picasso-inspired fashion show my clothes were unwittingly hosting. My paint-spattered ensemble could be the latest trend, a true avant-garde fashion statement.

As I attempted to regain my composure and locate my heart, which had seemingly taken a detour to my throat during the ladder acrobatics, a mischievous thought crossed my mind. I could only imagine how this daring feat would play out in the retelling the story—my brush with artistic greatness. Tales of my high-flying adventure would become the stuff of workplace legends, an epic saga to be shared around water coolers for generations to come. "Picture this—action heroes, move aside. This lifeguard-cum-Picasso had just claimed the title of 'High-Flying Painter Extraordinaire.'"

With my fifteen minutes of accidental artistic fame behind me, I knew it was time to bid adieu to my illustrious career as an avant-garde painter. As much as I relished the thought of becoming the next art world sensation, my recent gravity-defying performance had made it abundantly clear that the canvas and I were better off in separate realms.

The Avant-guard life was not for the faint of heart—or the drenched in paint. Hazard pay, it seemed, was not part of the artistic package. And while my clothes had made a valiant effort to become a masterpiece, I couldn't help but feel that the art world was just not ready for such an innovative fashion statement. Picasso may have pushed the boundaries of art, but I had pushed the boundaries of practicality and common sense.

And so, I hung up my paintbrush, bidding farewell to the wild world of artistic experimentation. My heart, now safely back in its rightful place, beat with excitement for the next chapter of my life. Who knew what other surprises fate had in store? One thing was certain—my artistic aspirations might have been short-lived, but the memories of that fateful day would forever remain etched in my mind, a testament to the unscripted comedy of life.

Fortuitously, right next to the Long Beach Arena, the construction of the Hyatt Regency Hotel was reaching its final stages. Recognizing an opportunity for a new chapter in my professional life, I decided to trade my paintbrush for a serving tray and apply for a much safer position as a banquet waiter in anticipation of the hotel's grand opening

As I donned my crisp white shirt and polished black shoes, I couldn't help but feel a sense of excitement and anticipation. The art of hospitality was a canvas of its own, and I was determined to leave my mark with the same fearlessness and gusto I had brought to the world of avant-garde painting. And with a sense of humor as my faithful companion, I was ready to embrace whatever masterpiece awaited me next.

While going through training and awaiting the Hyatt Regency Hotel's grand opening, I decided to embrace a plethora of opportunities. During the day, I adorned my apron and catered to the patrons of The Paradise Café, creating delightful experiences with exquisite dishes and warm hospitality. By night, I ventured as the bartender's assistant also known as a barback in the vibrant world of the Silver Fox, a local gay video bar just blocks away. It was there where laughter and good times flowed as freely as the drinks.

Juggling these two jobs brought an array of colorful experiences and a deeper understanding of the human spirit. The elegant conversations over candlelit dinners at The Paradise Café contrasted with the lively camaraderie and dancing at the Silver Fox. Each moment enriched my connection with people and taught me valuable life lessons.

However, the Hyatt Regency beckoned like a siren, promising better pay and more civilized hours—a beacon of hope for this weary traveler. But, as fate would have it, the old adage, "Be careful of what you wish for," was suddenly realized. All of a sudden, the hotel was open for business and we were so busy that I worked from 6 A.M. in the morning until past 1 A.M. the next morning. I was trapped in an endless loop of back-to-back shifts, like a hamster on a caffeine-fueled

Pushed Out of the Closet Without A Parachute

wheel. Days blurred into nights, and the concept of sleep became a distant memory, lost in the cyclonic world of overworked chaos.

Oh, the irony of wanting more and getting it all at once! My newfound fortune was a double-edged sword, slicing through my dreams of rest and relaxation. From the crack of dawn until the stars blinked out, I toiled away, making money but losing my sanity in the process. The Hyatt Regency became my 24/7 playground, and my bike was my trusty steed, carrying me into the abyss of endless shifts.

One night, as I embarked on another escapade to the Hyatt, I could feel the universe's mischievous grin. It whispered secrets of an extended journey, a never-ending quest beyond the confines of regular closing hours. Pedaling into the night, I had no inkling of the epic odyssey awaiting me, a journey that would take me to the very depths of exhaustion—a tale to rival those of ancient heroes.

So, there I was, a modern-day Don Quixote, tilting at the windmills of endless work hours, all while my trusty bicycle carried me into the heart of the bustling Hyatt Regency. The stage was set, the curtain raised, and my fate sealed as I embraced the adventure, one sleepless night at a time.

That night, as I embarked on my second shift of the day, I could feel the exhaustion settling in my bones like matzah ball soup in a bubbling pot. That evening, a Tuesday, there was a dinner event with a speaker at the Grand Hyatt Regency Ballroom. It was late on February 28th, but it wasn't the last day of the month due to it being leap year—oh, the irony! The dinner lasted longer than expected, and

Pushed Out of the Closet Without A Parachute

I hoped to sign out once it was over. To my dismay, I was assigned clean-up duty and had to stay with the crew until the speaker finished and all the tasks were completed.

Ah, the joys of being a banquet waiter, my fellow readers! I couldn't help but kvetch in my mind, longing for a moment to rest my aching feet. But there I was, like a true mensch, tidying up after the grand event, wondering if I'd ever make it back home to my bed. With each table I cleared, I muttered a little prayer, a plea for mercy from the heavens above, and perhaps a miraculous supply of caffeine to keep me going.

We were all exhausted, fatigue clinging to our weary bodies like a persistent shadow. The speaker at the dinner event seemed to have an endless supply of words, creating a hypnotic effect that threatened to lull everyone in the audience into slumber. Our collective yearning for respite grew stronger with each passing moment, as we longed for the weight of the day to finally lift from our tired shoulders

In the depth of this weariness, my co-worker Philip appeared like a savior, extending a much-needed invitation. Knowing of my connection to the Silver Fox, he suggested we seek solace and unwind with a nightcap before the bar closed. Though I was undeniably consumed with exhaustion, Philip's persistence broke through, and against my better judgment, I relented.

His southern twang intrigued me as he said, "Guntha, have you ever experienced the delights of an Alabama Slamma'?"

Pushed Out of the Closet Without A Parachute

I replied, "No, I don't believe I've had the pleasure."

With a playful gleam, he responded, "Well, my dear friend, allow me to introduce you to a heavenly elixir in a glass. You are destined for an unforgettable evening at the Silver Fox!"

Caught in the enchantment of his infectious spirit, I found myself surrendering, exclaiming, "All right, all right, let's finish cleaning up, and then we can go."

Finally, the speaker concluded his monotonous monologue, and the crowd hastily disappeared. Phil and I, in contrast, carried tray after tray of water glasses out of the room. Once the last glass was retrieved, we were allowed to clock out. Energized by a newfound sense of purpose, we managed to complete the task in record time. Now, side by side, Phil and I were ready to embark on our whimsical journey across town, seeking solace and comradeship in the warm embrace of the Silver Fox.

Although I wasn't one to indulge in heavy libations, my time at the Silver Fox often included the ritual of a flaming shot of Blackberry Brandy during the final hour. Occasionally, my fellow co-workers and I would venture out for an early breakfast, or delight in late-night bowling escapades. Yet, on this particular evening, the bar appeared eerily quiet, and our presence was a welcome sight for the few souls gathered there.

The night unfolded as a tranquil yet uneventful weeknight, and Philip and I relished the prospect of a leisurely evening ahead. Ever the intrepid explorer, Philip embarked on a personal odyssey, leaving no corner unturned in that cozy haven. When he returned, his face bore a delightful blend of excitement and agitation, like a child discovering hidden treasures within those familiar walls.

Curiosity piqued, I couldn't help but enquire, "Now, Phil, what has gotten you so riled up?"

With a flicker of excitement in his eyes, Philip replied, his accent betraying his southern roots, "Ya see them two gentlemen sittin' back in the corner over there?"

Peering in their direction, I casually responded, "Why, yes, those two distinguished gentlemen. What about them?"

What followed from Philip's lips left me questioning his sanity, "Well, darlin', that handsome fella sittin' there happens to be none other than Rock Hudson!"

Unable to suppress my laughter, I brushed off his statement with amusement. "Oh, Phil, you've got quite the imagination. You must be overly exhausted from work and just pulling my leg. Rock Hudson hanging out in this little gay establishment? That's a stretch! Here, let's have a quick shot of Blackberry Brandy to take the edge off this evening's mayhem at work."

To my astonishment, Philip agreed with a shot but drew out his response in true full Southern drawl, "OK, but I SW-EEE-AAA-RE it's true! I was his waiter when I worked at Inside Disneyland's VIP Club 33, the Holy Grail of Luxury for Disney Fans. And let me tell ya, Guntha, I was the best man for the job! Hold on tight, 'cause

I'm gonna go say hi and remind him of our meetin'. You better believe it, you're gonna be eatin' crow!"

With a mixture of disbelief and intrigue, I watched as Philip made his way toward the corner where he thought the famed Rock Hudson sat, ready to unveil the truth behind this unexpected encounter.

With skepticism and amusement, I anticipated witnessing Phil's inevitable embarrassment, convinced that he had mistaken the identities of those gentlemen. Engrossed in their conversation, accompanied by boisterous laughter and animated hand gestures that only Phil could pull off, he caught the attention of everyone in the vicinity. Among the voices resonating through the bar, one stood out—a deep, sultry tone unmistakably belonging to Rock Hudson. Could Phil possibly be correct?

Caught in my observation, the handsome, good-looking gentleman noticed my gaze and waved me over to join them. As I approached, my head still shaking in disbelief, Phil introduced me with his usual flair, "Guntha, my dear friend, allow me to present Mr. Rock Hudson and his esteemed companion, Mr. Dean Dittman. These gentlemen came to enjoy JoAnne Worley's performance at the Terrace Theatre here in Long Beach and thought to drop by for a drink afterwards. I've taken the liberty of ordering us a round of Alabama Slammas'. What say you?"

As Phil's arms moved about with the vigor of a flight attendant demonstrating safety procedures before a flight, I stood there, jaw agape, struggling to find my words. Finally, I managed to murmur, "How very delightful to meet you both. I'm Gunther."

Although my mind raced with curiosity, I managed to maintain my composure. I had encountered a few celebrities over the years, but never someone of such immense fame and global recognition. Yet, I wasn't the type to be starstruck or overwhelmed by their presence. As I stood there, engaging in conversation with Rock Hudson and Dean Dittman, one question nagged at the back of my mind: Why would Rock Hudson, a renowned figure, find himself in a gay bar like the Silver Fox?

Whispers of his potential homosexuality had circulated regarding Rock, but similar rumors surrounded other celebrities like Tom Cruise, John Travolta, and Hugh Jackman. In Hollywood, rumors were a currency unto themselves, carefully cultivated to appeal to all sides of the spectrum, if you catch my drift. So, while the thought lingered, I understood the complex dance of public perception and private lives played out in Tinseltown.

As I stood next to Rock Hudson and Dean Dittman, I warmly greeted them and extended a welcome to Long Beach. Curiosity getting the better of me, and I couldn't resist asking, "Have either of you ever been to the Silver Fox before?" Their response was an honest admission that this was their inaugural visit.

Intrigued by their choice, I inquired about the reason for both Rock and Dean attending "Gypsy," a musical comedy featuring JoAnne Worley. Dean explained that JoAnne, who was part of the play's cast, had invited them to watch her performance. Rock, with a smile, chimed in, "So, when JoAnne asked us to come to see her in the production, I couldn't resist. And let me tell you, she was absolutely wonderful."

Seizing the opportunity to share a glimpse of the bar's lively atmosphere, I continued, "Usually, this place is buzzing with excitement, filled with charming guys who gather to enjoy the latest videos. They even have a special night dedicated to the TV show Dynasty, where they screen previous season episodes, and the crowd erupts with laughter, playfully reciting the lines. It's truly a sight to behold, I assure you."

Rock Hudson, with his unmistakable voice, interrupted me, "I have no doubt that everything you've mentioned is true, but sometimes, all it takes is one attractive gentleman to appreciate the surroundings. And if I may say so, you happen to be as cute as they come."

As Rock Hudson complimented me, my cheeks turned as rosy as a ripe strawberry. It's not every day that a famous and attractive actor like him bestows such praise. I found myself at a loss for words, standing there like a bewildered fish out of water. Sensing my hesitation, Rock broke the silence and asked, "Gunther, if I may be so bold, what do you do here in Long Beach?"

Unsure of how much Phil had already shared, I responded, "Phil and I both work at the recently opened Hyatt Regency, just a short distance from where you watched the show tonight at the Terrace

Theatre. Additionally, I'm a recent graduate from the University of California, Long Beach."

Rock's curiosity persisted as he inquired about my major had been. Feeling a bit more at ease now that we had a dialogue going, I replied, "I was a music major with a focus on voice. Equally, a couple of years ago, I co-wrote a musical that I also performed in, all thanks to a grant from the city of Los Angeles."

Rock continued to show genuine interest, prompting me to share more about the musical. I obliged by saying, "Los Angeles was commemorating the end of the baby boomers by closing down several high schools in the Los Angeles School District. One of the pianists who works closely with Frank Pooler, our renowned choral director at Cal State Long Beach, approached me after hearing one of my original songs on guitar. His name is Vincent Jordan, a talented gospel pianist. He asked me to collaborate with him on the musical since he excels at composing music but struggles with lyrics. So, I've become his Bernie Taupin to his Elton John, so to speak. Our rehearsals took place at Excelsior High School.

With a pause to breathe, I continued, "And to top it off, I was one of the lucky ones who toured Australia with the University Choir and our jazz ensemble group, Voce. You might be familiar with the renowned Frank Pooler, our choral director at Cal State Long Beach. He mentored the Carpenters and helped shape their signature style— back when they were music students studying drums and piano respectively. It was Professor Pooler who encouraged them to sing and compose as well."

I continued, "Furthermore, Pooler co-wrote the holiday classic 'Merry Christmas Darling' with Richard Carpenter. Their success story has always been a great inspiration to me. It's incredible how their journey started right here in Long Beach"

Rock Hudson nodded, clearly intrigued by the connection. Encouraged by his interest, I added, "I suppose you could say their legacy lives on through me and Vincent Jordan, in a way. We performed to sold-out audiences," I joked. And continued in all earnest, "Actually, we had a captive audience with all the schools they were closing down, who got to see us perform. I believe three other schools closed, including Excelsior High School, and this was a way for them to bid farewell to an era. It was also a bittersweet tribute to the changes happening in our community. Subsequently, the title of our musical was 'Going Out in Style.'"

Rock smiled, appreciating the significance of the Carpenters' impact and the passion behind our musical endeavor. Suddenly, the atmosphere changed as a mischievous glimmer appeared in his eyes. With a playful grin, he encouraged me, "Why don't you give us a taste of the chorus, Gunther?"

Feeling excited and nervous, I couldn't resist sharing a snippet of our creation. I took a deep breath and launched into the chorus, pouring my heart into the lyrics. "We're goin' out in style, goin' to find out different ways, taking time to look back, on all our cherished days.

Pushed Out of the Closet Without A Parachute

Seasons spinning 'round and 'round, the years keep rollin' by, changes happening all the while, but through it all, we've got a smile, we're going out in style... I jazzed up the finale with a flourish of jazz hands, leaving Rock and Dean chuckling with delight.

As I finished, a wave of excitement washed over me. I realized that I had just serenaded Rock Hudson with a sample of our music. The evening had taken an unexpected turn, and I couldn't help but wonder what other surprises lay in store as I ventured further into music and storytelling.

Rock and Dean applauded me, their genuine appreciation fueling my excitement. It was a spontaneous moment I would have never attempted if the bar was full, but the emptiness of the place, and the lingering effects of the Alabama Slammer, plus the shot of brandy emboldened me to seize the opportunity. Rock, with a devilish twinkle in his eyes, inquired about my solo performances and whether I performed troubadour-style gigs.

Without hesitation, I replied, "Absolutely! I perform at parties, events, and even weddings. I can bring my guitar and create an intimate musical ambiance. If you'd like, I would be honored to come and sing at one of your parties." Rock studied my face, assessing my sincerity, and then surprised me with his response, "You must be clairvoyant... I'm hosting a party this weekend, and I would love you to come and perform. Would you be available?"

I was in a bit of shock trying to wrap my mind around what Rock had just asked me. Not that I couldn't perform, but how could

Pushed Out of the Closet Without A Parachute

he ask me to perform after just hearing me sing the acapella version of the chorus of my musical? But before I overthought everything, I answered, "Absolutely, I'd love to!" Rock quickly replied, "Fantastic, get all the details from Mr. Dittman. I can't wait to see you there. Excuse me for a few minutes, while I see myself to the men's room."

As Rock walked away, my mind still raced with a mix of excitement and disbelief. Was I being asked by Rock Hudson himself to perform at his party? It was a surreal moment, and I eagerly turned to Dean Dittman, who provided me with the specifics. To my surprise, the party would be held at Dean's house in West Hollywood instead of Rock's estate in Coldwater Canyon. I was given detailed directions and instructions: just bring my guitar, a selection of songs, and a warm smile would be enough.

At that moment, I realized that not only had I stumbled upon an incredible encounter with Rock Hudson, but I had also made a connection with Dean Dittman, a charismatic character actor known for his films like Bachelor Party, The Man Who Wasn't There, and Cheers. It was a unique opportunity, with unexpected friendship unfolding before me, and I couldn't help but feel that my life was about to take a thrilling turn into uncharted territory.

Once Rock returned from the restroom, the bartender announced the last call, so we concluded our libations. I realized the dire need for some shut-eye before my early morning shift back at work. Phil, however, was euphoric, floating on cloud nine. While I found myself in deep conversation with Rock, Phil reveled in mirthful banter with Dean, the two of them embodying the essence of colorful characters, both sharing the gift of animated articulation.

After such a fantastic night, we experienced a delightful release of pent-up energy. I however, found myself at the mercy of Phil's benevolence, relying on his graciousness to ferry me back to my trusty bicycle stationed at my workplace. The sun was preparing to paint the sky with its golden hues, heralding the arrival of morning in just a few hours. Undoubtedly, I would soon experience déjà vu as I made my way back to work for my morning shift.

On our journey back to the esteemed Hyatt, Phil, ever the inquisitive soul, commenced an inquisition, demanding intricate details of my discourse with Rock. With each revelation I shared, a crescendo of excitement coursed through Phil's being. "ROCK HUDSON HIMSELF, EXTENDING AN INVITATION FOR YOU TO PERFORM AT HIS SOIREE," he exclaimed, his voice resounding with disbelief, repetition underscoring his astonishment. With unwavering conviction, I reaffirmed my stance, responding, "Yes, and I'm totally freaked out about it."

Phil, an ardent advocate for loyalty, looked at me with passion in his eyes as he delivered a heartfelt reminder not to forsake his friends once I got famous, particularly the one who had introduced me to Rock's orbit. My words, filled with caution and tempered expectations, aimed to quell the flames of Phil's over-excitement. After all, for all we knew, Rock's overture might have been a mere gesture of benevolence, a fleeting spark destined to dissipate into the ether. Even worse, it may have been a joke, and I could arrive with egg on my face. But no matter what the outcome, Phil's faith in me and this extraordinary opportunity encouraged me to embrace the adventure with an open mind and a sense of encouragement.

In response, Phil unleashed a fiery tirade of impassioned pleas, entreating me to embrace a more positive spirit, to believe in the grand destiny unfolding before my eyes. He implored me to absorb the celestial convergence of cosmic forces, wherein this unforeseen moment had been ordained. "Do you not understand, Guntha? This is a divine intervention!" Phil beseeched me, his voice a symphony of Southern conviction. "Refrain from any doubt; you must believe! This Saturday, adorned yourself in your most dazzling outfit, capture the attention of all who lay eyes upon you!"

Phil continued, his animated arms adding even more enthusiasm to his words, "Heads shall turn, and whispers of intrigue shall fill the air, as they wonder, 'Who is this dashin' troubadour, stridin' in with his faithful guitar?' Why, they shall assume you hail from the distant shores of Europe or beyond, bearing the mantle of a renowned maestro, ready to weave an enchantin' spell upon their receptive hearts. And so, it shall be! But, just don't forget where you come from!"

I looked at Phil, my eyes filled with amusement and gratitude. "Don't worry, Phil, I could never forget my friends, especially someone as unforgettable as you," I said with a smile. "I'm excited about this party, and I promise to bring my absolute best and present my 'A game.' Moreover, I shall seize the moment and let fate fulfill its destiny. When the curtains rise on Saturday night, I shall stride into the room, radiating confidence and charisma. I shall be poised to captivate the assembled guests with a musical performance that they shall not soon forget.

And so, dear Phil, the stage is set for the next chapter of this extraordinary tale. The anticipation swelled within me, mingling with a tinge of nervous excitement. What lies ahead is uncertain, yet the prospect of performing at Rock Hudson's soirée beckons me toward uncharted territories. Wish me the best of luck, for I will need it to wow my audience, and make a favorable impression. I hope I have it in me to do the impossible… please keep your fingers crossed!"

We parted ways after Phil and I said our goodnights at the Hyatt, where my bike was parked. I don't even remember riding it back home, or how I stumbled into my room, my body a blend of exhaustion and exhilaration. The evening's events played on repeat in my mind like a captivating film reel. The encounter with Rock Hudson, the invitation to perform at his soirée—everything felt like a surreal dream. As I finally collapsed onto my bed, I was overwhelmed by a sense of disbelief and wonder.

I woke up in a daze with the alarm blaring, signaling the start of a new day. With a jolt of realization, I leaped out of bed, fully aware of the urgency to shower, knowing that I would have to make my way back to the Hyatt Regency as quickly as possible. Instinctively, I started getting ready and, at first, didn't even realize what day it was, where I was, or what had happened.

The night had been a sensory overload, and my body yearned for more sleep, but the responsibilities of my morning shift called. As I stood under the shower, the water cascading over me, I tried to relive every moment of the previous night at the Silver Fox. Was it all just a dream? I had to pinch myself, just to make sure I was awake and not still lost in the enchanting reverie of some unbelievable hallucination.

The reality of the day ahead hit me like a tidal wave. I needed to request some time off for the party on Saturday—a detail that had somehow escaped me in the deluge of emotions and excitement. I resolved to speak with Phil, perhaps swapping shifts with my biggest fan, who was sure to understand my desire to seize this once-in-a-lifetime opportunity.

As I hastily dressed and pedaled back to the Hyatt Regency, I couldn't help but feel an overwhelming sense of anticipation and nervousness. Performing at Rock Hudson's soirée was a thrilling yet intimidating prospect. Could I meet the high expectations and give a performance that truly fits the occasion? But I had a more immediate concern: Would Phil agree to switch shifts so I could make it to Rock's party?

Arriving at the hotel, I took a deep breath, ready to face the day with renewed determination. The events of the night before were an incredible gift, and I was determined to make the most of this rare chance. With each passing moment, the reality of what lay ahead sunk

Pushed Out of the Closet Without A Parachute

in, and I knew that my life was poised for a thrilling plunge into uncharted waters. As I stepped into the bustling world of the Hyatt Regency, I held on to the sense of wonder that had enveloped me. The little man in my head was telling me that this could be the beginning of an extraordinary journey, and all this due to a fluke and a lucky break. Who could have guessed?

Chapter 2: My Debut

As the week whirled by at the Hyatt, I found myself swept up in a flurry of special events and double shifts. Before I knew it, Saturday had arrived, and my excitement for the evening's party grew with each passing hour. Fate had a humorous way of intervening, as Phil and I, who had planned to switch days off, found ourselves working the morning shift together. Poor Phil, destined to brave the relentless second shift with only a two-hour break in between.

Undeterred by our demanding schedules, I decided to seize a moment of respite and grab a bite with Phil. Over lunch, we eagerly discussed the upcoming soirée—my musical performance, the perfect outfit I had to wear, and all the delightful details that awaited me at Rock Hudson's party. It was a welcome escape from the hectic workday, allowing me to revel in the anticipation of what the evening had in store.

With his charming Southern flair, Phil gestured with his hands, which acted as punctuation marks at the end of his sentences. A hand on his hip resembled a question mark, while his limp-wristed palms up, coupled with a tilted head, served as a precise period. There was no mistaking his body language—arms above his head with a downward gaze meant an emphatic "NO WAY," a combination of a limp wrist and hunched shoulders effortlessly conveyed his uncertainty with a touch of humor. Every unspoken gesture spoke volumes to Philisms; his presence painted our conversations colorfully.

And so, with his hands confidently on his hips—a signature stance, Phil began his characteristic questioning. "How do you feel, Guntha?" he asked, probing for my innermost thoughts. "Are you ready to dazzle them tonight, to own that stage and mesmerize the crowd?"

His inquisitive nature could make even the bravest second-guess themselves, but I mustered my courage and replied, "Phil, my dear, I'm treating this like any other gig and just being myself, singing my heart out. What else can I do? Hopefully, I'll leave them asking for more, and who knows, maybe I'll even land some referrals for future gigs. Tonight's the night, and you bet I'm ready!"

As Phil retired for a quick nap before his demanding second shift, I headed home to fine-tune my performance, practicing my songs on the guitar and solidifying my playlist. Thoughts swirled in my head, contemplating different scenarios that might arise during the evening, considering whether I needed to change the pace or add a surprise element. Over the years, I have played at a diverse array of gigs. Each one is etched into the tapestry of my musical journey.

One of the most remarkable moments in my early musical forays was when I played a solo for one of the Duchesses of England in an Accordion Recital at the tender age of six. The venue was none other than the former site of the Ambassador Hotel, with its fabled Cocoanut Grove nightclub. Oh, the memories! I have my father to thank for instilling in me my love of music and helping me navigate the years of accordion school in my youth.

As I journeyed into adulthood, my music carried me to increasingly diverse and cherished experiences. From the intimate ambiance of local bars to the joyous celebrations of weddings, I found myself sharing melodies that stirred hearts and created lasting memories. One unforgettable gig took me to San Francisco's Haight-Ashbury district, where the 'Summer of Love' resonated with every guitar strum. I also fondly recall thrilling a New Year's Eve crowd in a vibrant restaurant in Hilo, Hawaii, where the spirit of aloha infused every note. The islands' allure deepened as I joined a Hawaiian chorus, performing in Waikiki hotels alongside graceful hula dancers, each show a vibrant celebration of the rich cultural tapestry I'd come to cherish.

Among the various performances, one of the most defining moments was co-writing our musical "Going Out in Style" in 1981. It was a testament to my creative spirit and a collaborative journey that shaped my love for storytelling through music. Additionally, my classically trained days culminated in my Senior Recital at Long Beach State in May 1983. Standing on that stage, I felt the culmination of years of dedication and the profound realization that music was more than a passion—at that time, it was my life's purpose.

A notable adventure took me to Australia and New Zealand in the summer of 1983, where I performed with the University Chorus and Voce Jazz singing group. The journey was a testament to how far

Pushed Out of the Closet Without A Parachute

I had conquered my fear of singing in front of people. However, even with my growing confidence on stage, one obstacle remained: the persistent stage fright that accompanied the prospect of public speaking. It seemed no amount of musical prowess could shield me from the anxiety that crept in whenever I faced a sea of expectant faces. And so, with the challenge of addressing an audience still ahead of me, I pushed aside my worries and focused on the upcoming party of Rock Hudson's at the home of Dean Dittman, determined to give my all and dazzle them with my musical magic.

The hour had arrived, and as I stood in front of Dean's apartment building, a mixture of excitement and butterflies fluttered within me like a symphony of emotions. The directions had led me to this charming, well-preserved neighborhood, and a sense of anticipation surged through my veins as I readied myself to make an unforgettable entrance. Being early allowed me to absorb the ambiance and gather my composure before the soirée commenced.

The street exuded a captivating allure, with its vintage homes boasting meticulous landscaping and a touch of timelessness. The converted condos added a contemporary twist to the picturesque scene, creating a harmonious blend of the past and present—a fitting metaphor for the journey that had brought me to this momentous occasion.

Before I headed upstairs, I took a moment or two to gaze into the rearview mirror to ensure my appearance was on point, heeding Phil's advice to dress impeccably for the event. With a confident smile, I acknowledged how much Phil's influence had shaped my sense of style and presentation, but I, too, had my own unique flair, and tonight, I was "killing it."

"Inspired by Phil," I thought with a chuckle, acknowledging the charm and wit I had come to embrace through his guidance. "But I'll draw the line at having flight attendant hands," I added jokingly, not wanting to adopt Philisms penchant for grand gestures and gesticulations. I was content being my authentic self, embracing my individuality, and as I climbed those stairs, I felt like a force of nature, my own source of inspiration and courage… "Game face on… Grrrrrrr!"

With a deep breath, I reached the top of the stairs to Dean's second-story apartment. I was eager to embark on an evening that promised enchantment, togetherness, and the chance to showcase my musical prowess to the esteemed guests inside.

The door opened, and a man I'd never seen before greeted me quizzically as he eyed my guitar case. "Are you sure you're at the right place?" he asked curiously.

Without missing a beat, I replied, "I think so. Doesn't Dean Dittman live here? I'm Gunther, and I was asked to come here to be the entertainment for tonight."

With a chuckle, the man reassured me, "Oh, honey, I bet you are, and yes, you're definitely at the right place. But you can put that guitar in the guest room for now. This party hasn't started yet, and if I know Rock and Dean, it will be a couple of hours before it fully gets going. Why don't you grab yourself a cocktail? There's a bar set up on the kitchen peninsula. Rock is on the couch, and Dean is still getting ready... that Drama Queen."

I was taken aback by this stranger's candidness, but I followed his advice. I left my guitar in the corner of the bedroom (I never did get his name) and headed into the main living room, where I finally caught a glimpse of Rock Hudson.

As I stepped into the living room, I caught the corner of Rock's eye as he chatted with another gentleman when he quickly stood up. "Why, Gunther, you made it!" Rock exclaimed across the room, making a beeline towards me. He enveloped me in a bear hug that almost knocked the wind out of me as he continued, "I didn't think I'd ever see you again, and to be honest, I never expected you to follow up."

I grinned, "Of course, I'm going to show up if I say I'm going to. I put my guitar in the guest room for now, but where do you want me to set up, and when should I start playing?"

Rock chuckled surprisedly, "Now, Gunther, you just take a load off your feet. I know you've had a long drive from Long Beach, so get a drink, relax, and join us on the couch. I'll introduce you to people as they come in, and if you're still up for it, we'll arrange a time for you to sing once everyone's here."

Stammering slightly, I responded, "OK, whatever you think is best. I'm ready whenever you need me."

But Rock insisted with a firm tone, "You just go get that drink, and we'll take it from there."

As Rock returned to his chair and resumed his conversation with the other gentleman, I headed to the kitchen to grab a cocktail. The evening was off to an intriguing start, and I couldn't help but wonder what other surprises awaited me at this star-studded gathering.

I grabbed a light beer and settled into an empty chair across from Rock, who introduced me to his friend, David. Now, I didn't watch much TV when I was in collegeand fully immersed in all my singing and extracurricular activities. Yet, as I heard David's voice and the conversation flowed, it sounded familiar, and it also dawned on me that he looked very familiar. Ding ding, the lights went on. He was none other than Major Winchester from Mash. I later discovered his full name was David Ogden Stiers. Despite feeling slightly out of place, I sat and listened, intrigued by the star-studded company.

As the doorbell rang and more guests arrived, Rock stood up to greet a few until Dean walked out of the bathroom with a larger-than-life strut. Rock excitedly said to him, "Guess who made it?"

Dean replied with curiosity, "Who?"

Rock exclaimed, "Why, Gunther from the Silver Fox in Long Beach! Come say hi to him!" And just like that, Dean made a shortcut towards me, welcoming me with another one of those big bear hugs that seemed to be a signature of the evening. I was used to hugging close friends, but these warm embraces were on another level—not that I was complaining; it was all part of the unforgettable charm of the night. Two bear hugs in a row—but, now, who's counting?

As the room grew increasingly crowded, I was hesitant to occupy a seat when there might be others who needed it more. So, I stood and walked over to a group of people who seemed closer to my age. However, even in that crowd, I still appeared to be the youngest guest, aside from the enthusiastic young man who had greeted me at the door. He seemed to be a friend of Dean's, diligently running around the place, fetching more booze for the kitchen, and darting back out for whatever else the party required.

As I stood listening to the animated chatter, I couldn't help but overhear some folks discussing their work on the sitcom Mary Hartman, Mary Hartman. While I knew the show's reputation as a satirical soap opera that aired daily in weeknight syndication in the late '70s, I had never seen an episode. My TV viewing had been relatively limited, with my focus primarily on music and other artistic endeavors. Nonetheless, the lively conversation continued, and I recognized a few faces from various TV appearances and movies, though I still struggled to recall their names and specific roles.

Just when I began to feel slightly out of place, Rock made his way over with his trademark warm smile. "Are you having a good time, Gunther?" he asked, his presence instantly putting me at ease. I nodded with a smile, trying to emanate a sense of belonging. Rock had a gift for making everyone feel welcome and comfortable, and I admired his ability to connect effortlessly with people from all walks of life.

The apartment condo buzzed with laughter and lively chatter as the night progressed. The guests mingled, exchanging anecdotes and engaging in spirited conversations. I found myself moving from one group to another, savoring each moment and absorbing the vibrant energy of the evening. Despite my initial apprehensions, I was slowly finding my place between the celebrity-packed event, grateful for the opportunity to mingle with some of the entertainment industry's finest.

I couldn't help but feel a sense of wonder at how my journey had led me to this unexpected and exhilarating moment. The daunting prospect of performing for such esteemed guests no longer weighed heavily on my mind. Instead, I embraced the thrill of the evening, eagerly awaiting the perfect moment to share my musical magic and leave a lasting impression on everyone gathered at Rock and Dean's unforgettable party. With the night unfolding around me, a newfound sense of confidence washed over me, and I felt as if I were exactly where I was meant to be—among the stars, both celestial and Hollywood.

As the night unceasingly rolled on, I glanced at my watch and noticed that it was almost midnight—still, my performance hadn't even begun. Determined to take action, I searched for Rock, eventually finding him exactly where he was when I arrived. Leaning close, I whispered in his ear, "Is it time for me to set up and start singing?"

Pushed Out of the Closet Without A Parachute

Rock, who had been indulging in Scotch on the rocks—pun unintended—appeared slightly flustered but retained his charm. He replied, "Just reeeeelax and enjoy, Gunther. The party's too loud and crowded at the moment. Let's wait until it starts calming down a little. Hey, can you grab me another..." Before he could finish, I interjected, "Scotch on the rocks with a twist of lemon, correct?" His surprise was evident, and he chuckled, "Now, Gunther, you're a quick study. I guess I've underestimated you in more ways than one."

I retrieved his drink, all the while navigating the bustling party. I bumped into Dean again, who was fulfilling his role as the social butterfly and Rock's official greeter. Dean complimented me on my stunning appearance, noting that the entire room was curious about who I was and where I came from. I played coy and replied, "Oh, just a waiter from Long Beach who happens to play guitar and sing. By the way, any idea when it'll be all right for me to perform a few of my songs?"

Dean shrugged with a smile, "I haven't a clue, my dear, but right now, it's so loud in here that the only place you'd fit is out on the balcony, serenading to the coyotes. We'll have to wait and see a little later—maybe around 2-ish."

I couldn't help but ponder the idea of performing at 2 A.M. "Hollywood is certainly a different world," I thought, a mix of excitement and bewilderment dancing in my mind. Nevertheless, I decided to embrace the unpredictability of the evening and patiently await the perfect moment to share my musical talent with this glamorous and eccentric gathering. The city lights may have obscured the stars above, but behind the glitz and glamour, I was ready to shine and leave a lasting impression on Hollywood's finest.

The hours still seemed to drag on, but before I knew it, it was almost 2 AM with a small crowd lingering in the cozy condo. Feeling the weight of my upcoming shift in Long Beach, I approached Rock to let him know that I needed to head back and get some rest. As I shared my plans, Rock, with his newfound chivalry, quickly arranged a spot for me to sing and ensured everyone's attention was on me.

With hushed anticipation, I began with my original song titled *"The Whales,"* a somber yet powerful piece that conveyed a poignant message about man's impact on nature. The room fell silent, captivated by the performance unfolding before them. I became lost in the moment, immersing myself in the music, and for those brief minutes, it felt like the world disappeared, leaving only the melody and the emotions it evoked.

As I strummed the final chords, time seemed to stretch, making those three to four seconds feel like an eternity. Once I finished, an enchanting stillness enveloped the room as every pair of eyes remained fixed on my performance.

It starkly contrasted the bar gigs and New Year's Eve shows where I often felt like just another background element. But here, at this moment, I stood on a stage of captivated attention. The closing notes carried a somber poignancy, leaving an echo of sadness lingering in the air, as the song's powerful message about man's impact on nature resonated through the silence. The weight of that message hung in the air for an hour but was perhaps only a few seconds.

Suddenly applause, and as Rock approached me, he seemed still visibly moved. He expressed his genuine admiration and explained how he had underestimated me, thinking I wouldn't be good. "I'm in shock… I mean, you come here and play the guitar like that in front of people you've never met before and knock everyone's socks off!"

"I could never do that!" he exclaimed.

I still wasn't sure what was going on but answered, "What are you talking about? You're a famous actor who has been in front of many audiences and surely you've done this before."

Rock replied, "In front of cameras and on stage where the lights are so bright you can't even see anyone's faces, but Gunther I must apologize for not putting you on sooner. Frankly, I thought you wouldn't be any good, but you, my friend, are something special."

At that moment, I realized that Hollywood's lights couldn't dull the authenticity of my performance. I wasn't just a singer in the background anymore; I had taken center stage, and the response was exhilarating.

Dody Goodman, the familiar face from Mary Hartman, Mary Hartman, and Grease, approached me, inquiring about the song's origin. I proudly shared that it was one of my original creations, emphasizing my passion for writing and performing. To my astonishment, she mentioned her involvement with an animal rights organization and expressed interest in using the song in a commercial or for their cause. My heart soared, and without hesitation, I gladly gave my permission. After all, my goal was to reach as many people as possible, and if my music could contribute to a cause I deeply cared about, I considered it an honor.

As the room once again filled with lively conversation and laughter, I couldn't help but feel a mix of emotions. Playing only one song might have seemed unusual, but the party atmosphere still permeated the air. Yet, amid this exuberance, I experienced a newfound sense of belonging. Surrounded by Hollywood icons and new acquaintances, I discovered my authentic voice—as a singer and an artist with a meaningful message to share.

Even in those fleeting minutes, Hollywood had embraced me, and I knew I was no longer just a waiter from Long Beach; I was Gunther, the musician whose melody had the power to stir hearts and ignite change. The realization of this transformation filled me with pride and purpose.

Rock approached me and told me that the people were way too drunk, realizing that my artistry deserved a more sincere setting. He invited me to perform again next weekend for an hour, showcasing my crafted melodies to a room full of eager listeners. I graciously accepted, feeling honored by the opportunity. Still, I also knew it was time to bid farewell to the lively party and find some rest to recharge my soul, for such an enchanting evening (or should I say morning) demanded a well-rested soul.

With gratitude in my heart, I thanked Rock and said my goodbyes to the boisterous soirée. Rock's warm embrace wrapped around me as we exchanged parting words, and he whispered words that ignited a spark within my spirit. "You are a star, Gunther," he murmured with profound sincerity. "Believe in your light, for it will guide you far. And if ever you need a helping hand along your celestial path, know that I'll be there, eager to aid in your journey."

With a promise to call once I returned to my sanctuary, I set off into the nocturnal cityscape. Like nocturnal denizens, Hollywood creatures reveled in a world that thrived under the silver moon. How thrilled I felt to partake in and contribute to a nocturnal symphony, surrounded by fellow creative souls, dancing hand in hand until the break of dawn.

In my heart, I marveled at this chance encounter, knowing that fate had led me to the threshold of possibility. The following weekend held promises of melodies and dreams, and as I navigated through the labyrinth of streets, I couldn't help but embrace the belief that my life was about to change and change in the way I had only dreamed of. I wasn't sure if I was high on the evening events, but my eyes were wide open, and so were my hopes.

As I stumbled into my home, the clock taunted me with its nearly 4 A.M. display. The hour seemed too late and too early, making it inconvenient to reach out to anyone. I mustered the energy to leave a message on Rock's answering machine, again expressing my gratitude and ensuring him of my safe arrival home.

Exhaustion engulfed me as I collapsed into bed, anticipating that I'd sleep until noon, just in time to get ready, grab a bite to eat, and head to the evening shift at work. The knowledge of working with Phil again tempted me to keep him on pins and needles playfully. So, I decided to shut off my phone, knowing he'd try to call me in the morning. Sleep was my sole mission, and I surrendered to its call without hesitation.

It was already noon when I finally opened my eyes, though it felt like the crack of dawn after an eventful night. My body still groaned with exhaustion, but a refreshing shower and a hearty breakfast would rejuvenate me. I dialed Phil to assure him that I hadn't disappeared into the Hollywood abyss, leaving my day job behind.

Phil's voice echoed with agitation as he answered the phone, and I could almost picture his arms flailing in confusion. He vented his frustration, scolding me for not calling him right away. Calmly, I reassured him, recounting the late-night revelry and the resounding success of my whale song performance.

As the conversation continued, my excitement grew as I shared the news of the one-hour concert invitation for next week. I eagerly proposed a shift swap, and in typical Phil fashion, he playfully threatened to "own me." He humorously reminded me of our deep friendship and the bond we shared. His laughter and witty banter brought comfort, and I knew that if I got too high and mighty hobnobbing with the elite in Hollywood, I could always count on Phil to keep me grounded. After all, no matter how much success or fame I might achieve, Phil would be there to remind me of my roots and the true essence of who I am.

With the promise of a real chance to show off my talents on the horizon and the comforting familiarity of friendship, I embraced the joyous uncertainty of life, feeling grateful for the path that had led me to this remarkable moment. In one more week I could perform more than just one song and put on an entire music set to be heard.

In the days leading up to the weekend, my initial apprehensions slowly melted away. I anticipated an intimate gathering among friends, where candid assessments and creative insights would flow freely. With each passing day, I better understood the audience that would grace this musical soirée. It wasn't merely a casual party but a modest concert attended by individuals entrenched in the same industry that Rock had been a part of.

Before I knew it, another weekend had seamlessly woven its way into my life, and there I was, returning to the very place where I had found myself just the weekend before—Dean's apartment. It seemed that fate had an uncanny way of guiding my footsteps to this familiar threshold, as if there was a silent agreement between me and the universe.

However, this time, there were different people in the gathering of my intimate audience. The presence of Ross Hunter, the illustrious television producer renowned for crafting delightful comedies like "Pillow Talk," where Rock himself had starred alongside Doris Day, added an extra layer of significance to the event. He was also here with his life partner, Jacque. It's worth noting that marriage equality was not fully realized then, so we wouldn't use the term "husband" as we do today.

Rock had divulged to me that he and Dean had extended an invitation to Dean's agent, Dick Lovell, who boasted stronger ties within the music industry. Regrettably, Dick was entangled in prior commitments and couldn't grace us with his presence. Nevertheless, Dody Goodman and a selection of actors from Mash, whom I had the pleasure of meeting just the week before, were confirmed attendees. Dean's friends within the building, who had swiftly become my ardent supporters, were also set to join us for this evening of musical enchantment.

Armed with my faithful guitar, I took a moment for a quick tune-up, mindful of its jostling during the trip. Before delving into the music, I offered a brief backstory to the song I was about to perform, rather than commencing with "The Whale Song." I had reserved it for the finale, aiming to leave a lasting impression. I brought along my trusty boombox to accompany my guitar, which would harmonize seamlessly.

The night's opening song was titled "Without You," which was probably my most commercial-sounding song. Most of my compositions fell within the realm of love songs or pining for love songs. Among them were titles such as "Two Hearts," "Lost and

Lonesome," "In My Heart," "Close to You Again," "Make Believin'," "Forever Yours," "Someday," "Never Let Me Go," and a tune with a distinct Californian flavor named "Earthquake Surprise." Each song held its own story and emotion, ready to be shared with the intimate audience.

During the intermissions between songs, we took a brief break for me to provide a condensed biography of my musical journey, recounting how I had ventured into songwriting and even delving into the recent musical I had co-authored just the previous year. When someone inquired about the number of songs I had penned over the years, I had to confess that I honestly didn't have an exact count, but the total likely reached the hundreds. Some, I believed, were worthy of meticulous arrangements, while others might best be left in the archives, never to be heard again.

Following this interlude, I concluded the mini-concert with "The Whale Song." Dodi seemed particularly pleased when I announced the title. I decided to share the backstory of how this song came to be, leaving everyone in awe of the personal depth and meaning woven into each of my compositions. Life, as we all know, can sometimes be more prolific during certain phases and at other times lays dormant.

However, amid significant moments and unfolding events, where most would reach for a diary to record their experiences, I found my refuge in the language of music. Each song I crafted became a vessel, not just for lyrics, but for the emotions and atmosphere that

Pushed Out of the Closet Without A Parachute

enveloped me at those crucial junctures. "The Whale Song" is a poignant example of this phenomenon—an evocative composition that, whenever its notes resounded, unfailingly carried me back to that profound, life-altering instant.

Once I finished, thunderous applause truly overwhelmed me. I'm not typically the gushy type, one to let my emotions spill over in public. However, seeing some of Hollywood's finest react so passionately to my music, it all rushed to my head. I admit, I couldn't help but shed a few tears of joy and extend my heartfelt gratitude to everyone for their warm reception.

Rock and Dean, naturally, couldn't resist delivering their triumphant "Told you so" speeches. Yet, I still found it rather challenging to wrap my head around the overwhelming response. You see, while I had dabbled in playing music before, it was usually within the confines of my room, with perhaps a friend or two as my modest audience. Typically, I'd perform just one or two songs. On those rare occasions when I did venture to share my music at other gatherings, weddings, or similar events, I'd stick to well-known cover songs.

These were the easy-listening, melodic tunes of artists like Cat Stevens, Seals and Croft, and James Taylor, along with acoustic renditions of rock classics like Led Zeppelin's "Stairway to Heaven" and Jethro Tull's "Locomotive Breath." I'd always strummed other people's songs, never fully revealing my creations to the world. But tonight was an unmistakable turning point, the first occasion I chose to lay all my original music out in the open, so to speak, "putting it all out there."

I was curious to see what Ross Hunter and his partner, Jacque, thought. Though we had only been introduced that evening, I noticed them conversing with Rock, so I decided to approach. They congratulated me as I joined them, but I sought a genuine response, not just polite party banter. I pressed, "No, really, what did you think? Too many love songs, perhaps? Or in the words of McCartney, 'You'd think that people would've had enough of silly love songs... Looking around me, I see it isn't so...' But honestly?"

Ross uttered something to Rock that slipped past my ears, but it carried the essence of, "You weren't exaggerating about Gunther; he genuinely possesses that special something." Both Ross and Jacque conveyed their heartfelt appreciation for my music. Ross observed, "It felt like a journey back to the '70s, the era of Cat Stevens, Jim Croce, and James Taylor, where masterful storytellers ruled the music scene. Gunther, you possess a unique ability to immerse your audience in your songs. I've witnessed actors attempt a similar connection in their performances, but very few capture it as you do. You, Gunther, have it in spades!"

"Wow," I replied, my voice filled with nostalgia. "I often wish I had been born a decade or two earlier. In 1970, playing a party like this might have led to a record producer knocking on my door, eager to sign me for an album."

Pushed Out of the Closet Without A Parachute

Rock interjected, confident and encouraging, "Now, Gunther, don't underestimate yourself. There's always room for exceptional songwriters, especially those who can deliver their creations with the finesse you possess. In a setting like this tonight, you've managed to capture the attention of everyone in the room. I genuinely believe you have a promising career ahead of you if that's what you desire."

"Desire?" I exclaimed; my eyes filled with determination. "I've been dreaming of it since I was around twelve when I picked up a guitar. I had been playing the accordion since I was four, but I grew weary of performing on an instrument that felt stuck in the past. And now, I sometimes get that same feeling with just the acoustic guitar. But I'm eager to start arranging my songs. Hopefully, in the not-so-distant future, I'll acquire a mixing board to bring those musical visions to life and up to date."

During our lively discussion, Ross extended an invitation that hung in the air like a melody. "I'd love to have both of you over for dinner one evening," he proposed, his eyes reflecting genuine curiosity. "We could talk more about Gunther's music and simply catch up on life since Marc has been living with you."

Rock, ever the diplomat, responded graciously, "I'd be delighted to come, with Gunther, of course. Let's leave... 'What's his name out of the conversation."

Ross acknowledged the unspoken sentiments. "Well, I suppose that says it all about how things are going," he chuckled, his tone softening with understanding. "My apologies, I won't add any more salt to your wounds. Rock, we'll figure out a suitable day where Gunther can drive up from Long Beach."

I chimed in, eagerly, "That sounds wonderful. I'll just need to check my schedule in advance. I'm certain we can coordinate a date that works for all."

The remainder of the evening unfurled as a harmonious symphony of laughter and joy, with everyone immersed in the enchanting atmosphere. Compliments and positive feedback poured in, giving me a warm embrace of appreciation. This night had been an extraordinary gift, a moment I yearned to grasp and preserve. However, I couldn't overlook Dean and Rock's gatherings often stretched into the early morning hours, and the looming reality of an impending commitment playfully nudged my conscience.

With a tinge of reluctance, I bid my farewell, and as customary, exchanged those warm bear hugs with Dean and Rock. As I embarked on the drive home, the melodies of my own compositions resonated through the car. The a cappella renditions performed by none other than me. A surge of wild imaginings enveloped me, visions of hearing my voice possibly gracing the airwaves someday. The notion was nothing short of incredible and exhilarating! All it necessitated was the alignment of the right person, the right moment, and the right place in the grand scheme of things.

A chuckle escaped my lips as I contemplated the whims of luck. It was like lightning, I thought, never striking twice in the same spot. But perhaps I had ignited enough spark that would blaze its own path. I was eager to wait and see, recognizing that only time would tell.

Chapter 3: Rusty Pelican

As I embraced the Sunday morning shift at the hotel, my hands were full of responsibilities. Today, my task was to orchestrate a delightful coffee break for a large group of executives from NBC, leaving me to tackle it solo without Phil's company. The esteemed guests were busy planning events for the upcoming Olympics and sought the hotel's expertise in hosting special theme parties. It was the perfect opportunity for me to unleash my creativity, and so I eagerly presented my ideas for a Japanese theme, under-the-ocean theme, and a Roaring 20s theme.

The hotel's general manager swiftly greenlit my proposal, granting a budget of one hundred dollars per theme for procuring robust props. Time ticking away, I wasted no seconds, having already arranged the roll-in tables by 8 A.M. Glass racks were transformed into a cascading waterfall draped in artichoke-folded napkins and others in royalty-folded fashion, mimicking vibrant flowers to emulate a Japanese garden. To stay on schedule, I needed to head to Pier One as soon as it unlocked its doors at 9 A.M.

Despite my usual preference for biking, the weight of the props and time constraints dictated that I drive. My old Pontiac Tempest Le Mans, a trusty but fuel-hungry companion, fulfilled its purpose today. La Bamba, as I fondly dubbed my car, was a 1960s engineering marvel! This vehicle, a testament to GM's A-body platform, boasted classic design and performance enhancements.

Pushed Out of the Closet Without A Parachute

Picture me cruising in style, relishing every moment in this gas-guzzling beauty. La Bamba was my go-to ride for special occasions like this.

Allow me to entertain you with the charming backstory of how fate introduced La Bamba to me. In my previous rental, a sweet elderly lady was the proud owner, yet time's passage rendered her with little need for a vehicle. It appeared that the stars had aligned perfectly, gifting me a special price for this magnificent car with hardly any miles on it, barely even broken in. An actual chariot destined to accompany me on grand adventures like today. She became my trusty steed for the scavenger hunt to find grand props to impress.

At Pier One, I gathered Japanese umbrellas, artificial cherry blossom flowers, and a tablecloth from home section, intending to blend the Ocean and Japanese themes seamlessly. Starfish and abalone shells added captivating colors, solidifying my vision for the event. Laden, with all my props, I swiftly loaded up La Bamba and returned to the hotel.

Back at the Hyatt, I threw myself into completing my masterpiece. While food typically arrives thirty minutes before the scheduled 11 A.M. coffee break, I always aim for early deliveries to ensure ample preparation time. My foresight proved indispensable when, right on cue, they decided to start the break at 10:45 A.M.

The tables were grand, and I meticulously adorned the foyer, arranging dishes, glasses, and silverware with precision. Cascading glass containers served as towers for guests to gather their plates, creating an alluring culinary experience. Fresh fruits, juices, Danishes, pastries, croissants, and delectable breakfast desserts adorned the tables. As the guests indulged in the delicacies, I refreshed the displays, ensuring everything looked impeccable throughout the event.

The result was a resounding success, leaving the Heads of NBC thoroughly impressed. Considering this project was an improvised endeavor, the praises and commendations from my boss and the general manager filled me with immense satisfaction.

With the event's conclusion, my responsibilities extended to tidying up and storing the props in a secure, locked cage. With the success of my quick thinking and creative genius, I was hopeful that I would be picked to work with NBC during the Olympics and become their go-to person for future events. Nonetheless, I couldn't help but feel satisfied with being part of this spontaneous surge of creativity and hospitality.

By noon, my work shift had ended, and I felt fortunate not to have a double shift, giving me a chance to head straight home for a much-needed afternoon nap. I reached the condo, where I rented a room from another gay man named Pat Zega, a psychologist who owned this unit in a waterfront condo complex called The Portofino. Located in the charming Belmont Shore area of Long Beach, California, The Portofino was a classic icon with its water-view condos overlooking Alamitos Bay and its beach-close location only a few blocks from the sandy shores.

Pushed Out of the Closet Without A Parachute

Pat, my roommate, was what some would call very "sexually active" in the gay community, frequently dating multiple people at the same time. On the other hand, I had always been more focused on my career and staying fit. Having graduated from Long Beach State less than a year ago, I was eager to establish myself professionally, leaving little time for an active dating life or being promiscuous. However, I had been seeing someone for a few months, and we enjoyed each other's company whenever our schedules allowed.

Arriving home, I noticed a couple of messages blinking on my answering machine. With Pat out, enjoying his social escapades, I had the place to myself, and all I wanted was some undisturbed sleep. As I played the messages, I was thrilled to hear Rock's voice. At first, he expressed his happiness at my attendance at the party and praised my impact at both performances, saying, "Gunther, my friend, you made a big splash!" The warmth in his voice made my heart soar.

The second message brought an unexpected invitation—Rock had connections with some well-known restaurants in my area and wanted me to join him for dinner. He playfully added, "Hey Gunther, when I lived in Newport Beach, I had a lot of close connections with people, and a good friend of mine is the owner of the Rusty Pelican. I was heading down your way, hoping you could join me for dinner tonight. What say you? Talk to you later, love Rock."

I couldn't believe my luck. Excitedly, I replied to Rock's invitation, looking forward to what the night would bring. The idea of sharing a meal with Rock and enjoying the company of someone who believed in my talent and potential was both humbling and exhilarating. As I prepared for the evening, I couldn't help but wonder what new opportunities might unfold at the Rusty Pelican—a restaurant that had been out of my reach during my student days. It seemed to symbolize a new chapter, shimmering with possibilities and promising encounters.

A stunning outfit was in order, and my inner Phil voice whispered, urging me to "dress to impress." Yet, the lingering question remained: Did I possess anything worthy of donning at such an esteemed fine dining establishment? Hmm, this called for a phone call to Phil, seeking his advice and impeccable wisdom.

"Damn, Guntha... Butter my buns and call me a biscuit!" exclaimed Phil in sheer disbelief when I called him to share the news about my dinner date with Rock Hudson. He was excited for me and couldn't resist using another trademark, Philisms, adding, "I missed you today, and I hear you went totally Martha Stewart on us this morning at the Hotel!"

Phil laughed, adding, "Keep this up, and I'll have to take you back to Alabama on my next trip home!" I was honestly tempted to meet the family that had produced such a vibrant and colorful personality like Phil. But for now, I needed his fashion sense mixed with mine to create the perfect outfit for my evening with Rock.

"Phil, do you happen to have a fancy shirt that I could borrow for tonight, you know, something that will make a statement?" I asked. He pondered momentarily and then replied, "Guntha, we're both tall men, but you have much more muscles than I do. I doubt you'd fit in any of my shirts, but I have this particular one that's a bit baggy on me. It has a splash of nostalgic 'Saturday Night Fever' disco mixed with a dash of 1983's 'Maneater' by Daryl Hall and John Oates, topped off with this year's 1984 #1 hit 'Footloose' by Kenny Loggins. I'd dare to guess that putting you in this shirt will not only make a statement; it will make Rock's heart spin!"

I chuckled at Phil's shirt description but gently explained that he had the wrong idea about where things were going between Rock and me. I had no intentions of seeing Rock in a romantic light. After all, I was already seeing someone and knew Rock had someone living with him. While I admired Rock's handsomeness, I felt a stronger connection with him as a friend.

With his ever-optimistic spirit, Phil said, "Never say never, Guntha! Who knows, keep your eyes open, peeled, and skinned. Maybe you've been looking at things the wrong way."

I playfully retorted, "Enough, Phil! I need to take a power nap for a few hours. Could you come by around 6 P.M.? I must be ready by 7:30 when Rock is arriving at The Portofino to pick me up." Phil responded with an amused "Ah, hummm... eyes open, peeled, and skinned. See ya at 6!"

His quirky sense of humor always kept things lively, and I knew he'd be there to help me get ready for the night that held the potential to be fruitful for my musical career or, at the very least, forge a new and meaningful friendship with someone who could perhaps mentor me along the way.

After my power nap, I was fully refreshed and ready to face the world and my date with Rock. As I stepped into the shower, a sense of déjà vu washed over me, realizing I had already done this routine earlier in the day. Time seemed to warp, and I couldn't help but wonder if it was still Sunday. Nevertheless, by 6 P.M., I was showered, shaved, and ready for my close-up. I had to prepare myself for Phil's arrival.

A message on my answering machine informed me that Phil would run about 10 minutes late. In the meantime, I pressed a pair of my new black jeans and decided to don my cowboy boots, knowing they would make me stand out, even taller than Rock. Phil finally arrived, holding "the shirt" in his hand like a prized possession.

As he entered, Phil presented me with a spectacular shirt that perfectly blended casual and dressy elements. It exuded a beachy vibe with its bold, colorful linear stripes in teal, pink, red, white, and yellow shades. I knew the perfect accessory to complete the ensemble: a wooden Koa surfboard necklace, adding that quintessential bohemian flair. "George Michael, eat your heart out!" I joked, envisioning the final look.

I decided to wear the shirt untucked and open, sans undershirt, to enhance the relaxed beach feel. Phil watched me with wonderment as I talked to myself, putting together my outfit. His only comment was, "Oh my god, I've created a monster!"

Pushed Out of the Closet Without A Parachute

I playfully retorted, "Ha ha, takes one to know one!"

With the attire settled, I graciously dismissed Phil and tidied up the place before Rock's arrival. As I awaited our meeting, I grabbed my camera, determined to capture this memorable occasion, proof that Rock had visited my humble abode, or rather, the room I rented. The lyrics of Marvin Gaye's classic, *'Wherever I Lay My Hat (That's My Home),'* resonated as a reminder that true home is not a physical place but rather a sense of belonging and comfort.

Rock was remarkably punctual, arriving just before 7:30. As he ascended to the fifth floor, one level below the penthouse suites, he rang the bell. Welcoming him inside, I provided him with a quick tour of the apartment, and just then, my roommate Pat, just happened to walk in. The expression on Pat's face was a mix of disbelief and fascination, prompting me to explain, "I didn't get a chance to tell you earlier, but Rock Hudson and I have dinner plans for tonight, and he's here to pick me up."

With a knowing smile, he said, "I can see that."

I introduced Pat Zega to Rock Hudson, who said, "It's very nice to meet you, Pat." Rock and I exchanged warm glances, and he suggested, "Well, Gunther, we should get going, don't you think?"

"Of course," I replied, though I couldn't resist capturing the moment. I quickly snapped a photo of Rock in our living room, and then we made our way to his car, heading to the Rusty Pelican for what would surely be a memorable evening.

Pushed Out of the Closet Without A Parachute

We drove off for a short drive to Newport Beach and the Rusty Pelican. With spectacular, breathtaking waterfront views of Newport Bay and an eclectic menu of fresh seafood and tender steaks, it's no wonder Rusty Pelican became one of Rock's favorite places when he lived in Newport Beach. He also mentioned the late-night upstairs lounge, but I would have to pass on that tonight seeing that I had a busy week and another early morning schedule.

Our time at the Rusty Pelican was nothing short of delightful. We relished in each other's company, enjoying good food and drinks and endless conversation that seemed to stretch for hours. Laughter filled the air as I shared some of my silliest and dirtiest jokes with Rock, discovering how much fun he was to be around.

Rock opened up about his relationship with Marc Christian, admitting they were going through a rough patch. He shared how they met at the Sports Connection in Hollywood and how he was initially looking for a walking partner. As our conversation deepened, Rock revealed a vulnerable side, recounting his health scare in 1981 when he underwent open-heart bypass surgery, facing the potential of a fatal heart problem.

As Rock and I continued to chat, I found an opportunity to share my experiences as a fitness instructor and manager at Bay City Health Club in Surfside while attending Long Beach State. Working there also allowed me to run the aerobics program and teach classes, which I passionately juggled alongside my school schedule. Given his smoking and drinking habits, I felt, explaining the concept of aerobics and its overall fitness benefits might be helpful for Rock.

Rock seemed intrigued when I offered to take him through a beginner's aerobics class, and I could see genuine interest in his eyes. As we delved into our stories, I couldn't resist recounting my singing tour experience in Australia and New Zealand. I detailed how on a "free day," when we had no concert or rehearsal, I went out at a local Health Club and by chance met the owner. I mentioned that I had worked in various health clubs back in California to support myself during college and had become a popular aerobics instructor.

The manager was utterly captivated by the concept of aerobics. He couldn't contain his enthusiasm and urged me to demonstrate a class, which, in a serendipitous turn of events, led to a television appearance with over a hundred eager participants. My demonstrations impressed the manager, and he extended an extraordinary opportunity—an invitation to spearhead and oversee their aerobics program across Australia.

As exhilarating as this offer was, fate had other plans. Regrettably, I had to decline the proposition graciously and remain rooted in America due to circumstances beyond my control.

In the course of our conversation, it became increasingly evident that Rock and I shared more common ground than I had initially imagined. Our life stories wove together, taking unexpected twists and turns that ultimately shaped the individuals we had become. As we exchanged laughter and shared our experiences, an unspoken understanding seemed to develop, blurring the boundary that often separates celebrities from genuine friends.

Since Rock had opened up about his relationship with Marc Christian, I briefly mentioned that I, too, was seeing someone romantically, but I withheld the person's identity. Like Rock, my romantic interest was going through a rough patch—a divorce. However, unlike Rock, he had a young son and was going through a nasty custody battle, requiring us both to be discreet about our relationship.

As our conversation progressed, we unearthed unexpected commonalities, bridging the gap between our differences. With every passing moment, our friendship deepened, and I cherished the genuine and caring friend I had discovered in Rock.

If not for my early work schedule the next day, I would have gladly stayed out longer and enjoyed a nightcap with Rock. However, I was concerned that if he drank any more, he might not be able to drive home safely. We decided to call it a night, and Rock dropped me off at The Portofino.

On our way back, Rock had asked an interesting question: Had I ever slept with my roommate Pat? I didn't know what he was getting at, but I decided to be honest and told him that Pat and I were only roommates and that he was too old for me. I added that I usually preferred younger, blonde men. It was a moment of spontaneity, and I hoped my words hadn't offended Rock.

Trying to salvage the situation, I quickly followed my statement: "Now, I wouldn't sleep with someone I was living with unless we were in a monogamous relationship. Call me old-fashioned, but if I'm going to live with someone that way, we might as well get married, or at least sign up for a domestic partnership." I chuckled, hoping my attempt at humor would ease any tension.

Despite my candid response, Rock remained composed and replied, "Well, you've got a point there, Gunther." I was relieved that he didn't seem offended and that our friendship remained intact. We bid each other goodnight, grateful for our meaningful and enjoyable evening.

I stood in the parking lot at the bottom of my building, waving to Rock as he drove off. Before he left, I asked him to call me quickly to let me know when he made it home okay. I took the stairs up to the fifth floor, and as I walked into the condo, Pat and my good friend Philip were there, looking like parents waiting for me to return from my first date.

They bombarded me with questions, eager to hear all the "deets"—details in Phil-Speak.

"I never kiss and tell boys, so don't get your panties too tied up," I teased. "We had a nice evening and became better acquainted. That's all there is to it. I'm not sure what you're doing here, Phil, but we both have an early morning, and I don't know about you, but tonight I need a good night's sleep."

Pat chimed in, "Oh, Phil stopped by a while ago, thinking that you'd already be home, so I told him to come in and wait. I'm glad you had a nice time. I'm heading to bed as well. Good night."

With his hands in the air, Phil jokingly said, "I don't have to be asked twice. I know when I'm not wanted and when to get out of Dodge! We'll continue this conversation in the morning. We're both working on the same event, and I already looked up next week's schedule. Sleep tight, and don't let the bed bugs bite! I'll see ya at 7:30!"

With that, Phil made his exit, leaving me to finally wind down and reflect on the memorable evening I had spent with Rock. As I prepared for bed, I felt a sense of contentment and excitement for the friendship blossoming between Rock and me. Little did I know that this encounter would mark the beginning of an extraordinary journey with a Hollywood legend.

Chapter 4: The Kiss

The Rusty Pelican dinner marked the inception of many a rendezvous—a dance between Rock's visits to Long Beach and my drives to his Hollywood Beach stomping grounds. The ebb and flow of these encounters largely remained uneventful, but a handful stand as passionate brushstrokes, shaping the canvas of our blossoming friendship. However, before I paint those vibrant scenes, we must address the looming elephant in the room—the moment that laid bare the path we were destined to tread, one of treasured comradeship rather than romantic entanglement.

Instead of recounting every detail of a Friday night dinner at Long Beach's El Torrito Restaurant that followed my Rusty Pelican adventure, let me share with you the way I revealed it to my trusted friend, Phil. Picture the tale unfolding as a living conversation, filled with gasps of astonishment punctuated by Phil's lively reactions.

The morning that followed Rock and my El Torrito adventure. It was a precious Saturday when time seemed to relent in its grip, granting us a momentary escape from life's ceaseless demands. A full day off from work! It allowed me to powwow with Phil and give him his "deets" as I knew he would demand.

As the clock's hands pointed to 9:30 on that Saturday morning, sleep remained a distant companion, yielding to the rhythm of a day that had begun hours before. This was my designated day of respite, yet even in the absence of apparent obligations, my mind was entangled in the previous night's memories. Determined to break free from this cycle of thoughts, I reached for the phone and dialed up my old friend and fellow worker, Phil, a familiar voice I yearned to hear. The anticipation was tinged with good luck as I discovered that Phil, too, had been granted an unexpected day off from his usual endeavors.

"How about 8th Place Beach before the heat and hordes descend? Then, a leisurely late brunch at the Paradise Café?" I suggested, envisioning a perfect day.

Phil's reply was swift and unequivocal, laced with his trademark dry wit: "Did you really have to ask? You're like a mind-reader. Consider me onboard, and make sure your Hollywood adventures are primed and ready to spill!"

At 10:30 A.M., we sealed our meeting time, granting me the brief indulgence of a brisk shower and a hastily whirred smoothie. Opting for the bicycle was a decision with dual merit—a salute to conserve gas and a gleeful evasion of the automotive scavenger hunt masquerading as parking.

An ingenious stratagem, if I do say so myself. This could ensure I would outpace Phil's arrival despite his abode being tantalizingly closer to the sandy haven. This little-known gem, the 8th Place Beach, occasionally called Cherry or Junipero Beach by the uninitiated, reclined discreetly rightward from the hubbub of the famous stretch. Its quiet allure was crowned by the thoughtful addition of onsite restrooms and a lifeguard tower, a secret shared among the locals.

Pushed Out of the Closet Without A Parachute

This shoreline was more than a beach. It was an enclave, an unwritten destination for the LGBT community that gave it more privacy. An alternative universe, if you will, an escape hatch from the typical trappings of daily life. Belmont Shores, near Ripples, a popular dance club, attracted a larger gay crowd, but is often adorned by way too many, what Phil affectionately termed as "Twinkies" and "Cha Cha queens." 8th Place Beach was perfect for an uninterrupted conversation. It was tucked away from the grand stage, offering an ideal ambiance for an uninterrupted tête-à-tête.

After our heart-to-heart, Phil and I would indulge in a leisurely stroll along the coastline, a ritual culminating with a short ascent to Broadway. Guided by the promise of sustenance at the incredible Paradise Café, we would feast upon food and conversation, replenishing our reserves for the ensuing day.

However, before we surrendered back to the sun and beach, we'd make one last stop in Phil's playbook—the Mineshaft, a time-honored haunt that had acquired a particular corner in his heart. A glass of well-earned ale or two and a game of pool, I speculated, for after spending considerable time in Phil's vivacious company... a sip of something soothing was bound to become a necessity.

To my astonishment, the beach greeted me with a sight that could only be Phil's creation. He had outshone the sun with his pink oversized sunglasses, his beach towel billowing like a flamboyant flag of his presence. "Well, well, well, if it isn't Phil the Fabulous," I exclaimed, unable to stifle my grin. "Did you teleport here the moment I mentioned a beach day? Walk or auto?"

Phil's response, a perfect fusion of theatrics and wit, echoed across the sand. "Oh, Guntha, Darlin', no need to get your knickers in a twist. I channeled my inner you and pedaled down like the wind."

I paused for effect, my eyes narrowing in mock suspicion. "Wait a minute! That bike over there, adorned with pink streamers? It practically dances in a disco-like sway with the ocean breeze—even when standing still. That's your masterpiece, isn't it?

"I'm guilty as charged," declared Phil, fully embracing his role as a bicycle Diva. His hands came alive with an enthusiasm that could give a Broadway performance a run for its money. If he were in the water, I'm sure even the vigilant lifeguard would've dashed to his rescue, convinced he was in the grip of an epileptic seizure.

As he settled into a more controlled cadence of hand gestures, I eased into the sand beside him. Without skipping a beat, he fired off, "All right, spill the beans, Guntha. Lay it all out—the Rock saga, your flirtations with Hollywood, the crescendo of your music career. Don't hold back."

I couldn't suppress my chuckles at his rambunctiousness. "So, where should I start this narrative? These past few weeks have been a whirlwind, Phil. I swear, I could fashion a novella from all that's unfolded!" His eyes shimmered with an eager spark, though a hint of restlessness tinged his anticipation.

Pushed Out of the Closet Without A Parachute

He had been a part of the journey from the beginning. He was present the night we first crossed paths, privy to my debut performance and the West Hollywood soirée at Dean's house and in the loop about my escapades at the Rusty Pelican. However, the subsequent chapter of this culinary adventure remained an undiscovered realm for him.

An essential chapter lay shrouded, waiting for his discovery. The kiss I shared with Rock Hudson and its aftermath were certain to trigger Phil's characteristic reaction. I could already imagine his arm-flailing, shoulder-raising, eye-sparkling, and hat-tilting extravaganza—a spectacle that only he could orchestrate with such dramatic flair.

Phil urged me, "Pick up from where we left off—after your Rusty Pelican dinner with Rock. I'm practically on the edge of my seat to hear what transpired next." Sensing Phil's eagerness, I attempted to temper his excitement, suspecting that the unfolding tale might not match his anticipated scenario. Opting for a concise retelling, I aimed to shed light on the subsequent days with a touch of clarity.

"Rock called me and proposed another dinner in Long Beach," I recounted. "He left the choice of venue to me, but as you know, I'm not much of a foodie. I told Phil I was considering options like El Torrito in the Marketplace Long Beach or Panama Joe's in Belmont Shores. We settled on El Torrito since he was familiar with it. Dinner commenced, but the experience took an unexpected turn when some restaurant patrons recognized Rock."

Pushed Out of the Closet Without A Parachute

Phil was on the edge of his towel as I continued, "Rock displayed his finesse, summoning the manager and discreetly requesting a more private restaurant section. The staff obliged, granting us refuge from prying eyes and clamoring fans. In our newfound sanctuary, we savored a tranquil dinner, free from unwarranted interruptions. As our conversation flowed, I confided in Rock about the guy I had been recently seeing, candidly revealing that our relationship had hit an unexpected plateau."

Phil, exasperated, interjected, "Oh really... What was Rock's reaction?"

With a subtle smirk, I responded, "Rock's response was remarkably empathetic. I laid bare that the person I'd been seeing preferred to keep their identity hidden—a case of concealed feelings if you will. Following that disclosure, I opened up about my acquaintance and how he was embroiled in a custody battle over his young son. As fate would have it, I had the opportunity to meet the boy in person. The three of us—my friend, his son, and I—embarked on an adventure to Knott's Berry Farm not long ago. His boy is quite an endearing child, but the situation surrounding my friend was anything but charming."

"It struck me that the turbulent waters he was trying to navigate were well beyond my ability to calm. When I recounted my meetings with Rock Hudson and my performance at his event, my friend's reaction erupted like a volcano. Accusations were flung, transforming my artistic aspirations into battlefields, and he even insinuated that there were romantic designs between Rock and me."

Phil's eyebrows shot up in disbelief. "What on earth was he thinking? My goodness, he has no claim over you!"

"Get ready for this," I chuckled. "After my friend let loose a hurricane of emotional upheaval, igniting a melodrama that felt a bit exaggerated given the brevity of our relationship. It hit me that the drama scale was tipping alarmingly for the relatively short time we'd been dating. So, I confronted the situation head-on, expressing my genuine care for him but pointing out how the intensity and complexity were becoming overwhelming. I also apologized, recognizing the immense challenges he was grappling with during this period."

With Phil's curiosity piqued, he asked, "And then what happened?"

I suggested that we step back and reestablish our friendship, especially until he manages to untangle the intricate threads of his son's custody situation. I told him, "Who knows, maybe down the road, when things have settled, we can reconsider being more than just friends."

Phil let out a sigh that seemed to carry the weight of the world, "Well, Guntha, it appears you've stumbled right into a pot of boyfriend drama. I must confess, I'm practically perched on pins and needles to find out how this chapter of your tale comes to a close."

I shot him a wry grin, "As fate would have it, my dear Phil, there's a twist in this narrative. Following our dinner escapade, Rock decided to swing by my humble abode, though he opted to stay in the comfort of his car."

A hint of confusion danced in Phil's eyes, his voice edged with anticipation, "And do tell, why did he choose not to come up for a nightcap or some other indulgence?"

Ah, the unmistakable tinge of anticipation lingered in Phil's voice, yet it was time to peel back the curtain and reveal the heart of the matter. "Allow me to clarify and set the stage for you, Phil. Both Rock and I arrived at El Torrito in our respective vehicles, and given the Portofino's proximity, Rock entertained the notion of a brief stopover. Once we got to the Portofino parking lot, I exited La Bomba. I stole a glance at Rock, comfortably stationed in his Mercedes. With a subtle nod, he silently beckoned me over. Settling into the passenger seat, I caught a glimpse of Rock's uncertainty, a hesitation that unraveled his yearning for a more private exchange. You see, he inquired about the whereabouts of my roommate, Pat. Then upon learning that Pat was indeed home, Rock's reluctance to ascend revealed his thirst for an intimate conversation."

And then Rock's voice became more serious, though very sincere. "This evening, being in your company was a true pleasure— a welcomed escape from the turbulence I've been facing due to Marc Christian's influence on my life. But while I sat there, absorbed in your words about the man you're involved with, a singular realization struck me as I gazed at you: You wouldn't know love even if it were right in front of you." He bridged the distance between us with a determined tug, initiating a kiss so emotional and compelling that it left an indelible mark on my memory.

By now, Phil was on the edge of his seat, trembling with apprehension. "Holy Cow! What happened next? Tell me, hurry before I wet my pants in anticipation!"

"Phil, the kiss was an eruption of fervor, a fierce exchange that paradoxically bore an uncanny touch of familiarity. Almost as swiftly as our lips found release, Rock's voice, rife with curiosity, ventured, 'How did that feel to you?'"

A sly smile tugged at my lips as I mirrored his question, "Wait, you first, Rock. How did that moment feel to you?"

His response flowed without hesitation, "It felt as though I was embracing a family member—like I was kissing a brother or a sister. Tender, undoubtedly, yet lacking any sparks that ignite profound connections."

Echoing his sentiment, I unveiled my truth, "Indeed, Rock, that's exactly how it felt to me!

Following the path my heart laid bare, I poured out the depth of my emotions. "Rock, I hold you in the highest esteem, yet even the hint of romance remains elusive, like a distant dream. Understand, my admiration is bathed in genuine camaraderie; it's the treasure of our heartfelt bond that I hold dear. You transcend the role of a mentor; you are like a brother I've never had, a confidant and guide I've yearned for. Our conversations traversed the landscapes of life, love, and the elusive pursuit of happiness—dialogues my father and I were destined to remain strangers to."

"Rock, the object of my desire, remains a profound friendship. While I embrace you close within the haven of my heart, stepping into the realm of physicality could, perhaps, unravel the friendship we've woven. And truth be told, I don't see the possibility of romance ever blooming. Can you fathom such a notion? Does that make any sense, or does it paint me a complete fool?"

Rock appeared somewhat reserved initially, but the floodgates of his thoughts opened as he continued, "Gunther if I'm truly being honest with myself and with you, I must admit that I am drawn to you for a reason beyond physical attraction. I find solace in your presence, a reprieve from all the shit going on in my life.

You see, the situation with Marc has spiraled to an intolerable point. I'm at my wit's end, grappling with the challenge of extricating him from my home and my life. I made an egregious error when I allowed him to move in while I was away in Israel filming 'Ambassador.' Marc had initially told me he could organize my music collection and transfer albums onto tapes for analog preservation while I was gone. He had been staying at an older girlfriend's place, sleeping on her couch, and I thought little harm could come of it. Alas, my judgment was clouded.

Now, I want to be clear, Gunther. Initially, I found myself utterly captivated by your presence. But as our connection deepened,

I began to perceive the potential for something more profound that I hoped would turn into romance. Then and there I made it my mission to win your heart, my intentions perhaps skewed. Yet, as fate would have it, my intuition proved me wrong, and here we stand, at the precipice of this profound moment."

Initially, a sense of uneasiness held me back from saying too much. Having deflected Rock's romantic overture, I feared my words might be misconstrued, overshadowing my genuine care for him. Yet, his revelations shifted my perspective drastically, sparking curiosity and anger towards this Marc Christian figure. Despite never having met the man, the details Rock divulged painted a clear picture of his manipulative grip. Sensing Rock's unease, a nagging suspicion that Marc Christian threatened him spurred me to address the matter directly. With candor, I posed the question that lingered, "Rock, what hold does Marc have over you that prevents you from simply showing him the door?"

Rock's eyes took on an aura of painful sorrow. His gaze clouded with the weight of his emotions. He shook his head slightly, a struggle evident in his attempt to voice the words that had long been suppressed. "Marc threatened me in a way that has caused me to fear him," he continued, his voice heavy with the burden of the truth. "He threatened to expose my being gay, to use the National Enquirer as a weapon against me, revealing my secret to the world. I honestly feel trapped, unable to escape his coercive hold."

Pushed Out of the Closet Without A Parachute

Rock's pain was evident as he explained, "Initially, I did try to cultivate a genuine romantic connection with Marc, believing there was something there. But I was oblivious to his manipulative ways. Unfortunately, it took a while to recognize that I was being played." With a heavy sigh, Rock continued, "I grappled with a sense of emptiness after my previous relationship with Tom Clark had disintegrated. Time had eroded our bond, transforming us into different individuals. I opened my heart to the wrong person, and now I'm caught in a dreadful predicament."

My heart ached for Rock, and I grappled with the need to provide Rock with some form of solace amidst his evident agony. I understood that simply lending an empathetic ear might be the most immediate way to support him. At that moment, I ventured, "It sounds like Marc's motives might involve financial gain or an attempt to use your name to elevate his significance and notoriety. Have you considered seeking the assistance of a private investigator? Alternatively, could a settlement in the form of a legally binding agreement that secures his silence be a viable option?"

Rock appeared to grow more distressed, and I regretted causing him any further discomfort. I quickly backpedaled, saying, "Rock, forget I asked you that. It's your business, and I'm here to support you however possible. I understand why you often refer to Marc as 'What's his name.' He's nothing but a thorn in your side, and please, don't beat yourself up over this. You were taken advantage of, and I've been through similar situations. Once a viable solution reveals itself, you'll be able to put an end to this nightmare. I do think it's wise to keep a close eye on his behavior and activities, especially within your home."

Rock shared with me, "I do have staff members in my home who keep an eye on his activities. My butler, James, keeps me informed about everything, and my good friend and secretary, Mark Miller, operates his office from my house to monitor the situation. However, Marc still manages to come and go as he pleases, leaving us uncertain about his actions and intentions. This entire ordeal has shaken me to my core. I'd rather not dwell on it, which is why having you around has been a perfect distraction. Our time together is filled with joy and laughter, and I truly appreciate your talents—your songs, jokes, and most importantly, your friendship."

Phil's initial concern for my romantic escapades had transformed into a profound symphony of empathy for Rock's turbulent circumstances. With a wink and a nod, I underscored the hushed nature of my revelations. "Now, Phil, rest assured that the words I'm sharing about Rock are tucked away in the vault of confidentiality, my friend." Phil's nod resembled the sage agreement of two trusted confidants.

I leaned in and whispered to him, "I know this isn't quite the swoon-worthy tale you might have anticipated, but as they say, 'what doesn't break you makes you stronger.' Despite gracefully sidestepping Rock's amorous advances, I made sure to serenade him with the notes of my unwavering support and affection. My connection has evolved into something akin to having a cherished older sibling"

Phil's expression appeared as if he had momentarily slipped into a state of frozen astonishment, a momentary pause that might lead one to believe he had been ensnared by a curious sort of comatose state. Undeterred by his momentary stillness, I pressed forward with my tale, hoping to reanimate his features before any unintentional blueness could emerge.

"You see, my dear Phil," I reassured, "Rock and my bond was as clear as the sunlit sky. No ambiguity, no hidden agendas; we had flung wide open the door to a mutual recognition that Rock and I were destined to stand as steadfast comrades. And there's no flaw in that realization. In truth, it's a far more profound outcome than succumbing to the clichéd temptations that often pepper the landscape of the gay world. Authentic friendship—now that's a rarity worth treasuring. In our shared revelation, we both relish this newly discovered understanding, eagerly embracing the prospect of delving into even deeper realms of soulful connection."

Poor, Phil's dreams were thwarted as his imagination of conjuring a veritable fairy tale love story that could rival the most extravagant romantic novels had been tragically halted in its tracks. The vision of his dearest friend entwined in the arms of the iconic, rugged Rock Hudson—the embodiment of divine masculinity, a heartthrob immortalized on countless posters—forever vanquished. For Phil, this was the closest he had ever come to witnessing the metamorphosis of a cherished friendship into an intimate connection with the illustrious Mr. Perfect. Yet, as the narrative unfurled, the missing puzzle piece became painfully evident: the absence of that electric chemistry that sparks the flames of passion.

I told Phil, "Friendship is the better outcome! You see, in the realm of romance, without the flicker of chemistry, relationships often rest on the precarious foundation of other motivation. Some veer toward the path of those who employ connections for personal gain. The world is abundant with tales of affluent trophy spouses and companions—a testament to the transactional underbelly of certain liaisons. However, even in acquiring their desires, a hefty price is extracted: self-respect and self-worth are bartered away, the compromise to endure another's presence in exchange for status, wealth, or even a sliver of stardom.

Another impetus driving individuals into the arms of a partner is societal expectationsThe weight of family and friends presses upon some souls, urging them towards marital unions that aren't born of passion but rather a sense of duty. Matches that aren't born of passion but rather a prescribed narrative usually don't end well. Alas, both these pathways often lead to a life teeming with unhappiness, where the absence of love or chemistry cultivates an environment ripe for toxicity and discontent. It is no wonder that more than half of all marriages end in divorce."

I held no doubt that Phil, a perpetual optimist and a fervent supporter of faith, would swiftly rebound from his momentary melancholy and wholeheartedly celebrate my being okay as just Rock's friend instead of his lover. It was as if he'd witnessed a light bulb spring to life above his head, illuminating the profound truth that friendship itself can be a delectable feast. And when you blend the intricate dynamics of friendship with the hues of love, my dear friend, that's when you uncover the true treasure.

As the gears turned in Phil's head, I almost heard the cogs creaking as he muttered, "If that had been a snake, I'd be nursing a bite by now." The proverbial penny had dropped for Phil. However, I had a sneaky suspicion that an Alabama Slammer cocktail might add that extra zest to seal the deal, forever relinquishing his covert dreams of a romantic tryst with the chiseled deity, Rock.

And so, we left the sanctuary of our beach towels to embark on a stroll along the shoreline. True to his nature, Phil wasted no time transitioning into the role of a matchmaker. Just like a yenta, he eagerly pointed out potential matches for me on the beach.

"Oh, Guntha, feast your eyes on that strapping lad engrossed in a game of beach volleyball. He's looking at you like a thirsty traveler spotting an oasis."

I playfully gave him a stink eye before replying, "Oh, Phil, some things never change, and I'm thankful for that. But enough about dessert; how about we first savor lunch at the Paradise Café? Would that tickle you fancy?"

Chapter 5: Dean's Oscar Party

    Ah, it was that magical time of year, and on the 9th of April, what else could it possibly be but the 56th Academy Awards ceremony? You guessed it right. In 1984, the esteemed honor of presenting the Best Actress Award fell into none other than Rock Hudson's lap, joined by the fabulous Liza Minnelli, no less. It was Hollywood, and my friend Dean Dittman was at it again, throwing another of his legendary parties, as customary as Californian sunshine. Just nine days before, I had received my golden ticket and a special request to bring my trusty guitar along for the ride.

    Stepping into Dean's apartment was like diving headfirst into a whirlpool of party spirit. I scanned the room, eagerly searching for Rock, but Dean intercepted me with a warm but hurried bear hug. He was a man on a mission, scuttling about to ensure everything was just so.

    I offered assistance, but he playfully shooed me away, exclaiming, "No, no, Gunther, I've got it all under control. By the way, Rock's fashionably late. He'll swing by once he's all 'Tuxed Out,' we've timed his limo pick-up to perfection, synchronized with Liza Minnelli's arrival. They'll be strutting down the red carpet together, and I've got the TV tuned to the pre-Oscar coverage so we can all bask in his grand entrance! Now, you know where everything is, so feel at home. Drop your guitar in my bedroom, as we've got quite a few folks clamoring for an encore performance of 'The Whale Song' once Rock returns triumphant from the Oscars."

As I perused the familiar faces in the room, I couldn't help but notice a few partygoers who had graced us with their presence just the week before. And lo and behold, there was Dody Goodman, making a return appearance. The moment our eyes locked, she beamed and made a beeline for me.

"Why, hello there, Gunther! I'm delighted to see you again," Dody exclaimed. "I must tell you once more how much I enjoyed your singing last week, and I'm hoping you'll grace us with another performance tonight!"

Grateful for her warm words, I replied, "It would be my pleasure, Dody. Accordingly, I brought my trusty guitar just for that very reason. Now, Dody, I must say, I adored your performance in 'Splash.' You were positively hysterical! How was it working with Tom Hanks and Daryl Hannah?"

Dody's eyes sparkled with excitement as she reminisced, "Oh, both Tom and Daryl were an absolute delight to work with. It was a fantastic opportunity, and we had such a blast making that movie. But, Gunther, do you also dabble in acting?"

I chuckled and replied, "Oh, no, Dody. I've got a terrible case of stage fright, and I'm dyslexic, to boot. I'd probably end up reciting my lines backwards or something!"

We both shared a hearty laugh, and Dody leaned in, her words glowing sincerely. "You know, Gunther, I have a feeling you'd be marvelous at acting. The way you sing the 'Whale Song' with such passion... You would light up the screen!"

By then, my cheeks were blazing crimson, and I could feel the warmth in my face. "Well, for now, Dody, I think I'll stick to singing," I replied with a sheepish grin. Perhaps, if I succeed, I might give acting a whirl," I said with a hint of playful optimism.

Rock made his grand entrance, dressed to the nines in his stunning tuxedo attire. He headed straight in my direction to greet me. "Hey, Gunther," he said with a warm smile. "I'll only be here for a few minutes. I need to meet with Liza, but make sure you stick around for the after-party. I've got a surprise for you."

I nodded, fully intending to stay as long as I could. Unlike the previous weekend's escapades that had me up until 3 in the morning, I wanted to get some rest before my morning shift at the Hyatt Regency. So, I leaned in and whispered, "Rock, I'll probably need to take off around 1 AM"

Rock, however, was already busy greeting guests. Before he could go through the apartment, he announced, "All right, everyone, I'm off to pick up Liza. Once we've given out that Best Actress award, I'll be back with all the juicy backstage stories. Don't go anywhere!"

As the evening unfurled, guests mingled throughout the apartment with anticipation. A few had already crouched down in front of the television, poised for a night of glamour and glitz as Hollywood's brightest stars and nominees embarked on their iconic march down the legendary red carpet, all in anticipation of the 56th Academy Awards at the Dorothy Chandler Pavilion in Los Angeles.

You know, I've always been an ardent devotee of the Oscars. I've even been known to throw my own soirées, complete with mock Oscars bestowed upon those with the most astute predictions of the evening's victors. But this year, a different tune played. My days in 1983 were too consumed by classes and my senior recital, the final crescendo of my academic donning my cap and gown for graduation. And, now here in 1984, I was at one of the actual Oscar after-parties!

I had the pleasure of catching a few flicks, and out of the cinematic tapestry of 1983, "Terms of Endearment" was the masterpiece that struck a chord with me. Naturally, I was fervently hoping it would sweep the night, clinching the lion's share of Oscars. Imagine the sheer delight if Rock could be the one to bestow the Best Actress award upon Shirley MacLaine. With bated breath and fingers crossed, I nestled in to savor the unfolding spectacle.

Surrounded by buzzing excitement in the apartment, I, regrettably, missed the grandeur of the red carpet entrance. Nevertheless, a hush descended upon the room as Rock Hudson and Liza Minnelli graced the podium with their presence. As they descended the magnificent golden staircase onto the stage at the Dorothy Chandler Pavilion, Rock's towering height became evident, bestowing upon him a remarkable and imposing stature. Liza, dazzling in her enchanting purple gown, could barely reach the level of Rock's broad shoulders. Yet, together, they formed a captivating and dynamic pair, with Rock effortlessly radiating authentic professionalism, even when faced with the occasional hiccup, his natural spontaneity shined through.

He commenced with a witty quip, jesting, "There was nothing easy, except maybe reading these cards..." before seamlessly segueing into the scripted words on his teleprompter, which proclaimed, "Nothing easy about awarding an Oscar. Nothing easy about making a decision regarding five superb actresses." Together, they eloquently announced the nominees for the year: Jane Alexander for "Testament," Shirley MacLaine for "Terms of Endearment," Meryl Streep for "Silkwood," Julie Walters for "Educating Rita," and Debra Winger, also for "Terms of Endearment." The envelope was ceremoniously opened, revealing Shirley MacLaine as the triumphant victor! The room erupted with excitement, and we all agreed that Shirley's acceptance speech was one for the ages. It wasn't a rehearsed monologue but a genuine, from-the-heart, witty, and profoundly heartfelt moment.

Terms of Endearment won five awards, including Best Picture, Best Director, Best Supporting Actor for Jack Nicholson, Best Screenplay based on Material from Another Medium, and, of course, Shirley MacLaine's Best Actress.

Rock made a beeline back home right after the awards concluded, and I couldn't help but marvel at his swiftness. As the Oscars show came to its grand finale, a good portion of the crowd bid their adieus. It later transpired that most of the unfamiliar faces were fellow dwellers of Dean's apartment complex. Consequently, only a modest gathering lingered in the living room, eager to savor the juicy tidbits of information Rock had in store for us.

Dean didn't waste a second and asked the first question. His curiosity piqued: "So, how was Liza tonight? She looked absolutely stunning, but I couldn't help but notice her eyes seemed a bit, well, fuzzy." Rock's revelation sent a collective gasp rippling through the room, like a gust of Santa Ana wind sweeping through the Hollywood Hills. We were all captivated by the insider drama unfolding before us.

Rock shook his head as he started to divulge, a hint of surprise twinkling in his eyes as he began to unveil the evening's backstage secrets, "Let me tell you, Dean, Liza was floating like a kite the entire time. Meanwhile, I had to play guardian angel on the red carpet, fearing she might stumble into the Hollywood abyss. She popped a few pills in the limo, and who knows what else before that? It's a miracle we managed to present the award to Shirley without any crash landings. Shirley, on the other hand, was her usual stellar self—consummate professionalism at its finest. Ah, Liza, bless her heart; she has a lot of love, but she needs some professional help."

Rock's narrative continued, "Honestly, I was so entangled babysitting Liza that I barely had time to exchange more than a few pleasantries. We managed a few quick interviews, then were hurriedly whisked to our designated seats. The entire evening was plagued by a frantic scramble to make up for lost time as if they were trying to

Pushed Out of the Closet Without A Parachute

squeeze a full-length feature into a short film slot. The major awards, the crown jewels of the Oscars, like Best Actor, Best Actress, and Best Picture, were given mere moments in the spotlight. Johnny Carson valiantly tried to put a polished veneer on it, but beneath the surface, it was far from the elegant spectacle you'd envision."

I chimed in with my two cents, "Now, I must admit, while I haven't graced the Oscars with my presence, I once managed to snag a backstage pass to the rehearsals back in 1981. That was the very year they had to postpone the Oscars due to the shocking attempt on President Reagan's life. Every second was meticulously choreographed during those rehearsals, fitting snugly within the allotted timeframes. I had the pleasure of watching Dolly Parton rehearse '9 to 5' alongside her impeccable troupe of dancers. Dolly was the epitome of professionalism, and I even had the privilege of chatting with her afterward. I was truly impressed by her sincerity and wit."

"However," I continued, "Irene Cara was a different story. Much like Liza, she seemed to have taken a flight of her own. Irene was practically floating on her very own celestial cloud during those rehearsals, and remember, we're talking about rehearsals here. I can only imagine what she was like under the pressure of an actual performance. Yet, Irene ultimately triumphed with the Best Song award for '*Fame*,' and again tonight for *'Flashdance... What a Feeling.'* Sometimes, it seems winning has little to do with professionalism and everything to do with how the public, or in this case, the Academy perceives you on the screen. There could be thousands of feet of retakes on the cutting-room floor, but the audience remains blissfully unaware of the behind-the-scenes journey."

Rock displayed genuine interest in my encounter and remarked, "Well, Gunther, I've never had the pleasure of attending an Oscar rehearsal myself. As presenters, we're simply instructed to arrive at a specified time, and if any unexpected delays occur during the live show, we're left waiting in the wings. So, please share what a rehearsal is like and how you managed to chat with both Dolly and Irene."

"Well, folks, you're in for quite a long story, so I hope y'all don't mind if I spin the whole tale," I quipped, sensing eager anticipation from my audience.

Rock, the picture of intrigue, leaned in with interest while Dean chimed in with a hearty, "Please, do tell us everything."

"All right then, let me take you on a journey of pure chance, the kind that makes you believe in fate or maybe just knowing the right folks at the right time," I began, pondering where to dive in. "Rock, remember when I mentioned co-writing and co-starring in the musical I co-wrote back in 1981?" A nod from Rock confirmed his recollection.

"Right, so there we were, knee-deep in rehearsals for our little musical extravaganza, 'Goin' Out in Style,' and let me tell ya, we were running dry on flashy dance moves for our grand finale. Now, you remember Vince, the gospel pianist and singer I told you about. He's the one who roped me into this gig in the first place." I paused to set the stage. "Well, Vince had a buddy, a professional dancer named Randy. Now, names usually have a way of slipping my mind, especially when it comes to folks I met eons ago or just the other day at your fabulous shindig," I confessed, prompting chuckles all around.

"Anyhow, Vince gave Randy a call, and Randy had this genius notion to invite us to watch him rehearse for the Oscars, figuring we might pick up a step or two. To sweeten the deal, Randy rustled up some backstage passes, and we found ourselves as the sole members of the audience in the illustrious Dorothy Chandler Pavilion. We started by watching Dolly and her crew rehearse their toe-tapping number, '9 to 5'. When the dance troupe took a well-deserved 15-minute break, Randy whisked us away backstage, where all the dressing rooms were. Right then and there, just as if by magic, the one and only Dolly Parton sauntered down the hall with her lively entourage."

"Dolly, her signature charm dripping like honey, cast her sparkling blue eyes my way and asked, 'You're not one of my dancers, are you? I don't remember hirin' somebody as tall as you for my number.'"

"Now, I responded with a tad bit of surprise, 'Well, no, Miss Parton, I'm Gunther. I'm here with Vince, who happens to be friends with one of your dancers, Randy. Randy's kindly helping us with the choreography for a musical we've cooked up, and we've got some of the finest high school talent in all of Los Angeles County.'"

"Dolly, bless her heart, insisted, 'Now, don't be so formal, sugar. Just call me Dolly. It's mighty fine to meet y'all. I was just a teensy bit worried, you see, 'cause I couldn't recall hirin' a fella as tall as you. I reckon I don't even have a wig tall enough to dance with a chap like yourself.'"

"With a chuckle, I replied, 'Well, Miss Dolly, I surely wouldn't want to throw your whole act out of whack with my towering presence. I'd stick out like a giant sore thumb.'"

"Dolly let loose one of her trademark laughs, as sweet and genuine as Tennessee Moon Pie. 'Oh, sugar, I reckon you'd do just fine. Good luck with your musical darlin'. Right now, I've gotta get these poor feet out of these heels. They're murderin' me.'"

"In the wake of our enchanting rendezvous with the one and only Dolly Parton, our paths diverged, with Randy leading the way to the hallowed sanctuary of the dancer's dressing room. Ah, Randy, quite the charmer, yearning for a swift change into fresh attire, even if it meant donning a different leotard later. As the other dancers gathered around, their curiosity piqued by the whispers of the musical we were crafting, I couldn't help but be amazed that we had ignited their interest.

Intrigued, they had a thirst for a sample of our creation! They didn't need to ask Vince or me twice. News spread like wildfire of a piano tucked away in the lobby, and like a pied piper, we led the troupe there. The entire ensemble of Oscar's most nimble dancers followed suit, their reflections mirroring their enthusiasm in the lobby's glass, yet all doors leading outside remained stubbornly locked.

Then, seemingly guided by divine intervention, Vince's agile fingers graced the piano keys. He was a virtuoso, equally at ease with the language of jazz and R&B. The introductory chords exuded a sultry allure, and our harmonies melded seamlessly. As the initial notes reverberated through the lobby, an electric surge coursed through the assembled dancers.

In an instant, the room transformed into a stage, a canvas upon which their choreographic brilliance unfurled. Pirouettes whirled with the grace of dervishes, leaps defied gravity, arabesques and attitudes painted the air with a symphony of limbs, and adagio lifts and dips punctuated the performance. It was as though Bob Fosse himself had descended from celestial heights to choreograph this impromptu spectacle.

At that mesmeric moment, I couldn't escape the feeling that I was an integral part of this divine reverie. Our music and lyrics, crafted by Vince and me, breathed life into this euphoric display. It wasn't merely professional dancers gracing us with their artistry; it was the crème de la crème, the zenith of the craft, dancing to our melody within the hallowed walls of the Dorothy Candler.

No words exist to encapsulate the exhilaration coursing through us, a blend of awe, wonder, and sheer amazement. It was the extraordinary seamlessly woven into the tapestry of fantasy, a fusion of astonishing brilliance and spontaneous magic that left the lobby breathless, our souls intertwined in the ecstasy of the moment.

Randy and a handful of our fellow dancers were so profoundly touched by that impromptu performance that they generously volunteered to attend one of our rehearsals, offering their expertise to help the children with the show. Vince and I were left utterly dumbfounded, our hearts brimming with gratitude. We recognized that their involvement could wield a profound impact on these young souls, potentially altering the trajectory of their lives forever.

Jumping ahead for a moment, I can attest that these events left an indelible mark on the children. But that, my friend, is a tale for another time filled with its unbelievable magic and transformation.

"As we made our way back to the rehearsal, we once again found ourselves traversing the corridors of fame. This time, we bumped into another renowned singer, the youthful Irene Cara, known for her captivating role in one of my favorite films of the year, 'Fame.' It's fair to say that the contrast between meeting Dolly Parton and Irene Cara was like night and day.

In our initial encounter, Irene appeared somewhat paranoid, her demeanor clearly influenced by substances beyond the ordinary. I did manage to secure an autograph on my backstage pass sticker, but it felt as though she was physically present yet mentally adrift in some far-off place. She was there, yet not entirely present.

However, when she graced the stage alongside the dancers, a transformation occurred—a mesmerizing metamorphosis. Suddenly, she sprang to life, a phoenix rising from the ashes of her earlier demeanor. Her performance was nothing short of astonishing, a testament to her talent and the power of her craft.

Later, as Vince and I journeyed back to Long Beach, I couldn't help but reflect on the encounter. Irene struck me as a soul burdened with profound sadness. To possess such immense talent and yet be trapped by the dependence on a fleeting high or a substance, when the pure intoxication of merely being present at the moment was enough for Vince and me, left me with a heavy heart. At that moment, we felt like royalty, basking in the radiance of experiences that would forever be etched into our memories."

I couldn't help but notice that my story had grown rather long of the tooth, an indulgence I hadn't initially intended. With an apologetic smile, I turned to the patient souls who had remained, listening to my extended pontification. "I must confess," I began, "that I hadn't meant to dive into such intricate detail."

In response, Rock, his charisma undiminished, chimed in with his characteristic charm. "Oh no," he assured me, "we savored every moment of your tale. Your story, my friend, far outshines anything that transpired at the Oscars tonight. Believe me, my experience was mostly wrangling with the time police, who were determined to keep things moving, and trying to assist my co-presenter, who was, let's say, somewhat dazed and doped. Considering everything, she did a commendable job."

Dean, always the discerning soul, added his perspective, his intrigue kindled by my narrative. "It truly sounded like a magical moment to me," he reflected, "one that, if captured on film, would undoubtedly have merited its own award-winning honor and approval!"

Dean continued his inquiry, his words laced with a hint of theatrical intrigue, "So, what became of your musical? You mentioned that a high school performed it. Were you, perchance, a teacher or perhaps a student teacher?"

With a theatrical flair, I responded, "Oh no, we were commissioned through a grant generously bestowed by the Los Angeles School District to mark and commemorate the closure of several high schools in the early 1980s, a consequence of the declining population after the baby boomers had gracefully exited the stage. Our rehearsals found their home at Excelsior High School in Norwalk, yet auditions were open to the finest of fine-arts students from high schools scattered throughout the Los Angeles School District."

"Upon the culmination of our rehearsals, we embarked on a grand tour, a theatrical odyssey throughout the sprawling L.A. expanse, visiting all the high schools touched by the closing curtain. As for the exact number of performances, I must admit that time has dimmed that detail, but I believe we embarked on a two-week tour if my memory serves me true."

Pushed Out of the Closet Without A Parachute

I continued with pride, "We actually garnered quite a bit of attention from several newspapers in the sprawling Los Angeles area. Even the illustrious L.A. Times was kind enough to offer a favorable review. While I must paraphrase, for the exact words have since slipped through the sieve of memory, their sentiment was something akin to, 'This production, for a high school musical, far exceeded expectations and stood head and shoulders above many of the musicals this reviewer has covered this year.'

Needless to say, we played to packed audiences throughout our tour, and there was one show that we flung our doors open to the general public, a performance that swiftly sold out. We extended invitations to all our dear friends and family for that particular show, which turned into a truly remarkable experience for all involved."

The kids were exceptionally professional in their performance, and much of the credit goes to Randy and the other dancerswho generously shared their expertise in choreography and inspiring journeys of performing at the Oscars. Now, if you'll indulge me, let me share a profoundly moving story about one remarkable young boy that has stayed etched in my memory.

This boy, Johnny, expressed an impassioned desire to be part of our show during auditions despite facing significant challenges due to his handicap. At first, we were hesitant, uncertain if it was the right decision. However, when he began to share his story, it brought tears to our eyes. Johnny's way of speaking was slow and in fragments, not quite forming complete sentences.

Pushed Out of the Closet Without A Parachute

Johnny shared his heartbreaking story to us in the following way. My apologies in advance because I'm not an actor... But this is how I remember him telling Vince and me... "Last year I was approached... by a couple of mean kids... in school... that had a ggggun. I didn't think it was a real one... at first... but they demanded my lunch mmmmoney... I hadn't eaten for a while... because my mom is a drug addict... and she didn't have mmmoney for my food... I saved up some money... by collecting pop bottles and cans... to get enough to get a hot lunch at school... so I wouldn't give them my mmmmoney...so they shot me in the head... left me lying on the ground... thinking I was dead. The ggggun was pointed right at my head... somehow my skull prevented the bbbbullet from entering straight in... the bullet went around mmmmy skull... it lodged in the bbbback of my head... I mmmiraculously survived... after having mmmmany surgeries... I never fully recovered... but I'm trying rrreal hard... I'm trying to get away from my mmmmom... I don't know who my dad is... I'm trying to get adopted... Social Services... is helping mmmme... but I wanted to be in your show... I will do anything."

Vince and I assured Johnny that we would find a place for him in the play and asked if he could help backstage with the curtains. He was overjoyed, and his courage and determination truly touched our hearts. Additionally, we decided to dedicate our last show as a fundraiser for Johnny, aiming to assist him and other children facing similar challenges.

Pushed Out of the Closet Without A Parachute

The whole room had fallen into a deep, reflective silence. Rock, Dean, and the few neighbors who had remained were visibly shaken by Johnny's heartbreaking story. Rock broke the silence, his voice filled with admiration and gratitude, "I commend you and Vince for your unwavering dedication to those kids, especially to Johnny. Your story is truly one that deserves to be shared and thank you for opening your heart to us. I'll carry it with me always. Johnny's tale alone could serve as the foundation for a compelling film script and a deeply moving autobiographical narrative."

Dean nodded in agreement, still wiping away tears, "Indeed, non-fiction stories like this often find their way to Hollywood's doorstep. You can't even invent something so tragically poignant and yet so profoundly uplifting as this. I'm still touched, and it's a testament to the resilience of the human spirit."

I decided to relinquish the metaphorical microphone and let someone else have the floor. The party began to wind down as guests gradually departed, leaving just the three of us—Rock, Dean, and myself. It dawned on me that it was time to return to Long Beach. Glancing at my watch, I noted that it was already 1:00 A.M., and my trusty ride, La Bamba, awaited to ferry me home.

I bid my traditional farewell, but the middle of my Hollywood bear hug, I realized I wouldn't have the chance for an encore performance of "The Whale Song." Simultaneously, I recalled that Rock had alluded to a secret surprise upon my arrival, a revelation that had slipped our minds during the evening's overflow of emotions. I couldn't resist mentioning it, and Rock, still caught up in the moment, admitted, "Hold that thought for later. I'll share my surprise at a more suitable time. Tonight was quite eventful, and I understand you must get home."

    With heightened curiosity and intrigue, I left after our hugs and embarked on my journey to The Portofino in Long Beach. The late hour had the roads clear of traffic, making it a swift, contemplative drive, a blurred line between the late-night hour or early-morning hour, depending on one's viewpoint. One thing for sure, it was another memorable night, one that I surely would never forget.

Chapter 6: Brown Betty

There are certain times in a person's life, like the unforgettable time when my speedo decided to play the disappearing act during a high school water polo match. Picture this: you're gallantly climbing out of the pool, completely oblivious that your back end is enjoying its moment in the spotlight, while all that's left around your waist is a humble string, doing its best to salvage the situation. The crowd watching the game is left in a collective state of bewilderment, and it takes an excruciatingly awkward minute for me to grasp what has fully unfolded.

Your mortification battles with the urge to laugh it off, but alas, there are moments when even the best humor falls short. Yep, this little scene straight out of a sitcom happened to me! No comment on the specifics, please. And who, pray tell, could have foreseen that another such remarkable event was lurking around the corner, waiting to join the annals of my life's hilarities? All this when I had about as much foresight as a blindfolded squirrel.

Well, there I was, lounging at home, basking in the afterglow of my morning work shift's completion, when the phone chose that precise moment to make its presence known. And what a surprise it was to hear none other than Rock's unmistakable voice on the other end. It was a surprising call, especially considering it had been just a few days since the Academy Awards Party.

Pushed Out of the Closet Without A Parachute

As I listened, Rock began to unravel the secret he'd kept under wraps, which he and Dean Dittman had been cooking up, most likely with a side of liquid inspiration. They had embarked on a grand mission, you see: to introduce me to Dean's esteemed agent, the one and only Dick Lovett. Apparently, they wanted to see if he could arrange a performance by me at the Troubadour, a legendary venue steeped in musical history. They were fully committed to aligning the stars and my work schedule. As fate would have it, Saturday evening emerged as a perfect match, provided that the fabled work gods smiled upon me, granting a timely release from my morning shift.

As I hung up the phone, a cascade of memories swept over me, recalling my previous attempt to make a splash in the world of Hollywood's music scene. Unbeknownst to Rock, there was a chapter not too far in the past when I was summoned from the sandy shores of Hawaii to venture into a recording studio. Unfortunately, that venture turned out to be more of a misadventure. The whole escapade imploded spectacularly, with key players engrossed in their own line of "creative inspiration" that conveniently originated in lines of cocaine within the confines of Hollywood's Brown Derby's bathroom.

The once-promising opportunity disintegrated like confetti in a windstorm, and if not for my wisdom in clutching a roundtrip airline ticket before diving into that chaotic turmoil, who knows where I might have landed? That memory still reverberates, casting lingering shadows of uncertainty that I now needed to conquer in order to ensure that this time around would indeed be different.

Pushed Out of the Closet Without A Parachute

Surrounded by a flood of thoughts that danced through my mind, a lingering question persisted: Could success indeed be mine, a foothold in the capricious terrain of the music business? The absence of a backup band loomed like a specter, an imposing hurdle seemingly insurmountable in the presence of an eager audience and a majestic stage. Uncertainties gathered like mischievous spirits, casting their shadows over my contemplations.

Did I, in all honesty, warrant such a spotlight? Maybe it was a lesson life had diligently taught me: the true depth of the ocean remains a mystery until you summon the courage to dive headlong. And so, armed with my faithful guitar and a heart set with hope, I was poised to venture into the abyss of the unknown, fingers crossed for whatever surprises awaited.

Before anything else, the upcoming rendezvous with Dick Lovett took center stage, a meeting with the power to shape my melodic journey much like Rock's uplifting support. Could Dick perceive in me the same promise that Rock had keenly identified? This encounter balanced on the edge of becoming the turning point, a crossroads that might determine the path of my musical adventure.

I had to shelve thoughts of tomorrow's hopes and dreams. Instead, I needed to reel my focus back to the present, where the immediate reality insisted on honing in on, and navigating the week still left in April. The hotel reverberated with a fevered pitch, a buzzing excitement that intensified as preparations for the impending August Olympics escalated toward the anticipated electrifying crescendo. In the interim of this labyrinth of orchestrated unpredictability, NBC and other collaborators huddled for countless meetings, intricately fine-tuning the impending coverage that would enshroud the indoor volleyball matches set to unfurl next door.

Within this maze of pandemonium, there was one saving grace: I had already locked in an early spring vacation, a chance to reunite with my parents for Easter. This singular thought, akin to a life-saving buoy floating on the waves, would anchor me through the forthcoming weeks. It would be a constant reminder to endure the final stretch before the promised haven of rest and respite.

Looking ahead to the upcoming weekend, I found myself once again blessed by circumstances that played in my favor. They allowed me to slip away from my Saturday morning shift with enough time to hit the gym, savor a belated lunch, and relish in a refreshing shower.

This meticulous preparation was a deliberate effort to present myself in the best light for my debut appearance in front of Dean's esteemed agent. A quick confirmation call cemented our plans, and we collectively agreed to converge at Dean's apartment by 9:00 P.M. My La Bamba was fueled up and poised for the journey to West Hollywood, giving me a luxurious surplus of time for dressing and those final touches.

A brief power nap was on my agenda. However, my slip into a sound slumber took me by surprise. Upon regaining consciousness, the clock had stealthily leaped to 7:00 P.M., with just enough time for a quick dash of water on my face, a hurried toothbrush dance, and a rapid wardrobe change. I hurried out, a prayer to the traffic deities accompanied my exit, a desperate plea for an unobstructed journey through the intricate web of city streets.

My choice was to take La Cienega, sidestepping the dreaded 405 Freeway. To my delight, it proved to be a stroke of strategic brilliance as I deftly navigated through the urban maze. Like a well-conducted symphony, I arrived on Dean's Street with impeccable punctuality, the hands of the clock harmonizing with my intentions.

As I arrived, Rock welcomed me warmly and wasted no time. He urged me to start playing a couple of my top songs right in front of Dick. "Begin with *'The Whales*,'" he suggested, with a glint of excitement in his eyes.

Feeling the urgency, I grinned and quipped, "Could I grab a beer first?"

Rock responded graciously: "I'm so sorry. I didn't mean to rush you at all. I'm just very excited to have Dick here to listen to you play. As soon as you feel comfortable, you can begin."

I thanked him and said, "I just need a couple of minutes to wind down after dealing with L.A. traffic, but I'll be ready in about 10 minutes or so." In this friendly exchange, anticipation hung in the air, and even the bustle of Los Angeles traffic couldn't dilute the excitement.

As the sun descended below the horizon, marking the time at around 7:30 P.M., a delicate twilight lingered in the sky, casting a subtle and soothing glow. Simultaneously, I indicated my readiness to start. Positioned before Dean's sliding glass doors that opened onto the veranda, carefully arranged lighting provided ample luminance without intrusive harshness. Creating the right ambiance was paramount; I aimed to set the perfect backdrop for the somber notes of "The Whale Song."

Dean, Rock, and Dick settled into their seats while I positioned myself on a fold-out chair, poised to commence. "Before delving into the performance, I shared a brief narrative about the song's origin. It all began during my time in Hawaii, a chapter of life when I would frequently venture into the waves of Pohoiki Bay on the Big Island. On a day when the ocean's waves seemed larger than usual, likely due to an offshore storm that roared with primal force. I paddled out to the outer break, far from the shore, awaiting the following lineup of waves.

I positioned myself on my board, waiting for the next set of waves, my attention was drawn to a spectacle unfolding on land. Buses, laden with tourists, had converged at the Pohoiki loading dock and parking lot. Cameras in hand, they were capturing something remarkable. Little did I know, something equally extraordinary was unfolding beneath the water's surface.

Without warning, I found myself encircled by a pod of humpback whales. Initially, panic coursed through me, but my fear gave way to awe as a baby calf emerged mere feet from my board. In an attempt to communicate, I instinctively rubbed my surfboard with my hand, producing a squeaking, high-pitched sound. To my astonishment, the calf responded by looking directly at me.

Suddenly, on the other side of my board, the mother surfaced. Now her eyes as well as her calf's eyes, were focused on me, framed by the water's edge. In that instant, I sensed an understanding pass between us. She recognized I posed no threat, and in her gaze, I saw a friendly acknowledgment, a silent greeting that transcended species.

The pod, a congregation of perhaps five or six whales, swam around me. However, my focus remained fixed on the mother and her calf. Propelled by an inexplicable compulsion, I paddled closer, yearning to touch the magnificent creature. Yet, she eluded my touch, gracefully diving beneath the surface. Undeterred, I persisted, rubbing the side of my surfboard and producing more noises to recapture her attention.

Then, a mere ten yards ahead, she breached. With a majestic leap, her massive form soared from the water before crashing back with a magnificent splash. It was her goodbye to me, and as swiftly as they had arrived, the pod departed, leaving me immersed in an overwhelming sense of connection with the natural world.

It was in the depths of that encounter, "*The Whale Song*" began to form within me. The experience etched in me a profound understanding: we must embrace nature by experiencing it up close rather than perpetuating its destruction from a distance.

And so, on that Saturday evening, under the soft glow of the veranda lights, I shared this story through my song, hoping to ignite a similar reverence in the hearts of those who listened.

As I concluded the song, I let the last note of my guitar resonate, its fading echo tinged with a delicate tremor. Shifting my gaze toward my captivated audience, I was taken aback by an unexpected sight: Dean, wiping away a solitary tear.

"Terrific, Gunther," Dick's praise reverberated through the room. "You have a remarkable knack for crafting the perfect atmosphere for your songs. I could almost envision myself among those tourists, watching you beside the whales. Please, do continue."

I obliged by shifting to a more upbeat tune, one that carried bittersweet notes of nostalgia. I prefaced the song with a simple explanation: it wasn't written for a single individual but rather for the mosaic of memories and faces scattered through the chapters of my life, all those I had missed and yearned to see once more. The simple title was *Without You*.

As the final chord embraced the room, applause erupted, and Dick's impressed demeanor was unmistakable. Rock's words encapsulated the sentiment, "You've once again hit it out of the park, Gunther. But now, let's take a breather. It's time to indulge in some conversation and a few drinks to uncover Dick's thoughts on this captivating performance."

We savored our drinks, exchanged jokes, and dove into discussions about the contemporary music scene. Undoubtedly, the

Pushed Out of the Closet Without A Parachute

era of electronic music was upon us. Dominating the charts were the likes of the Thompson Twins, Depeche Mode, Duran Duran, Chaka Khan, and the industry-altering solo album by the young Michael Jackson. On the female front, Madonna had risen as a formidable force. Yet, amid this electronic wave, one ballad penetrated throughLionel Richie's haunting '*Hello.*' Dick's lamenting comment lingered: 'It's a testament to how star power can cut through the noise masquerading as music these days.'"

Dick offered insights, shedding light on the matter. He revealed that the Troubadour's present roster leaned heavily towards hard rock groups or artists in the vein of Depeche Mode. Regrettably, the troubadour-style singers of yesteryears no longer claimed center stage. Icons such as James Taylor and Carly Simon had ignited their journeys there, and the '70s showcased unforgettable performances by luminaries like Cat Stevens, Kris Kristofferson, Billy Joel, Van Morrison, The Pointer Sisters, Miles Davis, Leonard Cohen, and Bob Dylan. Even the comedic duo Cheech and Chong had their genesis at the Troubadour.

Today, however, the stage resonates more with acts like Guns N' Roses, and heavy metal ensembles like Metallica. Troubadour songs were once the voice of chivalry and courtly love, often shrouded in metaphysical contemplations. How could this revered haven have transformed into such a raucous Heavy Metal Den?

We found ourselves entangled in deciphering the ideal venue to highlight my talents. The flow of questions seemed endless, not requiring immediate answers, as we persisted into the evening. With each sip, the grip of the night grew firmer, causing time to elude our notice. Laughter resonated, blending with Dean's unusually animated mood. Then, almost as if orchestrated, an intriguing incident unfurled.

As laughter echoed and our our indulgence in drinks continuedour voices grew louder. In Dean's living room, there stood a cage typically home to a tranquil cockatoo. Yet, as Dean's laughter intensified, the bird's serenity shattered, replaced by ear-piercing squawks. In a scene that left Dick, Rock, and me simply amazed and shocked, Dean swiftly retrieved the unsuspecting bird from its enclosure. We exchanged glances, silently pondering the unfathomable fate that Dean might have in store for the innocent creature.

Our breaths held as Dean opened the freezer door, momentarily imprisoning the bird within its icy depths. Moments later, he released the bird back into its cage, its vocal cords seemingly frozen in place.

"Dean, what on earth possessed you?" Rock exclaimed, taken aback.

With a sly grin, Dean turned to us, his explanation steeped in dark humor: "There's a frozen turkey in the freezer, and I thought our feathery friend deserved a glimpse of its potential fate if it didn't shut up!"

Bewilderment transformed into uproarious laughter, each of us becoming an accomplice to Dean's peculiar discipline. In our shared mirth, I quipped, "Never find yourself on Dean's bad side, or you'll be next!" Everyone erupted in laughter, drunk on the moment, as we shook our heads in perfect unison.

The evening rolled on until it was the hour only bats and insomniacs would appreciate. "Dean, buddy, you were supposed to whip up dinner, weren't you?" Rock's speech had taken on a bit of a slur, a sure sign of too much merrymaking.

Suddenly, like a comedic superhero sensing the distress call, Dean leaped to his feet, arms flailing dramatically. "Hold on, folks! Dinner is about to make its grand entrance. I promise, just a few minutes!" With a wobbly grace that only an evening of libations could provide, Dean made his way to the kitchen. Meanwhile, Dick, Rock, and I were in the middle of spinning tales that might have made Mark Twain proud.

But then, as if the universe had scripted its own punchline, the most outrageous thing occurred: KAAAAPOOOOOOW! An explosion that rocked the apartment to its core, making us all jump like startled cats. Rock's eyes locked onto mine, and without missing a beat in panic, I burst out shouting, "What the fuck, what just happened, and where's Dean?" Not necessarily in that order!

In a surreal slow-motion sequence, Dean emerged from the kitchen, his cooking ambitions literally plastered all over him. Exploded brown bread clung to his scalp, dripped from his ears, and plopped to the floor. I couldn't help but blurt out, "Holy shit, Dean, are you okay?"

Pushed Out of the Closet Without A Parachute

With an expression hovering between bewilderment and relief, Dean replied, "My fat ass just saved my life! I put the unopened can of brown bread in the oven, turned around, and boom! The oven door flew off and bounced right off my, well, cushioned bottom."

Dick, seemingly the composed one, now resembled a character straight out of a slapstick movie. And then, despite our valiant efforts to maintain our composure, laughter erupted. Rock attempted to stifle it, but he couldn't hold back, and the room resonated with his infectious laughter that refused to be suppressed.

Rock struggled to get the words out, but eventually, he mustered, "Dean, my man, from this moment on, you shall be gallantly known as Brown Betty!" He declared between guffaws. And there we were, all of us, including the newly crowned 'Brown Betty,' doubled over with laughter, celebrating the hilarity that only such a ridiculous moment like this could bring.

Needless to say, "dinner" had been put on the back burner if there was still one was left! Yes, our grand culinary plans had taken an unexpected nosedive, resulting in a plateful of dripping disappointment. But hey, since the clock had spun its way into the uncharted territory of the early hours, Dean, now wearing the aftermath of his kitchen explosion like a badge of honor, boldly declared, "Well, why not rebrand this mayhem as a very avant-garde early breakfast?" His words hung in the air like visions of overcooked toast swirling in our minds.

Rock answered, "Perhaps we forget about anything that has to do with you cooking or fixing anything that has to do with food and get this place back in order."

With a nonchalance that could only be born from a night like this, Dean wiped away the tenacious remnants of brown bread that had somehow managed to weave itself into his hair. We exchanged glances, and a unanimous decision was reached: the kitchen, once a hub of culinary endeavors, was now a danger zone to be avoided at all costs. Even the previously squawking bird in the corner seemed to have reached a truce with its feathery fate. The avian eyewitness had endured an icy shock and a kitchen calamity that made the world wobble like a topsy-turvy amusement park ride. Yet, it perched stoically, the epitome of resilience in the face of our human-driven madness.

As I mentioned at the beginning of this tale, life often gifts us with moments that etch themselves into our memory, and the events of this evening are undoubtedly destined to be among them. While perhaps more deeply etched for Dean, I am convinced that each of us who shared in this escapade will forever carry the image of "Brown Betty," complete with dripping locks of brown hair and the enduring tale of a bird's frozen awakening. This one is unquestionably going into the annals of historical, or should I say, hysterical stories! The recollection of this night will forever linger, an indelible mark of hilarity and friendship that none of us will ever forget.

Pushed Out of the Closet Without A Parachute

As the first rays of daylight painted the room, an unspoken consensus seemed to settle upon us—perhaps the feathered observer had weathered our wild night better than any of us. Amid the lingering echoes of laughter, we acknowledged that this peculiar chapter was drawing to a close. However, before we departed, there was the task of restoring the apartment to its former state.

Summoning the courage to confront the aftermath of Dean's culinary calamity, I rose from my seat and ventured into the epicenter of the wreckage—his kitchen. And oh boy, what a sight awaited me! The explosion's pandemonium had transformed the room into a surreal gallery of brown bread art. It clung to Dean like edible confetti, adorned the ceiling like a strangely sticky fresco, and streaked down the walls as if the kitchen had been caught in the crossfire of a food fight between gravity and an overzealous chef.

With a resolute sigh, I located a towel and dampened it, gearing up to tackle the sticky masterpiece that adorned every surface. I approached Dean, my towering height seemingly an advantage in this gooey endeavor. "I'll take care of the ceiling, Dean. My long limbs might just come in handy," I offered, determined to alleviate at least a fraction of the mess.

Dean turned to me, his Southern roots lending his words a honeyed drawl. "Bless your heart, but please don't trouble yourself," he replied with a hint of resignation, and a smile tugged at the corners of my mouth. It was a mess beyond imagination, but Dean's spirit was unwavering, his humor intact despite the flour-coated debris. This was unquestionably ground zero of the culinary war, and we were determined to emerge from it with laughter.

Dean assured us that he had a cleaning crew scheduled for later in the morning, a team well-versed in handling the aftermath of such war zones. He explained that these specialists were accustomed to dealing with both routine cleanups and the aftermath of memorable events like our ill-fated cooking endeavor. Their imminent arrival brought a glimmer of hope, and despite the fact that their task was undoubtedly more challenging on this occasion, Dean's confidence in their abilities remained unwavering.

With a relieved sigh, I settled back into my seat, the remnants of my beer still comforting me. Dean's demeanor shifted from the jovial host to a man on a mission. "All right, my friend," he began with an air of seriousness, "let's cut through the mirth and get down to brass tacks about your singing career."

I couldn't help but chuckle. The late hour and the alcohol worked together to create a rather absurd scene. "Sure thing," I replied, my words carrying a hint of sarcasm, "because obviously, dissecting life-altering decisions at 2:00 in the morning after a night of drinking is the epitome of clarity."

Putting any joking aside, Rock and Dean appeared determined to have a serious conversation about my singing career. Dick, however, seized the moment to make a strategic exit. Before leaving, he approached me with genuine sincerity, his parting words carrying warmth: "Gunther, I genuinely enjoyed your songs and the time we spent together tonight. If there's any way I can help, don't hesitate to reach out. While The Troubadour might not be the perfect fit, as we all agreed, I'll ponder this further and either get in touch directly or through Rock if I come across any ideas." With that, we exchanged hugs and bid him goodnight as we accompanied him to the door.

Feeling my energy wane, I shuffled into the living room, prepared for a heart-to-heart with Rock and Dean. Seated across from me, Rock's words pierced the air, a clear-cut declaration. "You need to move to Hollywood, get yourself closer to the heart of the action."

My initial urge to defend my position was curtailed by Dean's timely interjection, offering his perspective. "Rock's got a point. Remaining in Long Beach and continuing as a waiter won't provide you the time necessary to scout out the right backup musicians—and I'm talking about the absolute best. It's what you need for a sturdy launch." He met my eyes, his gaze intense. "Don't doubt your talent, but you've got to offer a polished product, meticulously arranged and produced to perfection."

Rock jumped back into the conversation with enthusiasm, eager to emphasize the point. "You're spot on. We're talking about creating a demo, one that's the complete deal. Take *'The Whale Song'* for example—picture this: it starts with the eerie cries of seagulls, maybe even complemented by a playful concertina introduction to give it that unique old sailor's charm."

"It's so funny that you mention a concertina? Because I've begun working on an arrangement for *"The Whale Song,"* that starts with me playing an accordion solo…" I declared with a strong sense of determination.

Rock chimed in, his excitement impossible to contain. "Wait just a minute, Gunther, you're skilled with the accordion as well? Impressive, you truly are a man of diverse talents!"

I felt the need to outline my perspective and clarify the reasoning behind my decision to remain in Long Beach. I conveyed to Rock and Dean that I fully understood the importance of complete dedication, but I also shared that I had invested six years pursuing my music degree across different colleges. During that time, financial struggles were a constant companion. Student loans still loomed over me, and my current position as a banquet waiter surprisingly brought in substantial income compared to many of my peers. Some evenings, with tips included, I could earn up to $40 per hour or even more.

I outlined my strategy to navigate the impending summer Olympics, a commitment I had made to the Hyatt Regency, my workplace. I played a pivotal role as the intermediary between the hotel and NBC, who had chosen the Regency as their base during the Olympics. My responsibilities included managing their downtime, arranging coffee breaks, and attending to any additional needs they might have." Turning to Rock and Dean, I asked: "Would you be willing to grant me a window of a few months—maybe two to three—so I can accumulate a substantial sum? After that, I can confidently plunge into the next phase of my music career."

Pushed Out of the Closet Without A Parachute

During their lingering night-long revelry, I introduced the topic of a potentially life-altering decision, seeking their input and approval. Their responses were measured and understood, recognizing the sensibility of my proposed approach. A mere couple of months would stay the same trajectory.

Rock added, "This buffer time will enable us to chart a course and establish connections in the vibrant music scenes of Hollywood and Los Angeles." Overwhelmed with gratitude, I couldn't help but convey, "You both are incredibly generous, offering your support and championing my musical aspirations. This dream has been a lifelong pursuit, and I'm committed to pouring everything into it!"

As the first light of dawn began to tint the sky, the realization settled in that it was time for me to head home and catch some much-needed sleep. The torrent of thoughts of the past 24 hours had left me with plenty to digest. Between all the excitement, I remained grounded in the reality that the odds might not be in my favor, even with the backing of someone like Rock.

My experiences had already taught me that the music industry was unpredictable. It was a world where individuals with seemingly little to offer sometimes struck gold, leaving us to ponder, "How did they manage to be discovered?" Conversely, many talented souls toiled away, trapped in obscurity, working as waitstaff in the very heart of Hollywood or the broader expanse of greater Los Angeles.

The drive back home felt like a hazy journey, yet luckily, the roads were clear, allowing me to speed my way to Long Beach in record time. Oh, if only every commute could be this smooth! The thought brought a chuckle—hopeful thinking indeed! As I reached my destination, The Portofino by Alamitos Bay, a sense of comfort washed over me.

The sight of my abode was reassuring, prompting the question, "How could I possibly let go of this place?" The rent I paid Pat was incredibly reasonable, and the location was perfect. Proximity to the beach, my workplace, and Long Beach's lively gay establishments made it ideal.

Honestly, it was a fortunate arrangement I shouldn't take for granted. But my mind was abuzz, and sleep was a necessity. Tomorrow—or should I say later today, once I've rested— a different perspective would likely emerge. Isn't that the way life often unfolds?

Chapter 7: Revelations

As the novelty of mingling with a celebrity settled into the comforting rhythm of cherished friendship, life seemed to embrace a touch of routine. The initial awe that once accompanied Rock's presence now blossomed into an effortless closeness, where the star-studded allure blended seamlessly with the simple joy of being among friends.

On one awe-inspiring evening, I found myself invited to the magnificent residence of Ross Hunter and his partner, Jaques Mapes, to join an intimate dinner gathering with Rock. Ross Hunter, the iconic producer renowned for crafting light-hearted comedies and glamorous melodramas, stood as a luminary presence, primarily through his collaborations with Rock, which included cinematic gems like "Pillow Talk."

Jaques Mapes, equally gracious and cordial, completed the duo of hosts. While that evening offered a glimpse into a world of possibilities, it remained a singular, memorable encounter. As I strummed my guitar and shared my musical aspirations, I received invaluable insights. Yet, it was an ephemeral moment, a dream-catching glimpse into the entertainment industry.

Then, there were Dean Dittman's captivating dinner parties, which became a cherished ritual, where laughter and genuine connections became integral to my routine. The boundaries between celebrity and togetherness gently blurred, and the nights filled with true friendship's soothing comfort. It was in these moments, I realized the true beauty of knowing Rock Hudson, not just as the legendary Hollywood figure, but as a dear comrade who brought immense joy and warmth to our lives.

For example, at one of Dean Dittman's enchanting dinner soirées, what commenced as a night of musical interlude swiftly transformed into an unexpected mix of mirth and amusement. As was their custom, Rock and Dean, renowned for their late dining habits, set the stage for the evening's festivities. This time, I made a point to savor a small dinner before the soirée, arriving fashionably late in the heart of West Hollywood around 8 P.M. In addition to Rock and Dean, the guest list once again included the delightful presence of Dick Lovett, infusing the ambiance with a medley of vibrant personalities. My curiosity couldn't help but ponder whether he possessed any further insights regarding suitable venues for showcasing my musical talents.

As the evening progressed, libations flowed freely before dinner was contemplated. Rock's drink was usually scotch, and Dean would join him in savoring this potent elixir. They both attempted to coax me into trying something stronger, but I remained steadfast, nursing my beer, mindful of the responsibilities of having to drive home and how work usually awaited me early the next day.

As the evening continued to unveil its magic, conversations meandered through a delightful maze of topics, and I couldn't resist

Pushed Out of the Closet Without A Parachute

the chance to conjure captivating tales for my cherished friends. Laughter and cheer swirled around us like an intoxicating potion.

Amidst the merriment, Rock leaned in and, with a twinkle in his eye, asked me the origin of the jokes that had them in fits of laughter. With a mischievous grin, I replied, "Well, my dear friends, they come straight from the well of wisdom that is my 94-year-old neighbor."

I regaled the group with stories of my extraordinary neighbor, Virginia, a spirited woman well into her nineties who had journeyed through a life overflowing with fascinating experiences and, remarkably, had outlasted not one, not two, but five husbands.

In the thick of a chorus of chortles, I shared, "You know, when Virginia whimsically claimed to have outlived five husbands, what she meant, in her uniquely dramatic fashion, was that she only had four husbands but managed to recycle one of them in a second marriage!" The room was filled with a palable sencse of curiosity and fascination as I painted a vivid portrait of Virginia's enchanting gift for storytelling.

Virginia, a personality with roots in The New Yorker Magazine and a history that included residing in the enchanting realm of Malta, was an actual character in every sense. Stepping into her world was like entering a time capsule of elegance and flair.

Upon arriving at her abode, you'd find Virginia ensconced on a resplendent red velvet chaise lounge. She held a cocktail in one hand, and the other, a long cigarette holder, even though she rarely indulged in smoking. The effect was pure drama, a stage befitting a personality as theatrical as hers.

With a graceful gesture, she'd invite you to fetch a glass from her refrigerator's icy domain. Within, an assortment of frosty glasses awaits, ready to cradle your chosen libation. Once equipped with your glass and a carefully poured drink, you'd nestle in beside her, your curiosity piqued and your senses primed to savor the latest thrilling installment of her extraordinary life.

During each encounter, Virginia would sweep you into a lively conversation, immersing you in the intricate tapestry of her life. She had an uncanny talent for spinning yarns that ranged from the outrageous to the heartwarming. But her jokes truly set her apart—some of the cheekiest, most ribald humor one could conjure. Her spirit was akin to the legendary Sophie Tucker, and she carried those jokes with a mischievous charm that even Bette Midler would find inspiring.

Undoubtedly, Virginia had a repertoire of jests that could rival the most audacious humorists, and a few that could potentially turn the irrepressible Bette Midler herself a shade of crimson.

"Ah ha," quipped Rock as he said he would have to meet the infamous Virginia himself someday. I told him that you might be too big of a shock for her and cause her to "drop her martini olive right into her poodle's pompadour." The room erupted in laughter, thoroughly entertained by the comment I had shared unknowingly.

"Gunther, you sly devil," Rock said, wiping tears of laughter from his eyes, "I thought you were going to tell us something serious, but you got us good!"

And so, the evening unfolded, an enchanting tapestry woven with joy and laughter, destined to become an indelible hallmark of cherished memories. As the night continued to cast its spell, Dean was meticulous in ensuring that there wouldn't be a repeat of another "Brown Betty" moment, swiftly orchestrating the preparations for our dinner.

Surrounded by the vibrant atmosphere, I found myself entangled in a delightful conversation with Rock. We delved into the details of my upcoming Easter voyage to The Big Island of Hawaii, where my retired parents had chosen to spend their golden years in a house I had purchased while living there.

I recounted how, during my stint as a lifeguard, I had come to purchase a house on the Big Island, but decided to let my parents retire there, driven by the desire for further studies. I bid farewell to the tranquil shores of Hawaii and made my way back to California to pursue my education at Long Beach State.

Intrigued by the allure of Hawaii, Rock couldn't help but express a tinge of envy. He confided in me with a touch of humor that he could never return to Hawaii, alluding to what he audaciously called "the Jim Neighbors thing."

Curiosity piqued, I couldn't help but inquire, "What do you mean by 'the Jim Neighbors thing?'" Suddenly, a shadow of irritation and resentment washed over Rock's demeanor, though it was clear that his frustration wasn't directed at me, but at the media and a particular gossip columnist named Rona Barrett.

Rock shared a disturbing tale from the summer of 1971, recounting how a group of individuals with malicious intent in Manhattan Beach, California, had hosted a theme party and covertly circulated invitations for what was falsely billed as the wedding of Rock Hudson and Jim Neighbors. These malevolent pranksters had dishonestly leaked the invitation to the media, alluding to the two Hollywood stars without explicitly naming them. They used clever references like the "Rock of Gibraltar" getting together with someone akin to a "neighbor."

Rock proceeded to clarify that both he and Jim had vehemently denied the baseless rumors, but the damage had already been inflicted. From then on, their public appearances together fueled speculations, casting a shadow over their friendship and forever complicating his visits to Hawaii, where Jim Neighbors resided.

I offered reassurance, noting that Jim Neighbors maintained homes on different islands, Oahu and Maui, while the Big Island of Hawaii was substantially larger than the two combined. Hence, the chances of a serendipitous encounter were slim to none. However, I couldn't resist sharing an amusing story about Mr. Jim Neighbors.

In a captivating turn of fate, I recounted an unexpected run-in with one of Jim Neighbor's security guards during my days as a lifeguard in Hawaii. One evening, while on a date with this security guard, he received a security alarm call from Jim Neighbor's residence. Driven by curiosity, my friend insisted on checking it out, which led to an unexpected peek inside Jim's home. To my astonishment, we stumbled upon an elaborately decorated bedroom. It featured a canopy bed draped with yellow chiffon, a decidedly flamboyant decor, a stark departure from what one might expect for someone like Rock Hudson.

"But since I've never really seen your house yet, I expect that it will reflect your more masculine, or dare I say, macho qualities, am I right?"

Rock responded with a sly smile and a conspiratorial wink. His interest in the Big Island was clearly piqued; he leaned in and inquired, "So, pray tell, what does this enchanting Hawaiian haven offer, Gunther?"

Drawing upon my passion for this tropical paradise, I replied confidently, "Ah, trust me, Rock, you'd be utterly captivated. Around Easter time, my Easter Orchids bloom in a symphony of colors, their heavenly fragrance wafting through the air, enchanting every soul gracing our island sanctuary. You simply must join me and bask in the tranquility it offers. Fear not, for my parents are kindred spirits eager to embrace you with open arms, ensuring you feel as though you've found a true home away from home."

"Our humble abode rests on a sprawling tropical acre of land, seamlessly melded with a state forest reserve, where nature's embrace lulls you into serenity. Here, the hustle and bustle fades into oblivion, and the prying eyes of the press remain a distant memory. In this secluded paradise, the world's worries dissipate, leaving room for only unbridled joy and companionship. No distractions or unwanted fans to annoy you, Rock—it's a pure, unadulterated heaven," I enthusiastically shared.

Rock's eyes sparkled with the promise of this idyllic escape, and he seemed eager to embrace this serene refuge, far from the prying eyes of the world. With an open invitation to this tranquil retreat, I held hope that Rock might find solace and joy in this serene Hawaiian sanctuary, far removed from the clamor of Hollywood and the ceaseless gossip that all too often overshadowed the essence of his remarkable spirit.

As the evening flowed onward, Dean finally announced that dinner was ready. Anxious to assist in any way I could, I volunteered to set the table, and both Rock and Dick joined in, making it a collaborative effort. The tantalizing aroma of the meal permeated the air, heightening our appetites. The four of us soon gathered around the table, and our intimate dinner was a tapestry of delightful conversation and, naturally, infectious laughter.

Dean's home has always exuded warmth and thoughtfulness, and his hospitality knows no bounds. In a small gesture of appreciation, I brought a bouquet of gladiola flowers in a shade of green that perfectly complements Dean's apartment, which is adorned with various shades of green throughout.

Pushed Out of the Closet Without A Parachute

Dean has a spiritual side, and I sensed he might be a regular churchgoer. However, it wasn't until later in the evening, during a brief moment when Dean was in the kitchen, that Rock confided in me. He revealed that Dean was involved with the Hollywood cult church of Scientology, and he expressed his skepticism and disapproval of the organization, describing it as "all hogwash" and wanting no part of it.

According to Rock, "Scientology was nothing more than an invention of Ron Hubbard, and it was well known for its controversial status— oftentimes defined as a cult, a business, or a new religious hoax." Despite this, Dean seemed to have found solace in it, and while Rock did find some interest in the belief in reincarnation that Scientology shared, he like many others considered it "a ruthless global scam."

Therefore, in light of their differing perspectives, I chose not to judge, recognizing Dean's kind and generous nature. He had opened his home to us and treated us to a beautiful meal, and for that, we were grateful.

As we gathered around the table, giving thanks for all the blessings in our lives, Rock took a moment to express his deep gratitude for the skilled doctors who had given him a second chance through his quintuple bypass surgery. Our hearts swelled with appreciation as we reflected on the many things we held dear.

Rock, always the entertainer, couldn't resist adding a touch of humor, quipping, "Now get me another drink before I get too sober."

Pushed Out of the Closet Without A Parachute

Laughter filled the room, and it was clear that this evening was one to cherish. The sense of companionship was palpable, binding us in a moment of warmth and gratitude.

After the delectable dinner, I offered to lend Dean a hand with the dishes, leaving Rock and Dick to savor their drinks and conversation. Rock, however, appeared to be reaching his limit, his demeanor suggesting that he might nod off at any moment.

Sensing that it was time to say our farewells, I bid goodbye to Dean and took Rock aside for a quiet moment. In hushed tones, I reminded him about The Big Island of Hawaii, emphasizing that it might serve as the perfect escape from the ever-irritating Marc Christian, or as Rock disdainfully kept referring to, "What's His Name." Clearly exasperated by the situation, Rock concurred, saying, "Anything that will get me as far away as possible from that SOB! We'll talk later. You drive home safely, and we'll catch up tomorrow."

With warm hugs exchanged and hearts brimming with a sense of family, I began my journey back to Long Beach. The memories of the evening lingered in my mind—the stories, the laughter, and the jokes that had woven us into a tight-knit clan. However, as the miles passed under my wheels, my thoughts inevitably returned to the looming specter of work, and a sense of discontent crept in. The prospect of an early morning wake-up call the next day did little to lift my spirits, but such was life.

As I navigated the road home, I couldn't shake the hope that Rock might genuinely consider a rejuvenating getaway to The Big

Island. The tranquil allure of paradise had a remarkable way of washing away stress and troubles. Time spent in Hawaii, far from the tumult of everyday life, seemed like the perfect remedy for both of us. I carried an equal measure of concern and optimism in my heart, eagerly anticipating our following conversation and hoping that a tropical retreat would soon be on the horizon for Rock.

Interestingly, tonight's conversations didn't even touch upon discussing venues or anything related to music once we started talking about Hawaii. It just dawned on me while driving home that I completely forgot to delve into these aspects.

I awoke the following morning, an ungodly hour by my standards, and the day unfolded in a flurry of activity. Upon reaching my workplace, I was thrust into the role of orchestrating two major events that demanded meticulous preparation. On the bright side, these events would monopolize my day's focus, but on the downside, they entailed continuous and constant replenishment of fresh items.

Nonetheless, I embraced the challenge and pushed through the day, knowing that the group would depart by 2:30 P.M., translating into a relatively brief seven-hour workday with no evening shift looming on the horizon. Enmeshed in the nonstop rush, there was hardly a moment to catch my breath, let alone call Rock to inquire about his decision. I'd have to wait until I returned home.

The thought of my impending visit to my parents on the Big Island tinged me with a hint of concern. I couldn't help but wonder if Rock would make up his mind in time to secure a plane ticket. While

Pushed Out of the Closet Without A Parachute

I doubted it would be particularly challenging for him to procure a first-class ticket, given that he was traveling solo, the timing remained a critical factor, and seats tended to fill up, particularly around the upcoming holiday.

Upon arriving home around 3:30 P.M., I noticed several messages from Rock on my answering machine, each brimming with inquiries about my parents and the nitty-gritty specifics of the trip. It seemed that he was genuinely invested in every aspect of the journey.

With only the morning shift on my plate, I relished the luxury of a late lunch, taking my time to unwind and settle in for what I anticipated would be an extended conversation. It had become a cherished routine for Rock and me to spend three to four hours a week on the phone, simply reveling in each other's company. Our discussions spanned a broad spectrum of topics, whatever happened to cross our minds at the moment. These phone calls had evolved into a crucial element of our bond, bridging the physical gap that separated us.

This particular call had me revealing the history of my parents, ensuring that Rock fully understood that his visit would be met with open arms and never deemed imposing. I dialed Rock's number and was initially greeted by someone at his house, presumably Mark Miller, Rock's good friend who now played the role of his secretary. After a brief wait, Rock himself joined the call, slightly out of breath, but his cheerful tone conveyed his delight at my prompt response. I assured him that my busy work schedule had been the reason for my unavailability earlier, apologizing for not being home to answer his earlier calls.

Right from the outset of our call, I made it a point to emphasize that bringing someone along was a customary affair during my visits back home. I earnestly tried to put Rock at ease, assuring him that there was no need for him to feel the slightest imposition upon my parents. I told Rock, "My parents practically expect me to arrive with a different guest every time I return. It has become a delightful tradition, and my parents are always thrilled to open their home to new acquaintances and old friends alike."

I continued encouraging Rock not to worry, emphasizing, "Your presence would be warmly welcomed, just like any other guest I've brought along in the past. It's par for the course, and I want you to feel entirely comfortable about the whole arrangement."

Rock, seemingly more at ease, inquired about how often I saw my parents. "Usually," I explained, "I would visit my parents at least once a year, but circumstances had kept us apart since my last visit in 1981. Life became a never-ending sequence of events during my final years at school in 1982-1983, with my senior recital, various projects, and my graduation, which left me with limited time and resources to make the trip. So, the last time I actually saw them was on my way back from Australia and New Zealand after my musical tour with the Long Beach University Choir and the Jazz Ensemble Voce, which was indeed back in 1981."

"Ah," I continued, "I vividly recall back in '81, I felt a sudden burst of spontaneity and decided to invite a couple of my fellow members from the tour to join me in visiting my parents for a few days. The idea of surprising my parents with unexpected guests filled me with excitement. It was a bit like playing a game of 'Guess who's coming for dinner?' or, in this case, 'Guess who's coming to stay for a week?' Despite bringing along people they had never met before, my parents were always thrilled to have company and spend time with their son and his new acquaintances.

As I shared this story with Rock, he listened attentively and then inquired, "Now, Gunther, don't be upset, but you're telling me more about yourself than your parents. I'd love to know more about them. Are you very close to them? Do you have other brothers and sisters? You mentioned that your dad is retired, but what did he do for a living, and did your mom work too?"

I assured Rock that there was no need for me to be upset, and I apologized for unintentionally making it all about me. I then began to share an abbreviated version of my parents' story and how they came to retire in Hawaii.

I began recounting my parents' story from the very start and how they journeyed to America. "My parents' journey started shortly after World War II in Germany. Interestingly, my father had been married to someone else at the time. However, the country was so torn apart by the war that many people couldn't find their loved ones, and some believed their wives or husbands had perished. My father couldn't locate his first wife for over a year and presumed she was killed."

Continuing, I explained "That's when my father met my mother, and they decided to get married. Due to the scarcity of opportunities in post-war Germany, my parents took a boat across the Atlantic to New York. They ended up in Canada, where my father searched for employment. They lived in Toronto first and later in Winnipeg for a few years. During this time, my father found work in factories, producing various industrial items. A friend he met at work decided to head to the U.S. West Coast, where he assured my dad that better-paying jobs could be found. So, my parents moved to Los Angeles as well, and my dad quickly secured a new job as a tool machinist."

As I shared these intimate details with Rock, he occasionally interjected with affirmations like "yes" or "ah ha," assuring me of his genuine interest. I paused at times to ensure he was comfortable with the narrative, and he reassured me that he was deeply intrigued and eager to learn as much as possible about my parents and my upbringing.

Bolstered by his enthusiastic response, I continued, "Well, you see, my mom was informed in Germany that she couldn't have children. They had been trying but weren't successful. The doctors had mentioned certain medical issues she didn't quite comprehend. Nevertheless, both of my parents had accepted the notion that they would have each other and were content with that.

Pushed Out of the Closet Without A Parachute

However, destiny had a different plan for them. After they arrived in L.A., during one of the city's infamous heatwaves, something truly extraordinary occurred. According to the doctors, the intense heat triggered a change in my mother's metabolism, and like a miracle, she found herself pregnant with, well, me."

Rock asked me what year this was, and I continued, "So, I came into the world in Los Angeles, California, in 1956, at John Wesley County Hospital. My parents, who were renting at the time, were searching for a property to buy that was close to my dad's workplace but outside of the pricey Los Angeles area. They settled on Downey, California, a bedroom community, where I was raised until I left home at the tender age of sixteen."

Continuing with my tale, I explained, "I was a high school junior at Downey High School when I began lifeguarding in Huntington Beach, California. Without delving too deep into the nitty-gritty details, I'll just say that I wasn't getting along with my father, and we had significant disagreements about many things. Without burdening you with all the drama, I moved out with my parents' blessing to live with my lifeguard supervisor and his girlfriend."

I paused briefly and then redirected the conversation, saying, "I need to backtrack and share some intriguing revelations from my upbringing. To begin with, I had always believed I was an only child, but my father dropped a bombshell that altered everything I knew. You see, he discovered that his first wife was still alive, which was a shock to everyone involved. Furthermore, as a curious five-year-old,

I learned I had two half-sisters. Then, just a year later, I had the opportunity to meet them on my first family trip to Germany, along with other relatives I had never met before."

"In 1963," I continued, "my parents took me on a journey to Germany at the tender age of six. This trip not only introduced me to relatives on my mom's side but also unveiled a sorrowful chapter from my father's past. I discovered that my father had two brothers and that he, along with his brothers, had been abandoned by their mother and placed in an orphanage. My Onkel Otto, and my Onkel Emil, along with my father Alfred experienced the hardships of a tumultuous era in Germany, a reality deeply influenced by the shadows of World War II.

As I transitioned into adulthood I managed to maintain a cherished connection with certain relatives on my mom's side. Among them, my grandmother was a resilient soul who had experienced loss at an early stage when my grandfather departed this world while I was still a baby. During our family visits, we would pay our respects at his grave, a solemn reminder of his presence in our hearts.

In the company of my grandmother I developed a strong bond with my aunt and cousins, a connection that only grew with time. However, the path of my mom's side of the family wasn't without its share of heartaches. During World War II, my mom's brother, my uncle Hans, courageously served as a message carrier and miraculously survived the perils of war. Sadly, his life was tragically cut short in a devastating motorcycle accident shortly after the war ended.

His untimely departure left behind my Tante Elfriede and her three sons, my beloved cousins, who continued to carry their father's legacy. Additionally, during the trials and tribulations of life, Tante Elfriede had another child with a different man, and my dearest cousin Rosi came into this world. I've nurtured a close and cherished bond with her throughout the years.

However, the story on my father's side of the family took a different turn. Although I had the chance to meet both my Onkel Otto, who had lost his arm in the war, and my Onkel Emil during that 1963 visit, our paths eventually diverged. Regrettably, I've never heard from them or seen them again. On the other hand, my father managed to reestablish contact with his mother and began providing her with financial support. When my family returned to Germany when I was thirteen, we paid a visit to my 'other Grandmother,' and it turned out to be a rather tense and emotional encounter.

My father brought her a bouquet of long-stem roses, but her nerves appeared to have gotten the best of her. She cut and trimmed the roses incessantly, reducing them to four-inch stems. My parents decided it would be best for me to play outside for a while, and during that time, something transpired between my parents and my grandmother. By the look on my parent's faces, it was probably best to be outside and unaware of the details.

Pushed Out of the Closet Without A Parachute

Though I wasn't privy to the exact details of that encounter, I vividly remember my father's words delivered in his unique Germlish, a blend of German and English: 'I vill never give dat voman another cent, may she rot in hell!' It was evident the meeting had stirred up emotions and memories he had long suppressed. Perhaps, in some way, it may have offered him the closure he needed, even though it fell short of the reunion or resolution he had secretly yearned for. The intricacies of family relationships often leave indelible marks on our lives, shaping our perceptions and influencing our journeys in ways we may never fully grasp.

When my father discovered that his first wife was still alive, he was confronted with a flood of emotions and had to confront the haunting memories of the past. His first wife had fallen gravely ill, losing her sight and hearing, rendering her incredibly vulnerable. Despite the adversities she faced, my father felt compelled to seek answers to the mysteries that had long shrouded their lives. Unfortunately, their paths had diverged significantly, and their stories no longer aligned. Both my father and his former wife had forged separate lives by then."

As the weight of my storytelling settled, I emphasized that it was a dark chapter in my father's life, one he preferred not to revisit or dwell upon. I reassured Rock that my father's past remained a mystery, and it was a topic he continued to avoid, even to this day. However, I held onto the hope that, perhaps someday, he mightbe more willing to open up and share more about our family's history.

Pushed Out of the Closet Without A Parachute

Turning to my mother, I explained, "Ah, my mom's primary occupation, the backbone of our family, was that of a devoted housewife. She briefly ventured into the world of waitressing, but once she cradled me in her arms, her focus shifted entirely to raising me and managing our humble abode. From balancing the books to ensuring every corner of the house was in impeccable order, she embraced the role of a quintessential German housewife with grace and dedication.

You see, she embodied the essence of motherhood, a cherished tradition during a time when many women found solace in nurturing their homes. And let me tell you, Rock, her adaptation to the United States was quite different from my father's. English rolled off her tongue with ease, even though her accent often led to humorous situations. She gracefully navigated North American culture, whereas my father struggled, frequently leaving people bewildered by his attempts at communication."

As Rock listened attentively, I delved deeper into my childhood dynamics with my parents. "Growing up, it was far easier for me to communicate with my mom than my dad. To be honest, I often felt that my dad didn't quite understand me, and at times, I found it challenging to comprehend him as well. Despite my proficiency in German and fluency in the language, my dad's strict upbringing in the orphanage appeared to have left him with limited skills in expressing affection and connecting as a father, or at least the father I wanted him to be."

"Nevertheless," I continued, "there were moments that stood out, especially when my dad taught me how to play the accordion. Later, when I got involved in swimming, both my mom and dad would come to my swim meets and lend their support. My dad particularly enjoyed being one of the timers and indulged his fascination with stopwatches. He shared with me the skills he had acquired during his earlier jobs as a watch repairman before the war. My teammates always treated my parents kindly and often commented on how sweet they looked together."

"Despite these occasional positive moments," I added, "the dynamic within our household was complex. My dad considered himself the ultimate authority; his word was law, regardless of whether it was right or wrong. As I grew up more independent, clashes between us became frequent. I couldn't bear to be stifled by his old-fashioned beliefs and attempts to suppress my free will. Don't get me wrong—I understood the importance of rules and responsibilities, and I was a diligent student, completing all my chores and striving to be a model child. However, sometimes it felt like my efforts were overlooked, and I was treated as if I were the exact opposite.

The breaking point came when I was 15 years old, when my father and I had a major falling out that resulted in me leaving home and seeking refuge at a friend's house for a week. Throughout the ordeal, my mother played the role of mediator, bearing the brunt of our conflict. It became evident that I needed more freedom and independence, so I made my intentions known. I wanted to move out and take charge of my own life as soon as I could.

At this point, I was caught at a crossroads of ambition and adventure, and with my parent's permission I moved to Huntington Beach where each daybecame a new chapter in my life's story. With the taste of independence and the salt of the sea in my veins, I wholeheartedly pursued a career as a lifeguard, immersing myself in the vibrant and challenging world of ocean rescue. I was thriving in my element, relishing the responsibilities that came with the job, all while balancing my college studies.

As for my relationship with my parents, I remained connected to them through letters and occasional phone calls, but the physical distance between us meant that our bonds, especially with my father, were not as strained as they had once been. We found a way to connect without the constant friction we experienced when I was under their roof. My mother's unwavering support was a constant source of comfort and encouragement."

Rock was keenly listening, and I sensed a deep interest in my journey. It wasat this point, I decided to delve into the connection between my lifeguarding experiences and my eventual purchase of a house in Hawaii, a story I had longed to share.

Rock appeared slightly bewildered, curious about the sequence of events that led me to acquire the house in Hawaii. With a sly grin, I began telling this part of the story.

Pushed Out of the Closet Without A Parachute

"Well, it all started after I graduated with my AA in Liberal Arts from Golden West College in Huntington Beach. A year at the University of Irvine on a Water Polo Scholarship didn't quite cut it, and I found myself at Junior College, playing water polo, lifeguarding, and studying simultaneously.

My journey to the islands began during an Easter break when I visited my old surfing buddy, Mary, on the breathtaking shores of Mākaha, Hawaii. The University of Hawaii at Manoa beckoned, and a persuasive chat with the water polo and swim coach secured me yet another scholarship, leading me straight to Hawaii after finishing my time at Golden West.

After a year, the allure of the Islands, with its captivating beauty and distracting charm, prompted me to shelve my academic aspirations—the University of Hawaii at Manoa imposed restrictions—no simultaneous work and scholarship. Despite my frugal nature, the scholarship fell short of covering all my expenses. Practicality took the reins, and I found myself working as a full-time year-round lifeguard to make ends meet, temporarily putting my educational goals on the back burner. Life's twists and turns, it seems, had other plans for me.

As fate would have it, I encountered an unforgettable moment behind my lifeguard stand, where a real estate office was inside the lobby of one of the beach hotels. I kept my eyes open and inquired from time to time if there were any great entry-level deals. Then one day, I was in luck; a house situated in Leilani Estates on the Big Island, was brought to my attention—an ocean-view paradise resting on an acre of land.

Infatuated with the property, I took a leap of faith and made a somewhat audacious offer. Much to my astonishment, an elderly Portuguese woman who had recently lost her husband accepted it, but our agreement seemed lost in translation. Miscommunication ensued, and I found myself torn between elation and guilt. The woman had signed all the papers but wasn't aware of the terms and thought she was getting paid in cash.

After much heartfelt discussion with my parents, I managed to sway my father towards the path of early retirement. You see, he was grappling with the burden of high blood pressure and a condition called hammer toe. But after doing some research and inquiring, a revelation graced my path—a stroke of brilliance! Instead of the ordinary social security route, a clever maneuver presented itself. Medical leave, tailored to his health needs, would grant him the same monetary benefits as his full retirement while keeping the taxman at bay until my dad reached full retirement age."

Rock's fascination was palpable, and his gaze was locked onto me as if every word I spoke held a touch of enchantment. "Thanks to the symphony of timing," I continued, "my father, in essence, would be able to retire at the tender age of 52 due to his disability, receiving a sum equivalent to that of a 65-year-old collecting Social Security. The beauty of it? No taxes nibbling away at those precious earnings.

Pushed Out of the Closet Without A Parachute

Fortune pirouetted around us as my dear parents bid farewell to their cherished California abode—a treasure chest of memories and gratitude. This farewell untangled me from the remaining debt tethered to my new, humble homestead. A twist of fate and a stroke of luck—the stage was set for a win-win tale, with me and my parents as leading actors. I merely added my parents to the Grant Deed, and the house, now graced with 'Rights of Survivorship,' would belong to the surviving party in the event of a life's passage. Estate and inheritance taxes? No worries... No tax burden.

With the burden lifted, I temporarily resumed my lifeguarding duties on Oahu, cleverly securing California Resident status using my parents' former address—a masterstroke that unlocked the doors to my dream of attending Long Beach State, sweetened by a student grant. I made arrangements to rent a room in the Long Beach area and eagerly packed my bags, ready to embark on this new chapter just before the beginning of the fall semester. Ah, the fall of 1980, a time brimming with hope and anticipation.

Now anchored in Hawaii, I reveled in the perks it offered—the joy of seeing my parents in paradise whenever I returned. I had peace of mind that the house, vested in my name, would also embrace them through Joint Tenancy. A harmonious connection, ensuring that when one owner's melody reached its final note, their share in the property would seamlessly pass on to the other, the rhythm of our intertwined destinies playing on without having to go through probate or the court system."

Pushed Out of the Closet Without A Parachute

I pretty much covered all of Rock's questions, and I must admit, I felt my conversation flowed as smoothly as possible. While I did make a 'conscious' effort not to stray into unrelated tangents, I might have taken a few scenic detours along the way... okay, maybe more than a few—LOL! But hey, that's just part of my charm, right? Keeps things interesting!

I did most of the talking all night... but I had a mission, to ensure that Rock received the insights he sought about my parents and upbringing. As it often did, our phone call continued for over an hour, a testament to the deep connection and bond we had already nurtured.

So, I concluded my sharing of the background information, "In the end, fate, chance, and a bit of audacity paved my path to obtain the serene house on the Big Island. Life's unexpected threads were woven together into a fateful moment. I can't lie; it was one hell of a journey, but I would do it again in a heartbeat."

Rock expressed gratitude for the detailed narrative and confessed he hadn't anticipated such an intricate story. With a genuine curiosity, he posed one last question, "Gunther, what should I bring for your parents? What would truly light up their day?"

I responded with honesty and a touch of sentiment, "Our company and a warm, heartfelt hug, my friend; that's all they desire."

A gleam of excitement resonated in Rock's voice as he assured me, "I can offer that in abundance!" With logistical details aligned, the only pending query was the timing of his arrival in Hilo, on the serene shores of the Big Island.

Chapter 8: Off to Hilo

As the week quickly slipped away, my eagerly awaited trip to Hawaii was now just a day away. Fortunately, I had been working tirelessly, pulling off three consecutive double shifts and racking up plenty of overtime, ensuring I only had the morning shift on Thursday. This precious time would allow me to pack my belongings, get a fresh haircut, and do all those little things we do to look our best when reuniting with loved ones. After an exhausting week, I couldn't wait to board the plane and catch some much-needed sleep during the flight.

As the dawn of Good Friday, the 20th of April approached, I found myself filled with eagerness and a dash of trepidation. I mean, come on, it's not every day you get to jet off to Hawaii with a legend like Rock Hudson in tow, right? Sometimes, I had to pinch myself to ensure I wasn't simply imagining this wild and fabulous adventure. But here I was, all set and ready to go, embarking on an escapade that felt like a delightful twist of fate and a splash of theatrical flair.

Ah, of course, there was a slight wrinkle to my plan. I would have to channel my inner travel agent and make the trip back to Hilo to pick up Rock, for he would be arriving on a different flight scheduled to land around 6 P.M. But hey, not really bad news, this just meant I'd have some cherished time with my parents before Rock's arrival—an opportunity to let my parent know how I met Rock and reassure them that he was a genuinely nice man who expected nothing more than their authentic, down-to-earth selves. And let's be honest, having a Hollywood heartthrob like Rock Hudson at our doorstep is enough to make anyone's palm a little sweaty with anticipation and excitement!

I decided to give Rock a call to see if he was prepared for our upcoming Hawaiian vacation. I picked up the phone, and to my delight, Rock answered—quite a surprise since someone else in the house would usually always grab the phone first. "Hello, Rock Hudson's residence, how can I help you," he cheerfully greeted. I couldn't resist a playful remark in a sweet Southerner's voice, "What are you doin' answerin' your phone? Are you fixin' to fly the coop?" After a moment of laughter, Rock recognized my voice. "Oh Gunther, it's you, you jokester," he said warmly.

Rock inquired about my trip preparations, asking, "Are you all packed and ready to leave in the morning?" I confirmed my readiness for our island adventure, prompting me to share a helpful piece of island-savvy advice. With a consoling tone, I said, "Well, there's no need to bring a whole bunch of clothes, and my mom has us covered! She's more than willing to take care of our laundry while we're there, so don't hesitate to reuse your clothes and pack light. We'll be deep in 'nowhere's land,' and the chances of encountering anyone other than a few locals are slim to none, unless we decide to venture into Hilo."

As the designated tour guide, I continued with a hint of playfulness in my voice, "Now, I've got this nifty tour guide flag I can carry so that you won't lose sight of me during our island adventures.

Pushed Out of the Closet Without A Parachute

And as for the dress code, there is no need to fuss with tuxedos or fancy gowns here—just a bathing suit or some comfy shorts and a T-shirt will do the trick, and don't you dare forget your tennis shoes. That's what we call Big Island formal wear, my dear!" I couldn't help but chuckle at the comical image in my mind, picturing Rock, the epitome of Hollywood elegance at 6'5", standing tall in his laid-back island attire. Oh, what a delightful sight that would be, a true fusion of styles fit for the Big Island stage!

Rock, never the minimalist, assured me with his signature charm that he'd be traveling light, with nothing more than a carry-on in tow. And the steadfast plan? To spend the entire trip gallivanting in his bathing suit, embracing the island spirit with unwavering dedication. "If I forget anything," he chuckled, "well, I suppose I'll just have to go without, or better yet, I'll make it a shopping adventure and grab a shiny new replacement!"

Of course, I couldn't resist a teasing remark, "New one of what?" I inquired with a wink, already savoring the playful banter that defined our friendship.

And that's when Rock unveiled his grand strategy, "You know, a fresh pair of socks or underwear, just in case those daring sharks decide to stage a clothing raid!" We both burst into laughter, our spirits dancing lightheartedly across the phone lines.

"Oh, fear not," I replied, my voice brimming with confidence, "I'll be your trusty tide pool lifeguard, keeping those sharp-toothed rascals at bay. But beware of the crafty brine shrimp lurking in the thermal ponds—they're tiny tricksters who can sneak up your legs, looking for a nest!" Rock's laughter resonated like a symphony, his infectious spirit lighting up the conversation.

"Darn those pesky shrimps!" he exclaimed, ever the quick wit, "Perhaps we can round up a few and throw them on the 'Barbie'!" Now we were both in stitches, the sheer joy of our pre-Hawaii rendezvous lifting our spirits.

"Rock, my dear friend," I said through joyful tears, "let's save this comedy routine for Hawaii, shall we? I've got a million tasks to check off my list, and I can't focus with all this laughter shaking my core. Really!" We shared a final moment of mirth, knowing that our island escapade was mere hours away.

With warm farewells and promises of "bon voyages," we gracefully concluded our conversation, hearts aflutter with the excitement of our imminent journey to paradise. I couldn't wait to embark on what I'd hoped would be an unforgettable adventure on the Big Island, a journey filled with the promise of new experiences and beloved memories.

At the crack of dawn, well before the sun even considered rising, I found myself faced with the Herculean task of getting ready when I just longed for a few extra hours of sleep, but alas, the call of paradise couldn't be ignored. With all the necessities carefully packed and lined up like loyal soldiers by my bedroom door, I tiptoed around, trying not to wake Pat, who had already bid me bon voyage with a sleepy smile.

Pushed Out of the Closet Without A Parachute

La Bamba served as my go-to ride for this special occasion. As I packed my gear into La Bamba's capable trunk, I said a silent prayer, whispering to the car gods, "May you continue to be my loyal companion and deliver me safely to my destination." Oh, the memories we had already shared, the roads we'd traveled, and the escapades yet to come! With a touch of humor and a dash of hope, I revved the engine, ready to embark on this thrilling journey to the islands. But first to the airport, and then I'll let United Airlines take me the rest of the way!

So, with a mixture of excitement, nerves, and sheer giddiness, all wrapped up in one, I was finally on my way. I chuckled to myself, thinking of the adventures that awaited and what events could surprise me on this visit. The airport—the mere first stepping stone to my island paradise, my home base, and divine harbor. The journey had begun, and I was ready to embrace every twist and turn with arms wide open, fueled by laughter and the sheer joy of living. Hawaii, here I come, with my trusty La Bamba and the prospect of an unforgettable rendezvous with the one and only Rock Hudson!

Ah, those good old days of air travel, where the emergency aisle was a coveted spot for us taller folks, ready to leap into action if needed. I chuckled to myself, knowing that I'd manage to doze off as soon as I settled into my window seat, flight pillow, and noise-canceling earphones at the ready. A few hours of blissful sleep awaited me, well-timed around the breakfast service. Ah, the perks of yesteryear when even the economy class enjoyed a taste of the good life with in-flight meals, though not quite as fancy as the first-class fare with a touch of liquid courage! Of course, for an extra cost, you could buy an alcoholic beverage, but with traveling alone... how much fun would that be?

As I dozed off for my customary nap, my mind couldn't resist the notion of time zone calculation, a dance of hours blending and bending in the vast sky. Seven A.M. plus nine and a half hours meant our arrival at 4:30 P.M. California time, and with the three-hour time difference, we'd gracefully touch down around 1:30 P.M. in the heart of Hawaiian time. Aha! The mystery is solved. I'd have a delightful four and a half hours to spare before returning to the airport for Rock's arrival. Ah, time—always the elusive trickster, but now tamed and on my side, I could now rest easier.

The hum of the jet's engines and the air pressure change caused me to fade away until we hit a little turbulence, and I checked my watch. Almost an hour and a half in flight, and the in-flight service was about to begin. I started thinking about what I would do right after we landed and before I had to turn around and pick up Rock. A stop at the supermarket might be a good idea, I thought, to ensure we have everything we need for a wonderful time together on the Big Island.

The notion of a market run with my parents tickled my soul, knowing they'd already showered the cupboards with plenty of snacks, as parents do when their children return home. (Even though I wasn't a child and well into my twenties.) What things do I possibly still need to get?

Pushed Out of the Closet Without A Parachute

A couple of days ago, I had asked Rock if I should get some Scotch for his enjoyment, but his easygoing response melted away my concerns. He reassured me that he'd happily enjoy whatever my parents preferred. "And what do they like," he asked? Basically, the sacred beverage that runs through their veins like a divine ritual—coffee! They seldom drank alcohol, but once in a while, they'd indulge in soft drinks and the occasional Hawaiian fruit juice, though coffee remained their holy grail.

As for me, I'm the odd one out, sipping on plain water all day long, shunning coffee, tea, and soda like a rebel against caffeinated conventions. But hey, an Arnold Palmer can sometimes hit the spot, that delightful dance of iced tea and tangy lemonade, a perfect companion for the tropical breeze. Sweet or not, it was time to embrace the flavors of the islands, inhale the scent of plumerias and pineapples, and let the unhurried pace of paradise guide us through this extraordinary time.

And, as my thoughts meandered through the planning trivia, I suddenly realized I was overthinking everything! It was time to surrender to the charm of island time, that magical tempo where life unfolds effortlessly. If we really needed something, the local grocery store in Pahoa would be our oasis. My parents were no strangers to frugality, adept at stretching a meal's leftovers for days. However, I had no doubt my mother already had a culinary masterpiece planned each day for us, her loving touch gracing our plates with the essence of homecoming.

Pushed Out of the Closet Without A Parachute

Alas, the joy of coming home, especially around Easter, with all my Easter orchids in bloom, filling the air with their heavenly scent. It adds to Hawaii's tropical paradise, and I can't wait to reunite with my parents and introduce them to my newest best friend, Rock. With a movie on the flight to keep me entertained and a delightful meal to savor, the hours simply melted away, and before I knew it, we were fast approaching our destination.

As we started our descent, the excitement swelled within me. In just about twenty more minutes, I would behold the familiar sights, smell the sweet Hawaiian air, and be surrounded by the distinctive volcanic earthy aroma that only the Big Island could offer. Oh, how I missed that scent—it touched my senses, reassuring me that I was indeed back home, where my heart found solace and serenity amidst the enchanting beauty of the islands.

As I gazed out the window, attempting to spot a glimpse of the islands, the plane's angle denied me the view, leaving only the fortunate ones on the other side with the majestic scenery. Yet, the aircraft was circling, and soon, the iconic landmarks of Mauna Loa and Mauna Kea, shaping the Big Island's landscape, came into view. It's incredible to think that beyond the familiar Hawaiian Islands, a new addition, Lo'ihi, is gradually forming, destined to debut on the world stage perhaps ten thousand years from now. Nestled about twenty miles southeast of Kilauea volcano on the Big Island, Lo'ihi already boasts its name, patiently biding its time in the depths of the ocean.

Pushed Out of the Closet Without A Parachute

As we continued our approach, the vision of Mauna Loa and Mauna Kea became clearer, guiding us towards Hilo. Surprisingly, the town appeared free of clouds and rain. At the same time, the volcanic peaks remained crowned with a ring of clouds, channeling the tropical rains to transform the once barren black lava into a flourishing haven of greenery. The lush tropical plants thrived in the fertile soil, among the richest in the world, ready to embrace any seeds that dared to take root. Enriched with nitrogen and perfectly drained by the porous lava, the soil nurtured the growth of thriving trees and abundant vegetation, painting a breathtaking portrait of nature's unyielding strength and resilience.

As we descended to a lower altitude, the landscape unfolded before me, revealing the patchwork of houses and lush papaya plantations. In the distance, the airport came into view, a familiar sight that marked the gateway to the island paradise. Our flight made a graceful turn, veering towards the coastline of Hilo Bay, and I could see the rugged rocks of the shoreline passing beneath us, a visual cue that our touchdown was imminent.

With a gentle swing of our wings, we glided over a vast field, swiftly transforming into the airfield. In the blink of an eye, the tires made contact with the runway, and a chorus of screeching announced our arrival. The captain expertly reversed the engine thrusts, slowing the aircraft down as I felt the force pushing me forward in my seat, a reminder of the rapid deceleration. We had landed, and as I glanced at my watch, I adjusted the time back three hours, from 4:30 P.M. to the local time of 1:30 P.M. The moment I had been waiting for was finally here—I was about to reunite with my mom and dad, and the thought of seeing them again filled my heart with joy.

Undeniably, the agony of waiting to disembark is a universal experience of air travel that knows no bounds. It's a quintessential part of the journey that tests our patience to the limits. As the minutes tick by, you can almost bet that someone's overhead bag will jab into your head, side, or body part, leading to a comical dance of dodging and maneuvering. And, the wails of babies, their tiny ears feeling the discomfort of decompression, filling the cabin with their cries, as we all yearn to finally set foot on solid ground and bid farewell to the metal tube that carried us through the sky. The waiting game felt never-ending, but the anticipation of getting out at our destination grew stronger with each passing moment.

I remember the days when they used a ladder to empty the plane from both the front and back, and it did feel more efficient, but progress has its quirks, I suppose. Now we must wait, row by row, until it's our turn to disembark. At least I was seated in the middle of the plane, just above the wing, making the wait a tad more bearable.

As I stepped towards the opened door, the irresistible scent of island air caressed my senses, a blend of earthy volcanic essence and the sweet fragrance of plumeria dancing in the humid breeze. The airport itself felt more like an open oasis, with roofs but no walls, allowing the air to circulate freely around us. It was comfortable, not too hot or cold, and I felt the warm embrace of Hawaiian soil beneath my feet once again. The Big Island, with its lush greenery and perennially pleasant weather, welcomed me back home, and I couldn't wait to find my parents and begin our joyous reunion.

As soon as I reached the escalator, taking me down to the ground level, I spotted my parents waving eagerly, their faces beaming with joy. A wide smile stretched across my face, and my heart warmed at seeing them. I was my mother's only child, and although my father had other children from before World War II, he had never raised them as he did me. Our journey through life had its share of ups and downs, especially during my tumultuous teenage years.

Reflecting on the past, I remembered when I was coming of age, discovering my path, and learning things beyond my father's comprehension. Growing up, he was raised in an orphanage and only attended school until about the sixth grade, a life different from mine. But with time, my love for both my parents deepened, and now that I was living my own life, our bond grew more robust than ever.

As I approached, hugs and kisses enveloped me in their warm embrace. It had been far too long, and the feeling of seeing them again after being apart for so long was indescribable. The love and longing in their eyes mirrored my own, and everything felt just right for that moment. Yes, it had been way too long, and I missed seeing them so much!

Of course, my mother asked the typical questions about how the flight was and how I was feeling, but I knew the elephant in the

Pushed Out of the Closet Without A Parachute

room had to be let out right away. I couldn't resist teasing her, "So, aren't you itching to hear how I became friends with Rock Hudson?"

She looked me in the eye and with her familiar German accent, trying to be polite and not pry, said, "Vell, I didn't want to be rude und I thought you would tell me when you were ready."

I hugged my mom affectionately and assured her, "You could never be rude to me, you know that, don't you?"

I started to share the story, "So, it all started when my friend and co-worker Phil asked me out for a nightcap after a long and tiring event we had worked on. We went to this bar, and to my astonishment, there was Rock Hudson, sitting with his friend Dean Dittman. At first, I couldn't believe it, but Phil told me they had met in the VIP lounge in Disneyland, and they both remembered each other. Phil is quite a memorable character, to say the least.

As we got talking, I mentioned to Rock that I had graduated from Long Beach State with a degree in Music, and I recently co-wrote and starred in a musical. Turns out, we had both starred in musicals, and that's where our connection started. But it didn't stop there; we soon discovered we had many other things in common.

Well, one thing led to another, and Rock asked me to come play at one of his parties. Now, I've played at several of his gatherings, and we just became good friends. Surprisingly, really good friends. We talk on the phone a lot, and he's become a mentor to me, a great listener, and someone I can always count on. And, of course, I lend my ear to him as well. It's just one of those rare connections that happen in life, and I feel so grateful for our friendship. You'll understand better once he is here." I explained to my mother, hoping to pique her curiosity about meeting my dear friend, Rock.

With limited time on our hands, I quickly inquired if my parents had already done the shopping in town. I hadn't notice any shopping bags when I packed my suitcase. My dad, in his usual mix of English and German, confirmed, "Oh, yaaa we did dat gestern," meaning they had done it yesterday. Then my mom, ever the thoughtful one, asked, "what does a big movie star like Rock prefer to eat." She had stocked up on what she knew I enjoyed, but I let her know that Rock enjoys home-cooked meals and is fond of red meat, especially steak.

I suggested stopping by the meat market in Pahoa or the supermarket in Hilo to pick up something special, like a few cuts of filet mignon. So, we ended up at the KTA Superstore parking lot, and the sight brought back memories as if it were yesterday. My mom, being her caring self, expressed her concern about spending too much money and insisted that I didn't need to go all out for them. But I wanted to do something special, so I went into the store to get three filet steaks—one for each, including Rock. The thought of that surprise made it even more meaningful. As for myself, I couldn't resist picking up some Mahi Mahi, a personal favorite of mine, for dinner. The anticipation of our meal was making my mouth water already.

The drive back home, with no traffic and sticking to the speed limit, usually took about 40 minutes. We didn't talk much during the ride. I felt myself dozing off a little, tired from the early start and the time change. Checking the clock, I realized it was already 2:15 P.M., which meant it was 5:15 P.M. in California. My mom asked about Rock's arrival time, and I mentioned that his flight was scheduled to land at 6:00 P.M., leaving me just a couple of hours at home before I had to head back to the airport. It would be a late dinner for my parents, but I assured them that Rock and I would be fine, especially if we managed to avoid any stops along the way. With that in mind, my mom said she would time dinner around 8 P.M. so Rock wouldn't feel too rushed.

Once we got to the house, I unpacked my things and let my mom know that I would give my bed (an old water bed frame in which we put an excellent Tempur-Pedic mattress) to Rock, and I would take the couch sleeper bed. She told me whatever I wanted to do was fine with her. With that settled, I told her we could catch up later, longing to take a leisurely stroll among the loving embrace of our cherished plants. My mom, anxious to cool off a little, mentioned she and my dad were about to dip into the above-ground Doughboy pool, inviting me to join in the aquatic fun. Politely, I declined, already devising plans to introduce Rock to the thermal hot spring pools nestled in Isaac Hale Beach Park by Pohoiki Bay.

As I wandered the familiar grounds, my gaze landed upon the easter orchids, tenderly tied to the fern trees adorning the driveway. Some appeared slightly parched and wilting, so I swiftly retrieved the hose and nurtured them back to life, eager to share their vibrant bloom and enchanting fragrance with Rock. My parents, masters of the green thumb, had transformed the once-wild expanse below the house into a flourishing vegetable garden teeming with luscious pineapples, verdant green beans, plump tomatoes, and an array of delightful lettuces.

Yet, this was merely the beginning of our abundant paradise. When I acquired the property, it already had a multitude of fruit and nut trees—avocado, mango, papaya, guava, and the magnificent macadamia nut—each day felt like a veritable feast of nature's bounty. Among the treasures were a couple of orchid trees adorned with glorious flowers in bloom, a dazzling sight to see. Ah, the mornings were a divine treat, savoring a heavenly breakfast; freshly picked avocado on toast (actually, the ripe ones would usually be lying on the ground), complemented by a protein shake infused with the essence of our very own freshly frozen mangoes. I found it to be a delightful indulgence and a perfect start to the day!

Time always goes too quickly when you're having fun, and working in the yard always brings me joy! As I tended to the plants, finding delight in nurturing the easter orchids and marveling at the flourishing vegetable garden, my mom's call brought me back to the present. It was almost time to embark on my journey to the airport, where I would eagerly embrace my dear friend Rock. Putting the hose back in its place, I readied myself to depart, but not before checking in with my parents to see if they needed anything.

With warm smiles, they assured me they were all set, but my mom had a brilliant idea. "Why not get something special to drink with dinner?" she suggested.

Ecstatic with the notion, I replied, "You're absolutely right, Mom! This calls for a celebration, and I'll pick up a bottle or two of wine to complement our meal." My parents rarely indulged in wine, typically saving it for special occasions like Christmas dinner, but tonight was an exceptional night that deserved to be marked with something extraordinary. The anticipation of tonight's gathering filled my heart with excitement and joy!

My mom stopped me just as I was about to step out the door, a little surprise in her eyes. "Oh, I almost forgot," she said with a smile, "I made a special lei for Rock from our plumerias in the garden. Let me grab it for you. I put it in a plastic bag in the refrigerator." I thanked her warmly and rushed up the stairs, sparing her the effort of coming down. Her thoughtfulness was touching, and as I held the lei in my hands, I knew it would make Rock feel genuinely welcomed. I had planned to stop by the lei stand near the parking lot, but her gesture was even more special. Our home-picked flowers always had an extra touch of scent, perhaps because they were freshly plucked from the trees thriving in our soil enriched by volcanic ash and pumice.

Back at the airport, I found myself on the other side of the reunion, eagerly gazing up at the skywalk, awaiting Rock's arrival. With perfect timing, he appeared before me, his radiant smile

Pushed Out of the Closet Without A Parachute

illuminating the space, adorned in a dashing Tommy Bahama Hawaiian shirt and shorts, carrying a modest carry-on, as promised. I knew his housekeeper, James, must have handled the packing, as Rock had mentioned during our phone call last night. Yet, what mattered most was that he was here now, and I hoped this trip would grant him the much-needed solace from the pressures of Hollywood, the Marc Christian fiasco, and the weight of the burdens that had plagued him of late.

As soon as he saw me, his eyes lit up with joy. I knew I had to start this adventure on the right note, so I blurted out, "Welcome to Hilo and the Big Island!" He greeted me with a warm hug, and I asked how pleasant his flight had been. I thought to myself, "I'm sounding more like my mother every day."

I couldn't help but continue with my lively demeanor, "Oh, did you see the other side of the airport? There's a company that does skydiving lessons. Additionally, there was a woman nervously waiting at the airport for her husband to return from his skydiving lesson. The pilot approached her, saying: 'I'm sorry, but there's been an accident. I must inform you I have some bad news and some good news. The bad news is your husband fell out of the plane. The good news is he had his parachute on. In spite of wearing the parachute, I have more bad and good news to inform you about.' The woman was beside herself and begged him to continue. 'The additional bad news is that your husband hit the ground before his chute could open.' The woman gasped for air as she uttered, 'Oh my God!' The pilot continued, 'Well, the good news is we hadn't taken off yet.'"

We both burst into laughter, and it was the perfect icebreaker for the start of our time together on the beautiful Big Island.

I gave Rock the scenic tour around Bayfront Park in Hilo Bay and the charming old town. It was a quick detour, but the sights were delightful, and I knew Rock would appreciate the beauty of our little corner of paradise. Soon, we turned south towards Leilani Estates, where my parents eagerly awaited our dinner arrival. As we drove, I mentioned that I needed to make a quick stop to grab a couplebottles of wine. To my surprise, Rock piped up, "Oh, Gunther, let me come along and help pick them out. By the way, what's on the menu for dinner?"

I happily shared with him that my mom was preparing succulent filet mignon for him and my parents, while I would savor a delicious Mahi Mahi.

"Sounds fantastic," Rock replied, ever the gourmet enthusiast. "How about a red wine for your parents and me and a white for your fish?" he suggested.

I confessed, "I prefer red wine, especially a fine red Burgundy when I have salmon, but a vibrant Pinot Noir would make a perfect pairing with Mahi Mahi."

Rock was impressed by my knowledge of wine pairing based on the type of fish and proposed, "Let me select the maker of the wine—I know a couple that I think you'll love."

"Absolutely," I agreed, "I trust your taste entirely. Just one thing, though—I hope no one recognizes you in the KTA Supermarket. Hilo is a sleepy small town that rolls up its doors at 7 P.M., so we should be able to sneak in unnoticed." To my relief, the store was nearly empty, and we managed to slip in and out without any commotion and undetected.

As we cruised into the quaint town of Pahoa, Rock couldn't help but express his amazement, "You weren't kidding when you said your house is in the middle of nowhere. This town has only about ten buildings, which all look rather weathered and worn." He swiftly counted them off, "A post office, a small market, a church, a school, a gas station, and a couple of other buildings... Oh, and I even spotted a sign pointing to the dump."

I chuckled, knowing he was getting a taste of the rural charm of Pahoa, and I replied, "Yeah, it barely qualifies as a town, but hidden in the back is a wonderful natural food store where I once worked for a short while during my time here. Most folks tend to drive into Hilo, where there are a couple of supermarkets like the KTA we visited earlier. Trust me, out here, we won't be bothered. It's a peaceful haven, far away from the hustle and bustle of city life. You'll see."

As we finally drove up to Malama Street, we found ourselves descending the long, winding cement driveway to my humble abode, perched high on cinder blocks with a breezeway underneath to combat the relentless humidity of Hawaii. Fortunately, the ever-present Tradewinds gracefully swept through, while the single redwood walls stood resilient, shielding the house from wood rot and mold. The enchanting drive down the driveway was flanked by majestic King Palm trees, clothed in a blanket of ground cover and adorned with little yellow flowers whose names eluded me momentarily. And there, in the middle of this botanical haven, clumps of towering Ohia trees soared skyward, some reaching an astonishing height of over 70 feet, while a few showcased the delightful sight of wood roses blooming on their magnificent trunks.

As we approached the house, the driveway gently curved into an "L" shape, guiding us towards two garages that, in this tropical paradise, did not need conventional doors—nature's embrace served as a benevolent shelter from the elements. This section of the driveway was gracefully adorned with fern trees, lovingly attached by my rejuvenated Easter Orchids, now gloriously blooming. The sun descended towards the horizon, signaling the approaching spectacle of the mesmerizing sunset. I couldn't help but urge Rock to quickly head upstairs so we wouldn't miss this breathtaking event. From my deck facing west, we were blessed with a view of the vast ocean, awaiting the spectacular sight of the sun bidding its farewell as it gracefully dipped into the embrace of the majestic Pacific.

Heading up the stairs, a round water catchment tank embraced by lush tree ferns and exquisite orchids comes into view. The curved walkway leading to the stairs is adorned with a grand orchid tree, resplendent in its full bloom. The air is filled with a delightful, almost jasmine-like fragrance, adding to the enchantment of this place. Rock gazes around with awe in his eyes and utters, "Gunther, you weren't kidding, this is an absolutely stunning place. You said it was a simple house, but this exceeded my expectations. It's all about the location, and you, my man, have chosen the most magical spot."

I smiled, proud to share this hidden gem with my dear friend, and said, "Hold on, Rock, just wait until you see the view from the deck on the other side. We are connected to a vast forest reserve, and the entire stretch of trees and wilderness behind the house, all the way to the ocean, about two or three miles away, is protected and designated as a forest reserve. Nothing can be built or turned into farmland there, ensuring its natural beauty remains untouched. However, I have to admit, there are a few local pot growers who sneak in and plant their harvest somewhere within this massive forest to cultivate their prized Kona Gold.

In any event, picture, if you will, the saga of Malama Street, where the unexpected takes flight! As the sun's gentle embrace painted the horizon with hues of gold, a sudden whirl of helicopter blades pierced the tranquility, signaling the arrival of federal law enforcement. With their keen eye from above, they stumbled upon a clandestine secret—a grand crop of six to eight-foot pot plants, mysteriously thriving in the lush embrace behind my parents' retired haven. Bewilderment engulfed my dear parents, their minds swirling with questions, 'Vat in the world are they doing? Are they goin' to arrest us or something?'

Yet, with gracious hearts, my parents offered the authorities their consent, allowing the feds to sweep away the leafy intruders. 'Mein Gutness,' my mother muttered. 'It was like a scene straight out of Hawaii Five-0, an unexpected brush with the law right in the presence of our peaceful refuge.' And as the chopper took flight, the echoed iconic line, 'Book 'em, Daniel,' seemed to ripple through the air."

Rock and I couldn't help but burst into laughter, our spirits lightened by this quaint episode in a sleepy town that didn't fail to surprise us. As we turned the corner, the sun dipped below the horizon, casting a golden glow over my parent's home. They were enjoying their usual coffee, savoring the last moments of light, and, of course, it was a reasonable time for my mom to indulge in cigarettes, her simple pleasure in the serenity of Malama Street.

As I caught my parents' attention, I proudly announced, "Mom and Dad, I'd like to introduce you to Mr. Rock Hudson."

In his gentle way, Rock stops me before I can continue, "Oh Gunther, please let your parents call me by my real name, Roy Sherer. It makes me feel like I'm with family, and I already sense a connection, even though we've just met."

"Absolutely, Rock... I mean Roy," I said, amused by the slip.

As introductions were completed, I could have scripted what my mother's next question would be, and as expected, she asks, "Oh, und how was your flight, was it good?"

Pushed Out of the Closet Without A Parachute

Roy gives me a corner-eye look and smiles, replying, "I had a wonderful flight... but, what should I call you? Gunther only introduced you as 'mom and dad.'"

I chime in, "I'm so sorry, Roy. This is my mom, Erika, and my dad, Alfred, best known as Rickey and Al."

As Roy settled in next to my mom, it was as if two kindred spirits had found each other. He pulled out one of his cigarettes and politely asked, "Is it okay if I join you in smoking?"

My mom responded warmly, "Vell, of course. Make yourself at home, und don't hesitate to ask if you need anything. Günther mentioned how you two met and have become good friends?"

Roy glanced at me, and I chimed in, "Oh, I only gave them an abbreviated story; my mom will remember it better if you give all the details."

Roy gave the more detailed version of our meeting at a bar in Long Beach recalling how he invited me to perform at a party he was hosting the following evening. "Gunther came to perform, and I haven't been able to get rid of him since," Roy joked, leaving me with a playful "Ha Ha Ha" under my breath, as the laughter filled the room. Even my mom found the humor in the friendly banter.

The evening exceeded all our expectations. It felt as if Roy had been part of our family for years. My mom prepared a fabulous dinner, and we relished every bite, especially with the exquisite wines Roy had picked out. They complemented the meal perfectly. For dessert, my mom served a delightful medley of local fruits from the garden, topped with vanilla bean ice cream. To my surprise, my dad brought a bottle of German Gewürztraminer to accompany the sweet treat.

As we finished our desserts and shared the bottle of Gewürztraminer among the four of us, Roy took charge and playfully announced, "Come on, Günther, you and I will do the dishes so your parents can relax after putting all the work into such a great meal!"

My mom was astonished, remarking, "I never knew a movie star who washes dishes."

I couldn't resist adding, "Well, Mom, you've never known a movie star before, period!" Laughter filled the room, and I could tell that my parents really liked Roy.

When we were done doing the dishes and Roy sat out on the porch with my mom for another cigarette, I thought how fun it would be to drive down to the thermal tide pools next to Pohoiki Beach. The full moon was on the 15th, but it was still big enough to give us enough light to walk the path into the jungle to the most magnificent brackish water pool that existed, surrounded by jungle plants and exotic lush covering.

My parents had their regular routine of watching old movies and lounging in their recliner and declined, but my mom said, "You two go and have a good time; we are too tired and will relax here." Roy was game, so we both put on our surf shorts, grabbed a couple of beach towels and candles and were on our way.

We still had a little red wine left, so I brought that, and we made our way down the windy road to Pohoiki, which happens to be one of the most beautiful drives I have ever been on. Huge monkey-pod trees line the road and create a canopy of coverage—the canopy can grow nearly equal to the height of the tree. As we ended up at the boat ramp to Pohoiki, the surf breaking over the rocks was almost iridescent in the moonlight. I thankfully brought a flashlight to help guide us into the jungle behind the beach and soon found the pool luckily uninhabited and to ourselves.

As we immersed ourselves in the soothing waters, memories of the thermal tide pools came rushing back, and I couldn't help but notice that the water felt hotter than I had remembered—or perhaps it was just the elapse of time. The temperature usually hovers around 100 to 102 degrees, influenced by the amount of rain and freshwater that enters the pool.

As we settled into the pool, Roy casually rested his arm on a smooth rock in the corner, only to be jolted up by an unexpected sensation. "Oh, those are the brine shrimp. I warned you they like to explore interesting places!" Roy soon realized that a simple swipe of the hand could brush them off without any fuss. As we chuckled about the friendly shrimp's peculiar cleaning habits, it was evident that we were in for a relaxing evening, surrounded by the lush jungle and the comforting warmth of the brackish waters.

As the evening drew to a close, the warmth of the tide pools and the last sips of wine began to take their toll, leaving us both feeling a pleasant weariness. The anticipation of an exciting day exploring the area ahead of us nudged us to seek a good night's rest.

Pushed Out of the Closet Without A Parachute

I eagerly shared my plans for tomorrow—a grand tour of the Kilauea Volcano and the magnificent Hawaii Volcanoes National Park. My parents revealed that we had just missed the recent eruption of Mauna Loa and Kilauea, a breathtaking spectacle that took place from March 25 to April 15. Regrettably, we had arrived just five days after the eruption had ended, missing the chance to witness the awe-inspiring lava flowing in the night. I recounted my previous experience with the lava flowing into the ocean when I lived here. I told Rock, "the mesmerizing glow created a captivating and eerie ambiance that left a profound impression on my soul. Though we missed the eruption this time, will still have fun exploring the exciting volcanic wonders at the park."

As we drove back to the house, Roy shared his observations about my parents. He remarked that my father seemed reserved and didn't reveal much of himself, making it hard for Roy to get a read on him. On the other hand, he saw an unmistakable resemblance between my personality and my mother's. He praised her for being kind, gracious, funny, and intelligent, adding that she was in great shape for her age—an inspiration in many ways.

I agreed with Roy's assessment and acknowledged that my father's limited English proficiency might have contributed to his conversation reticence. Despite his linguistic challenges and relatively limited education, my father was a man of strong beliefs, and once he held a conviction, it was challenging to sway him. Regardless of the supporting evidence or knowledge you possessed, it did not affect the persuasiveness of your argument. I shared a humorous anecdote about when he mistakenly believed that running the microwave would damage the TV due to interference. Despite my attempts to explain the truth, he remained steadfast in his belief, a testament to his unwavering and sometimes stubborn nature—typical of his German heritage.

    As we settled into the house, we found my parents in front of the TV, on the verge of dozing off. They stirred as they heard us come up the stairs, and we all agreed it was time to call it a night. I showed Roy to the bedroom where he would stay for the visit. With only one full bathroom in the house, we'd have to manage the shower schedule, but it was nothing we couldn't handle. I suggested Roy take the first shower, and I'd follow once he was done.

    After Roy and I showered and were ready for bed, we bid goodnight to my parents, who were settled in for the night. As Roy walked into the bedroom, my mom couldn't help but express her surprise at Roy's genuine kindness and politeness. She admitted that she had expected a movie star to be more self-absorbed, but Roy had proven to be the opposite.

    I smiled, pleased that they had hit it off so well. I then asked her how Papa felt about Roy, and she replied, "You know your father, he's always set in his ways, and no one really knows what he thinks." We both chuckled in agreement, knowing my dad's opinions were always a mystery. With that, we bid each other goodnight and drifted off to sleep, excited for the adventures that awaited us in the morning.

Pushed Out of the Closet Without A Parachute

Very early in the morning, before anyone else was awake, I sneaked down into the garden to gather some fresh fruit and veggies. The scent of wild orchids, heliconia, red ginger, and the blooming torch ginger greeted me as I carefully plucked them. I had to wash them off with the hose, as some ants had already discovered the sap dripping from the large ginger bloom and were relishing it.

However, in my haste to be discreet, I forgot that using the water would trigger the pump, which filled the house with water from the catchment tank. I feared I might have awakened everyone in the house. Sure enough, not long after, I could hear footsteps moving about. My attempt to be quiet had failed, and breakfast time had begun. On the bright side, I had found three perfectly ripe avocados that would be perfect on my mom's homemade bread, toasted, of course!

As I joined Roy and my mother on the patio, both of them smoking again, I proudly presented the armful of goodies I had picked from the garden. Rock admired the assortment of flowers I placed in my mom's favorite vase, a Mother's Day gift from years ago. My dad was still in the shower, but Roy and my mom were delighted to see the huge avocados I had found. "These will make a fantastic addition to our breakfast," my mom remarked with a smile.

Breakfasts in my family were typically a German-style affair, with a table full of choices to pick from. Alongside the cereal and yogurt, I had already set out, I laid an assortment of sliced meats, cheeses, and now the fresh avocados, mangoes, pineapples, guavas, and a couple of papayas that would need another day or two to fully ripen. The table was a feast of tropical delights, and I knew my parents would appreciate the effort to create a special breakfast to start our day.

We had an excellent breakfast, and to my surprise, Roy even had more coffee than my parents, if that could even be possible. I wanted to see if my parents wanted to come along for a trip to the Volcano House, but they declined, having seen it so many times already this year with the eruption. This would allow Roy and me to have more time to ourselves, but I just had to double-check if he was interested or would rather lounge around and relax.

Roy had only one concern: whether our trip to the Volcano House would take up the entire day, or if he could find time to read and relax. I assured him that we'd likely have an early lunch at the Volcano House and be back home before 1 P.M., which sounded perfect to him. The morning would be filled with exploration, followed by a leisurely day in the sun and enough time to read a script he had brought along.

The day unfolded according to plan, and we found ourselves back at the house after a delightful walk on the rim trail around the Halemaʻumaʻu crater and a light lunch at the Volcano House, considering we were still pretty full of the generous breakfast spread. Roy thanked me for showing him around and expressed how much he enjoyed our morning together. Then, with a hint of curiosity, he asked me about my plans for tomorrow, Easter Sunday.

Pushed Out of the Closet Without A Parachute

I replied that I yet to make definite plans and was open to suggestions. I mentioned that if he hadn't been with us, I probably would have taken my parents into Hilo for brunch or something of that sort. To my surprise, Roy immediately said, "Gunther, I insist on taking you all out for brunch tomorrow, to the nicest place possible. It's the least I can do for you and your parents for hosting me and letting me stay here." His genuine kindness and generosity truly touched my heart.

There aren't many choices, but I told Roy, "I do know the Hilo Hawaiian Hotel offers a great brunch, but I don't know if we can still get a reservation."

Roy told me not to worry about it and would make arrangements but wanted to know what time. I told him that they prefer earlier brunches than most people. I suggested, "How about 10:00 or 10:30?"

He answered, "Perfect. We'll let them know later tonight." At that point, we kicked off our flip-flops, grabbed a couple of coolers, and lounged on the sunny side of the deck to get some much-needed color and R&R.

I woke up to the unusual sound of squabbling mongooses, their chatter breaking the usual serenity of the wind rustling through the trees. Startled for a moment, I noticed that Rock and my dad were conversing on the covered deck where my parents were relaxing. Suddenly, they appeared to be heading off somewhere, so I inquired, "Where are you two headed?"

Pushed Out of the Closet Without A Parachute

Roy explained, "Your dad told me about a petrified forest and some lava tubes in the area, and he wants to show them to me."

I sensed that my dad had cornered him, so I playfully said, "Are you sure you want to go? I know you wanted to read that script you brought."

Roy chuckled and replied, "No, that's perfectly fine. I read enough of the script to know it's not for me. It's for a possible TV show, and I'm not interested. I promised to look at it, and now I have, so I'm good. You enjoy the sun, and we'll be back shortly."

I turned to my dad with a teasing smile and warned, "Now, you be nice to Roy. Don't lose him in the petrified forest or leave him in a lava tube!"

My dad looked at me puzzled until he finally caught on that I was joking, and he playfully retorted, "Yah yah yah!"

As my dad and Roy headed off to explore the petrified forest and lava tubes, I spent some quality time with my mom in the Doughboy pool. We chatted about life, my work, and my plans now that I've graduated from college. I confessed that I didn't have a definitive plan yet, and the hotel business wasn't my long-term goal. I shared with her an intriguing offer I had received to work as an Aerobics advisor in Australia, with enticing perks like a car, a house, and a generous salary. I explained that I had gone as far as obtaining a resident visa and confirming my sponsor, the manager, and part-owner of multiple health clubs in Australia. This was a necessary process if you possessed a skill set that Australians living there couldn't provide.

However, the opportunity fell through when my sponsor got involved in a smuggling scandal. Despite the setback, it got me thinking about a potential career in the fitness industry, which resonated with me. Still, I needed more time to piece together a solid plan for my future.

We were in the pool for longer than I expected, and I wanted a quick shower before Roy, and Dad came back. I expected to see them home once I was ready, but they still weren't back. It was well over two hours since they left, and my mom and I were starting to get worried. Could my dad have gotten lost? Or worse yet, could someone have fallen or gotten hurt?

I know it sounds silly, but I was genuinely concerned. I took an additional hour before they finally came driving in, and as soon as they were within earshot, I immediately grilled both of them, "Where have you two been? I thought you would be gone for maybe an hour or two at the most."

My Dad responded, "I waz just showing Rock, ah, Roy, around—herumgeführt mit ihm." Meaning he just drove Roy around showing him places.

Roy grabs me and whispers, "Your dad was so nice to show me around, but he kept saying something about this and that... Gunther, I couldn't understand a single word he said, so I just kept nodding my head and said Ya Ya Ya."

Pushed Out of the Closet Without A Parachute

I laughed and replied, "Oh my God, Roy... I'm so sorry."

But Roy quickly reassured me, "No, please don't be sorry. I truly relished the opportunity to get better acquainted with your father. He's undeniably old-school but incredibly sincere, and yes, 'VERY GERMAN!'" We both shared a hearty chuckle, fully embracing the distinctiveness of my dad's character. I could almost picture Roy attempting to decipher my father's earnest yet slightly cryptic German explanations, nodding as if he comprehended every word. It was akin to a delightful scene in a charming comedy, a snippet right out of a film titled "Rock Goes to Hawaii." ...So, stay tuned for more captivating highlights in next week's episode.

We decided to have a barbecue on the grill outside, keeping things casual with paper plates, and sat outdoors while enjoying another gorgeous sunset. As we savored our food, we found ourselves discussing and solving the world's problems, and of course, Hollywood couldn't be left out.

My dad, being the curious type, wanted to know all about making a movie and the tremendous effort it takes to get everything just right. Roy, ever the entertainer, switched into his Rock personality and regaled my parents with tales of modern filmmaking, contrasting it with the old studio days when stars were carefully groomed and crafted.

My dad was utterly captivated, and Roy thought it would be fun to show him some examples of filmmaking. He asked me if there was a Blockbuster or another place to rent the DVD "Das Boot." None of us had seen it yet, so we were all intrigued.

Roy explained, "It's a 1981 West German war movie directed by Wolfgang Petersen. It was adapted from a 1973 German novel based on his World War II adventures aboard the German submarine U-96." The mention of a submarine and World War II caught my mom and dad's attention, and we all agreed to try and grab the movie the next day.

It was an opportune moment for Roy to suggest treating us to a special Easter brunch at the Hilo Hawaiian Hotel in the morning, followed by the possibility of grabbing the movie on our way home. My mom, taken by surprised by the grand gesture, responded, "You don't have to do that."

However, Roy quickly retorted, "I would truly love to take you all out for allowing me to come here and sharing your lovely home and hospitality with me. It would genuinely make me happy to treat you." My mom, flattered and deeply humbled by the invitation from a Hollywood movie star, graciously accepted.

As for the evening entertainment, much to my chagrin, my father insisted on sharing some cringe-worthy home movies. I immediately protested, not wanting Roy to witness my rather awkward younger self. "Please, no way! Roy has no interest in these potentially embarrassing home movies. Let's opt for board games instead!" I exclaimed.

Pushed Out of the Closet Without A Parachute

Yet Roy enthusiastically chimed in, saying, "Oh, come on, Günther. Your parents want to regale me with tales of your youthful adventures. I'd love to witness them, and we can always play games afterward."

In response, I conceded with a hint of apprehension, "All right, if I can survive the embarrassment!" I added with lighthearted jest, "You just wait, Mr. Sherer: I'm going to find a way to get back at you for this!" Laughter filled the room at my expense, but I mentally prepared myself for the impending revelation of little Günther in various escapades, from swim meets to lifeguarding at the beach and even playing the guitar with my once bleach-blond long hair back in the early '70s.

The looming specter of those home movies was more tormenting than a sunburn on a hot summer day. Roy's relentless enthusiasm for witnessing those candid glimpses from my past only heightened my dread. I clung to the faint hope that, just maybe, those movies had been misplaced or miraculously disappeared over the years, sparing me from the humiliation of revisiting my younger, less refined self.

Among the reels of footage, there existed a particularly cringe-inducing moment, a memory when a group of cheerleaders playfully toilet-papered our house and delivered homemade cookies ahead of a giant water polo match. As I watched, I couldn't help but wince at the sight of my younger self, a bumbling figure in that awkward situation.

"Enough of this, please! It's like nails on a chalkboard to me. I implore you, let's cease this," I earnestly begged my parents.

Fortunately, they agreed to end the parade of my youthful escapades. Instead, my father suggested we embark on a board game adventure with "Mensch ärgere Dich nicht." It was a game Roy wasn't familiar with, so I provided a translation of its name, which meant "Hey Man, Don't Get Angry." This German game has been a part of my life since childhood. I couldn't believe they had the actual copy from when I was a child, and it was barely holding together.

Roy was intrigued and expressed, "Let's play! I'm quite the card and board game enthusiast—playing games like this with friends is truly one of my favorite pastimes." My dad beamed excitedly, as my mom cleared the table and presented the game. As I gazed upon the vintage board, a wave of nostalgia washed over me; it appeared just as it did when I played on it as a child, but now carried a subtle whiff of age, a testament to the years it had spent in Hawaii's humidity and dampness.

Interestingly, Roy got addicted to the game, and we played "Hey Man, Don't Get Angry" four times in a row. Everybody, but me, won at least one game, but I got more enjoyment from watching everyone else win, especially Roy! He won two games (beginner's luck), and when he celebrated his victory, he did it with such gusto. "Yay, I won... I won... How do you like that," he cheered, making the game much more fun than I ever remembered it being.

Pushed Out of the Closet Without A Parachute

During the game breaks, Roy shared some stories from his childhood, which unfortunately weren't filled with as much joy. His father had left the family, and his stepfather had a cruel streak, taking it out on both Roy and his mother. My mom was horrified and couldn't fathom how anyone could be so cruel, especially to a little child. I thought this might lead my dad to open up about his difficult childhood, but he remained silent.

Not wanting to dwell on somber topics and dampen the evening, I quickly broke the ice with a joke. Laughter filled the room again, and we all continued, enjoying the night to the fullest. Surprisingly, we didn't get to bed until after midnight—a first for my parents since moving to Hawaii. They told me they had the most fun they've had in a long time, and I couldn't have been happier to have Roy there to bring so much joy to my family.

Pushed Out of the Closet Without A Parachute

Pushed Out of the Closet Without A Parachute

Pushed Out of the Closet Without A Parachute

Pushed Out of the Closet Without A Parachute

Chapter 9: Big Island Easter

We slept in much later than I ever expected, but it turned out to be a relaxed start to the day, leaving us plenty of time to get ready for Easter Brunch in Hilo. Church wasn't our tradition, but we had our unique way of celebrating the holidays, and this year, thanks to Roy, we had a special occasion at the Hilo Hawaiian Hotel.

As my parents bustled around getting dressed for the outing, I had already done my morning workout, a short jog, and attended to my orchids. Roy was on the porch, enjoying a smoke. As I walked onto the deck, I asked if he had showered already. He assured me he was the first to shower, and I was the last one left to get ready.

With about twenty minutes to spare, I checked if the bathroom was free. My mom had just finished up and kindly offered to use the other half-bathroom, urging me to go ahead and shower. In a mere ten minutes, I was all freshened up and quickly dressed in my only pair of long pants, which matched nicely with a Hawaiian print shirt I had also brought. With everyone ready, we set off for our Easter Brunch adventure in Hilo.

Precisely forty minutes later, we arrived at the hotel, and to my surprise, the parking lot was packed. I shared my concern with Roy, hoping that we wouldn't have to wait in a long line for brunch. But Roy, ever the smooth operator, reassured me, "No need to worry. I called ahead, and they've already prepared a special table for us."

Pushed Out of the Closet Without A Parachute

My mother was thoroughly impressed, never having experienced such personalized service before. As we stepped inside, it was like stepping onto the red carpet. The staff greeted us with utmost warmth and professionalism, addressing my mother as "Mrs. Fraulob" and attentively asking, "How can I help you, Mr. Fraulob?" Of course, Roy was treated like the star he was, with waitstaff expressing their excitement, "Mr. Hudson, we are so happy you joined us today. How can we make this brunch extra special for you?" It was clear that we were in for an unforgettable Easter Brunch experience.

With the cat out of the bag, the restaurant was abuzz with excitement, and all eyes were on us. My mother looked slightly overwhelmed by the attention, and people started approaching us, asking for Rock's autograph. He graciously signed a couple, but the requests just kept coming. My parents were in disbelief, realizing the true extent of Rock's fame and the constant attention he must receive.

My mom couldn't help but ask, "How can you always deal with such a fuss? It must drive you crazy."

Roy remained composed, displaying his trademark patience and humility. He explained, "Unfortunately, this is the price of being famous and recognized wherever you go. That's why it's such a blessing to spend time with you, where I can escape the public eye and enjoy this tropical paradise you live in."

During all this commotion, my mom sighed, "My oh my, I could never handle being famous."

Pushed Out of the Closet Without A Parachute

I couldn't help but smile and reassure her, "Don't worry, Mom, I don't think you'll ever have to deal with that!" We shared a light-hearted chuckle as the hotel staff started to serve the exceptional Easter brunch, with Rock's star power casting a magical glow over the entire experience.

With our meals quickly served, we relished the advantages of having connections as our dishes arrived promptly after ordering. However, dealing with the enthusiastic fans was a different story altogether. They just kept coming, and it got to the point where Roy had to kindly put his foot down, saying, "I'll be happy to sign autographs once we're done with brunch. For now, please let us enjoy our meal."

The manager, who had been so attentive to our needs, quickly came to the rescue, ensuring we wouldn't be disturbed any further. They stationed employees on both sides of our table to intervene if anyone approached. With the fan frenzy at bay, we finally had the opportunity to dig into our fabulous meal. The food was so delectable that we could feel our stomachs about to burst with delight.

Roy gracefully excused himself from the table, disappearing into the crowd of fans eagerly awaiting him outside. My parents and I exchanged worried glances; the gathering in front of our hotel was a sight, especially for a tranquil town like Hilo. Excitement was rippling through the air, making the scene almost surreal.

Acting swiftly, I seized a few "to-go" cups and signaled to Roy that we needed to make a hasty exit. While I hastened to fetch the car,

Pushed Out of the Closet Without A Parachute

Roy navigated the crowd of admirers adeptly, edging closer to the wide-open door. It was like a suspenseful scene plucked from "McMillan and Wife," and my parents, left bewildered by the unexpected turn of events, experiencing an Easter brunch like no other.

Once safely inside the car, I sped off, assuring my parents that I would be the only one stepping out when we reached the video rental place to grab the DVD. I had called ahead to ensure they were open, and thankfully, they were ready to accommodate our little adventure.

The car ride back was a relief, and the quiet allowed Roy to let out a long sigh, releasing the pent-up anxiety and stress from the unexpected fan encounter. My parents and I were grateful for his kind gesture, assuring him that we would never forget this extraordinary Easter brunch.

Still in shock, my dad made a humorous comment, saying, "I'm surprised they still remember you. You aren't working anymore, are you?"

Roy and I exchanged amused glances before Roy explained that even though he might not be filming a new movie at the moment, he still receives residuals whenever his past movies play anywhere in the world. My dad was new to the concept of royalties, and he seemed perplexed by the idea.

Roy's words carried a mix of determination and passion for his craft. "I recently worked on The Ambassador, a thrilling film shot in Israel. It was a great experience, and I plan to keep working as long as

I can," he said. "I've also spent some time touring onstage, performing in plays like Camelot, James Brown's Body, and I Do! I Do! Since you watch TV, you might have caught me in the 1982 crime drama series The Devlin Connection on NBC, where I played alongside Jack Scalia. Unfortunately, they had to cut the show short due to my heart surgery and the writer's strike, but I still believe it had potential."

Roy leaned back, his eyes filled with hope and excitement for the future. "I'm keeping an open mind and staying optimistic. I want to find a project I truly enjoy and feel passionate about. So, I'm reading scripts and waiting for the right opportunity to come my way. It's all about timing and the love for the work," he concluded with a smile.

I skillfully maneuvered into the video store's driveway, finding it conveniently empty. With the open sign beckoning, I swiftly grabbed "Das Boot" and dashed back to the car, feeling victorious like a seasoned treasure hunter. "Well, that was a breeze. Thanks to Easter, I had the whole store to myself," I declared triumphantly.

My mom sighed with relief, "Thank goodness, we've had enough excitement for one day."

Eager to prolong the blissful day, I suggested taking the scenic route home, and everyone agreed. Our next stop was Rainbow Falls, a hidden gem on the outskirts of town. Its beauty was breathtaking, the falls shimmering like liquid diamonds under the radiant sun. We strolled along the stone path, capturing the magic in photographs. The moment was pure poetry, but as we headed back, I noticed everyone's eyelids drooping, yearning for a well-deserved power nap once we returned home.

I carefully ushered our way back to Leilani Estates. The majestic row of King Palms greeted us, swaying gently in the breeze. Quietly glancing at the rearview mirror, I couldn't help but smile at the heartwarming sight of my fast-asleep companions, like they were in a sugar-induced coma after a wild glucose high. With a gentle touch, I coasted the car with the engine off into the garage, and they remained blissfully unaware until we came to a peaceful halt.

"Wake up, everyone. We're home," I said gently so as not to startle them. No one had a clue where we were until they got their bearings and realized we were already parked in our garage. I chuckled and informed everyone that I would prepare some papayas, cleaned and sliced with a hint of lemon for a zesty pick-me-up, and bring them to the back porch for us to enjoy while we all relaxed.

"Coffee, anyone?" I asked, and everyone let me know their preferences. Some things never change, do they? Roy with sugar, no milk; my dad black; my mom with a little milk and a dash of sugar; and me, water! LOL, I do enjoy the simple things in life the best!

The deck transformed into a haven of relaxation, laughter, and delightful conversations as we indulged in our beverages. I cherished moments like these the most, surrounded by loved ones, basking in the warmth of each other's company. The trade winds blew gently, and our Ohia trees and Norfolk pines, which I had planted when I first moved in, swayed along with the rhythm of the breeze. With beauty all around us, we relished the tranquility and found solace. Life may have twists and turns, but in the company of dear ones and the taste of nature's bounty, we understood that we should be eternally grateful for our gifts and never take them for granted.

That evening, we embarked on a culinary adventure, deeming it "clean out the fridge" night—a moment of gastronomic spontaneity. I turned to Roy, inquiring about his appetite, but he graciously declined, still full from our marvelous brunch earlier. With the kitchen at our disposal and many delectable ingredients, everyone could concoct their individual delight.

In a burst of creativity, I seized my parents' homegrown butter lettuce, a trove of treasures, to craft a tropical salad masterpiece. A medley of flavors danced on my plate as I artfully arranged fresh papaya, succulent pineapple, and tender leftover chicken from last night's BBQ. My culinary curiosity also led me to discover some other items in the produce bin I hadn't noticed before. "Are those yellow and red peppers in the fridge homegrown bell peppers?"

My mom told me they were indeed and added a nice splash of color to my creation, nurtured by my parents' green thumbs. I topped it off with a Raspberry Vinaigrette and paraded my production before everyone.

"Would anyone else like me to conjure up another culinary marvel for their banquet?" I playfully quipped, hoping to ignite their appetite for adventure. Alas, there was no interest; everyone seemed content with casual munching on chips and nuts—a laissez-faire dining affair for the evening. Yet, as I savored every succulent bite of my tropical salad, I couldn't help but relish the joy of culinary discovery. How often does one savor such homegrown exotic tastes in such a divine and organic place? These bell peppers, lettuce, and fruits were all nurtured in nitrogen-rich lava soil, basked in the tropical sun, and nourished by pure rain. They all carry a natural elegance orchestrated by nature's hand.

The sunset had been another beautiful work of art, and now Roy was thrilled with debuting "Das Boot," eagerly prepping things for my dad to notice about the filming of this masterpiece. Roy's fascination with the ingenious method of shooting the movie was palpable. As the film unfolded, he couldn't help but marvel at the seamless camera work. He followed the action within the cramped confines of the tiny submarine, moving from cabin to cabin or section to section through a very narrow hole that only a small person could easily fit through. The technical wizardry behind capturing the unfolding drama with those large cameras left Roy captivated and eager to share the intricacies of the process with my dad. Were they on a track? Perhaps a cleverly devised gurney or a swing of some sort? It was indeed a feat of camera genius, making "Das Boot" a film to be remembered for ages.

We all settled into the cozy living room, with Roy and I perched on the couch and my parents comfortably reclining in their chairs. As the movie began, the suspense and intrigue immediately captured our attention, punctuated by thrilling action scenes that left us in awe of the masterful camera work that Roy had mentioned. However, amidst the high-stakes drama, a new soundtrack emerged—the gentle melody of snoring.

To my surprise, my mom and dad had dozed off, snoring away in harmony with the intense submarine action. Embarrassed by their unintended slumber, I turned to Roy, feeling the need to apologize for the impromptu snooze-fest. But, ever understanding, Roy reassured me, "No need to apologize for them, my friend. They must be quite exhausted, and it's entirely understandable."

As the movie continued, we couldn't help but snicker each time one of my parents caught their breath and snorted another loud snore. It was a comedic twist to our movie night, adding a touch of levity to the high-stakes drama. "Well," I thought, "it is what it is!" And we enjoyed the film and the company, appreciating the moment's uniqueness.

"Das Boot" was undoubtedly a cinematic masterpiece, and it has the accolades to prove it. The film's gripping storytelling, outstanding direction, and meticulous attention to detail earned it well-deserved nominations for six Academy Awards, including Best Director, Best Screenplay, Best Cinematography, Best Sound, Best Film Editing, and Best Sound Effects. In 1983, it won Best Foreign Language Film.

The following day, my mom & dad graciously apologized for nodding off during the movie and vowed to watch it again now that they were well rested. True to their word, they gave it another go, and this time, they were equally captivated by the film's brilliance. They showered Roy with gratitude for revealing so many intricate details that made the movie even more fascinating—a shared moment of cinematic appreciation brought us all closer together.

As we discussed the day's plan, I suggested heading down to Black Sand's Beach for a delightful beach day. The agenda was set—pack a delicious lunch, enjoy a refreshing swim, and perhaps even try bodysurfing. For my mom and dad, there would be ample shade, with park benches and tables to relax in comfort. However, I knew we needed to get there early, for Black Sand's Beach was a popular destination, attracting BBQ enthusiasts and sunset admirers later in the day. But have no doubt, we'd be back well before the crowd descended, leaving us with plenty of cherished moments to bask in the sun and savor the magic of the beach.

As we arrived at the beach, a crowd had gathered, marveling at the impressive swell. The waves were calling to me, and excitement coursed through my veins. Oh, how I wished I still had my surfboard with me! Alas, it became evident that only the shorebreak was surfable, and regulations prohibited the use of boards in that area anyhow. Undeterred, I couldn't resist the allure of the waves.

"Come on, let's go!" I rallied, hoping to encourage my companions to join in the ocean's embrace. However, they chose to stay on the shore and observe from afar. My dear mother, ever the worrier, voiced her concern, urging me to be careful. But there was an indescribable connection between me and the sea—as if I had once been a dolphin or some other sea creature in my past life. The ocean felt like my true home.

Without hesitation, I leaped into an oncoming wave, feeling its invigorating rush envelop me. As I caught my first wave, its face was perfect, offering me a thrilling ride. With only one fin at my disposal, I relied on my skills to navigate and stay on course. The wave carried me along its sharp left turn, and I expertly skimmed its face, using one hand as a rudder to steer. The ride was brief, with the wave inevitably closing out, but I swiftly veered off the lip and swam back out to where the sets were forming, eager to seize another exhilarating moment in the dance of the sea.

As I glanced back towards the shore, I saw Roy and my parents comfortably settled under the shade of the palm trees, watching me with affectionate eyes. They knew how much I had missed the sheer joy of surfing, a passion that had once filled my daily life. In those days, if the surf was up, you could bet I'd be out there riding the waves with pure contentment for hours. But as life progressed, responsibilities took precedence, and the carefree surfing enjoyment became a rare luxury.

Yet, vacations meant letting go of those worries and embracing the thrill of being alive. So, with a renewed sense of freedom, I showcased my skills, executing a graceful flip as I dropped into a wave that turned out to be the ride of the day, carrying me all the way to shore. It felt like I reclaimed a piece of my soul that had been temporarily tucked away.

Pushed Out of the Closet Without A Parachute

With the wave's adrenaline still coursing through my veins, I dashed out of the water and approached Roy. I inquired if he'd like to explore the other side of the bay, where the waves were calmer and more suitable for a stroll. He explained that due to his heart surgery, he would be limited to walking along the shore. I eagerly offered to accompany him, and his face lit up with gratitude. Together, we set off on a gentle adventure, savoring the beauty of the beach, the sound of waves lapping against the shore, and the feeling of sand beneath our feet.

As we strolled along the shore, I couldn't help but inquire about Roy's feelings. Was he genuinely enjoying our laid-back beach day or secretly yearning for the glitz and glamour of a luxurious hotel? Roy's response put my worries to rest as he expressed his genuine delight. He shared how being with my family, without any hidden agendas, brought him immense joy, and he even wondered what life could have been like with a loving family like mine.

In turn, I opened up about my challenging upbringing, explaining that my relationship with my father was far from perfect. I, too, had moments of anger and pain that I had to navigate. The problematic circumstances led me to leave home at a young age to lifeguard in Huntington Beach, creating a distance between us for several years. However, I persevered, achieving my educational goals and finding success through water polo and other endeavors. My accomplishments eventually bridged the gap, and I purchased the house where my parents now lived, even though they ended up selling their home to pay off the remaining amount, turning life's lemons into sweet lemonade.

Roy's eyes locked with mine, and he admired how I fearlessly frolicked in the surf, embracing my natural athletic abilities. He saw in me the spirit of a dolphin or a fantastical sea creature, entirely at home in their watery domain. He applauded my diverse talents, excelling at whatever I set my mind to, and praised me for achieving greatness beyond mediocrity. Seeing a reflection of himself in my younger persona struck him how alike we were. He acknowledged that talking to me was effortless, as if we were kindred spirits.

His words echoed my thoughts—as if we were attuned to the same frequency. It felt like fate had brought us together, and there was a profound reason for our encounter at this precise moment in our lives. Like souls cut from the same cloth, we had walked similar paths, and finding solace in each other's company was exactly what our hearts yearned for.

We returned to my parents' side and indulged in a few more delightful hours, engrossed in conversation, savoring the turkey sandwiches my thoughtful mother had prepared and quenching our thirst with the refreshing soft drinks from the cooler. The day had been nothing short of extraordinary, and it struck me that mid the fun and good times, no one had caught on to the fact that Roy was the legendary Rock. Perhaps the subtle use of his real name veiled his identity, but regardless, it resulted in a perfectly splendid day for Roy.

The relaxation in his eyes and the genuine joy he exuded was a priceless sight to behold.

I couldn't help but take pride in my small role in adding tranquility to his life and allowing him to bask in the present moment. My mind couldn't help but wonder, contemplating the potential of our friendship and how it might evolve in the days to come. Time would reveal the path we were destined to tread together, but little did I know that in just over a year, unforeseen events would change everything.

Life's unpredictable twists led Roy on a journey he could never have anticipated, a battle against his mortality that would test his strength to the core. As he retreated from the world, I couldn't help but wonder if I had unknowingly done something wrong. But it wasn't about me but about Roy's struggle to face the inevitability of life's end. A battle he courageously fought, even though the odds were stacked against him.

In the following days, we embarked on more thrilling adventures. One of the more memorable days was when we dove into the enchanting thermal tide pools. There, the merging of cold ocean waters and warm brackish water created a mesmerizing sight of tropical fish and provided an enjoyable escape under the radiant sun. While resting on smooth lava rocks, Rock surprised me with a poignant question: "Gunther, have you ever experienced a love so profound that it left you yearning even after it ended?"

I took a moment to ponder what constituted true love, and my mind wandered back to a significant chapter in my life. I recalled a young man named Donn, whom I met on Oahu while working as a lifeguard. At the same time, I still had braces on my teeth, which made me feel somewhat insecure about my appearance. However, when I encountered Donn, I was captivated by his godly charm, and we soon found ourselves immersed in a whirlwind romance.

"We met at Hula's; a charming bar nestled under the grandeur of a Banyan tree in downtown Waikiki. After exchanging phone numbers, our connection quickly blossomed, and fate seemed to align our paths perfectly. Coincidentally, this was also the time when I was scheduled to have my braces removed. The transformation was remarkable—I felt a newfound confidence with my new radiant smile, and Donn was utterly smitten. He saw me as the epitome of charm and beauty. Our first date took us on an enchanting journey of dinner, dancing, and laughter, setting the stage for the magic that was about to unfold.

As the moonlight embraced us, we embarked on a moonlit hike up a mountain trail, guided solely by the celestial glow. The world around us seemed to fade away, leaving only the two of us basking in the beauty of the starlit sky. On the peak, we found a flat rock adorned with a cozy blanket, the perfect sanctuary for our souls to intertwine. The stars above bore witness to the profound connection that ignited between us, transcending the need for words. It was a love unlike any other I had experienced, one that stirred my spirit and awakened my soul to a depth I never thought possible.

However, our relationship was far from smooth sailing. Even though we both knew we loved each other, Donn had a stronger love for drugs. It started with occasional marijuana and Quaaludes, but it soon progressed to more dangerous substances like cocaine.

Eventually, I discovered, in a heart-wrenching way, that he was involved in both taking and dealing heroin. I couldn't bear to watch him descend into the clutches of addiction, and with a heavy heart, I had to step away from the relationship. Despite our deep affection for each other, I knew I had to prioritize my well-being and make one of the most challenging decisions of my life to move on. I desperately wished I could have saved him, but sometimes, specific paths are beyond our control, and fate takes its course."

Since then, no one has come close to igniting a love within me that matches the depth of what I would call "true love." Although I cherish the memories, I have grown wiser and understand the importance of finding love in its purest form—one that is nurturing and stands the test of time. As I shared my story with Rock, there was a sense of catharsis, a release of emotions that had been dormant. At that moment, I knew our bond was more profound and that Roy better understood my journey.

I asked him the same soul-searching question: "Who, if anyone, held the title of love of your life?"

With a contemplative glint in his eyes, he began recounting the numerous souls that had graced his journey. "Well, Gunther," he started, the timbre of his voice filled with reminiscence. "I have loved many people, including my dear wife Phyllis, for almost three years. But you see, those connections bloomed from infatuations that slowly evolved into a more deep-rooted friendship.

Ah, there were almost seventeen years when I was entangled with a man named Tom Clark. It all commenced as compatibility with fringe benefits; later, it metamorphosed into a professional association, and I hired him to be my agent. Yet, sparks never truly ignited the soul's inferno and were a mere flicker in that realm of partnership. We danced the intricate dance of lovers but never truly felt the symphony of passion in our hearts. Instead, we bickered and sparred like an old married couple until that fateful day when we knew we had reached the end and had enough. Oh, there were luminous moments of joy and darker shades of trials, and while I yearned to believe the scales tipped in favor of bliss, in the end, there lingered a sense of yearning, an intangible essence that was elusive."

I nodded as I listened to Roy, understanding his sentiments all too well. "I know exactly what you mean; it was the same for me," I admitted with a sigh. "I'd meet someone and become fascinated with them, but once we finally were together, the spark wasn't there, and I, too, felt that there had to be more. Maybe you and I are in love with the challenge of finding love so much that..." I paused, reverting to that memorable evening at El Torrito Restaurant in Long Beach and "The Kiss."

"Well, like what you told me after that night in Long Beach when you kissed me and said, 'You couldn't even see love if it stared you right in the face!'" I continued with a question, my voice tinged with curiosity, "Do you think that is our problem? Or are we too jaded and can't settle for what is good, even though it is not perfect? Does anything I'm saying even make any sense?"

Roy looked blank, his thoughts mirroring my own perplexity. Neither of us wanted to dwell on the matter any longer, so he shared his belief: "Gunther, when true love comes, I believe we will just know it, just like you had with Donn so many years ago. It happens naturally, and you realize this is the person I want to spend the rest of my life with."

"Absolutely," I replied, finding comfort in his words. With that, we returned to the house and prepared for dinner.

As we got ready to head home, I couldn't shake the bittersweet feeling that this was Roy's last full day on the island. The week had flown by, and though I still had four days left, I knew it wouldn't be quite as fun without him here. My parents, who were back at the house, had decided not to join us at the thermal pools, so I thought, Maybe we could bring them a little treat from Pahoa.

On our way back, I suggested a quick detour to the quaint local town. The charming general store there looked like it might topple over at any minute, but it was all part of Pahoa's organic charm—the little slice of paradise I called home. As we drove, laughter and jokes filled the car, and I couldn't resist slipping in a banana pun, asking Roy, "Why do bananas never get lonely?"

After our earlier deep conversations, I half-expected some profound insight, but he just replied, "I have no idea at all."

I enthusiastically delivered the punchline, "Because they hang out in bunches!" Buh, dump, dump! But it only earned me a laugh from myself. Undeterred, I continued, "So, now you know why bananas use sunblock here in Hawaii, right? That's because otherwise, they'd peel!"

Roy couldn't help but chuckle, shaking his head. "Okay, that's just getting desperate now," he teased.

"What? Wasn't it appealing enough?" I retorted, grinning.

"Stop already," he said, still laughing. "Why is your side-splitting?"

With a grand flourish, I replied, "Because I find it a-peeling!"

We both laughed heartily, cherishing these lighthearted moments that made our time together unforgettable.

As we strolled into the picturesque town of Pahoa, a weathered fisherman caught my eye, proudly displaying his daily catch on ice in front of the store. A magnificent Mahi Mahi seemed to beckon us among the glistening treasures of the sea. "What do you think, Roy?" I inquired with a sense of culinary adventure.

With a glint of excitement, he replied, "This would undoubtedly make a splendid meal, and my, what a beauty!"

Succumbing to the temptation, we secured the prized fish and decided to explore the local general store, which greeted us with a delightful clutter that defied order. After navigating the labyrinthine

Pushed Out of the Closet Without A Parachute

aisles, we settled on the fish alone, and as we made our exit, Roy couldn't help but chuckle, "That must be the most unorganized store I've ever set foot in! Finding anything in that disarray is a conundrum. And, my dear friend, you were right—the place seems like a nostalgic relic on the brink of whimsical collapse."

"Ha ha," I added, "It's been exactly like this since I resided here, and that was at least four or five years ago."

When we arrived with the enormous Mahi Mahi, my mom's eyes widened in amazement, exclaiming, "Oh my, this fish could feed us for an entire week!"

With his curiosity, Dad wondered if we had ventured for a fishing trip off the Pohoiki coast. I playfully replied, "As much as I'd love a fishing adventure with Roy, we stumbled upon this beauty right by the quirky general store, and we couldn't resist." I then turned to Roy with a mischievous grin, suggesting, "You know, we should take a photo of you holding the fish, and we'll say you caught it. It'll be our little fisherman's tale!"

Roy chuckled heartily, replying, "Oh, trust me, no one would buy that fish story. Everyone already knows that fishing isn't my cup of tea!"

We all laughed, and I continued, "Well, you could have told them about the one that got away, and this one here is just its little brother." With a plan in place, I assisted my mom, and we grilled half of the fish while preserving the rest in the freezer for another delightful feast.

Pushed Out of the Closet Without A Parachute

We dined like royalty that evening, savoring every delectable bite of the Mahi Mahi. Our unanimous agreement resonated—it stood among the most exquisite fish dishes we had ever experienced. The flavors gracefully danced on our taste buds, painting a succulent masterpiece. Collaborating with my mom, we conjured a Pineapple Chutney that perfectly complemented the Mahi Mahi's essence. It entailed fresh crushed pineapple, seedless golden raisins, brown sugar, white vinegar, salt, ground ginger, cayenne pepper, ground allspice, ground cloves, ground cinnamon, and chopped almonds.

This blend of elements harmonized seamlessly, creating a compelling melody of flavors. The pineapple's inherent sweetness elegantly intertwined with the subtle warmth of the spices, while the raisins contributed a delicate fruitiness. The addition of chopped almonds offered a gratifying textural contrast. This chutney, a true masterpiece, stood as the Mahi Mahi's perfect counterpart, enhancing its depth and complexity. Accompanied by sprigs of asparagus and a side of garlic-infused Hawaiian Bread, our delectable endeavor encapsulated the essence of our time together: a blend of exceptional cuisine, shared moments, and treasured companionship.

Alas, it was our last evening together, and I felt sad that our excellent adventure was about to end. I insisted that Roy and my parents return to the porch and enjoy the last of the sunset twilight as I took care of the dishes and cleaned everything up. My mom and Roy had settled into their routine in the corner with folded garden chairs facing each other, smoking and, as they say in Hawaii, "Talking story." They would chat for hours and say nothing. Solve the world's problems with nobody listening. Roy had become family, and I could tell my parents loved him. Even my stoic German dad liked having him around. I could tell he really got a kick from all of Roy's Hollywood film stories.

As the hours slipped away, we collectively decided to bid the night farewell and seek the embrace of our beds, ready to continue our journey with the dawn. Just like that first morning upon our arrival, my mother's promise of yet another traditional German breakfast awaited us, now enriched by locally grown, soft-boiled eggs. The thought of such a hearty morning spread was enough to lull us into sweet dreams as we surrendered ourselves to sleep.

However, my journey of restlessness led me on a gentle stroll up the driveway, drawn to the allure of the moonlit night. The air held a touch of magic as I reached the summit of the street, only to be beckoned back by a sight that stopped me in my tracks. An elegant and mysterious owl gracefully glided into the outstretched arms of an Ohia tree, taking refuge within a hollow in its branches. It was the elusive Hawaiian Short-eared Owl, known as the Pueo, a rare treasure in a world increasingly marked by habitat loss. My heart raced with excitement, eager to share this enchanting encounter. Yet, as I returned, the snores filled the room, and my tale would have to wait for the morning's light.

The last to slip into the embrace of slumber and the first to greet the timid rays of morning light, I tiptoed into the kitchen like a whisper, orchestrating the morning's breakfast ensemble with the finesse of a seasoned conductor. I aimed to set the stage for breakfast in perfect harmony, ensuring my mother would be greeted by a tableau of culinary delights, leaving her only the task of timing the eggs to her liking. The minutes ticked by silently as I pondered how long she preferred her eggs to be boiled, a culinary alchemy I was determined to master.

As the sun rose, casting its golden glow upon the horizon, the house stirred. The gentle hum of anticipation permeated the air as each soul prepared for the day ahead. With Roy's flight scheduled for the afternoon, there was no urgency to rise early. Yet, the rhythm of time seemed out of sync, my internal clock urging me to seize the day and wring every drop of adventure from it.

The shadow of departure cast a veil of melancholy over an enchanting vacation, a kaleidoscope of shared moments that would forever be painted onto our hearts. The morning breeze swept swiftly, carrying the awareness that farewells were imminent. As we readied Roy's suitcase, my parents stood resolute in their desire to see off this newfound companion who had graced our lives.

As we recounted the occasions that had seamlessly come together into a colorful collage of memories, laughter rippled through the air Roy, typically composed, conveyed his gratitude with heartfelt sincerity. In their customary warmth, my parents expressed their appreciation in the local farewell greeting, "Mahalo for visiting us! We enjoyed meeting you so much und spending time with you." We drove up to the drop-off area parking lot at the small Hilo airport, and all stepped out to see Roy off with hugs and kisses.

Roy began to make his way toward the airline check-in, and as he ascended the escalator, my dad's voice echoed, "You have a good trip home, und come back und see us again… You don't have to have Günther mit you!' My dad couldn't resist his playful spirit, 'Don't worry about the money. You can stay mit us for free!'"

Roy chuckled warmly, offering a collective wink of connection before he vanished from view. This moment marked the conclusion of a marvelous week during which Rock Hudson, our cherished guest, painted a spellbinding chapter of his presence onto the canvas of our lives on the enchanting Big Island.

P.S.—One week after Rock's return to Los Angeles, my parents were pleasantly surprised by two packages bearing his thoughtful signature. To my father, Roy gifted a substantial needlepoint kit featuring an image of a woman engrossed in sewing or needlepoint herself. To my mother, Roy presented a magnificent, large crystal apple that gleamed with exquisite craftsmanship.

These gifts revealed Roy's boundless kindness and generosity and his remarkable thoughtfulness. In today's fast-paced world, where the hustle and bustle of life often overshadow these simple gestures of connection and warmth, Roy's sending such beautiful gifts resonated deeply.

I refrained from disclosing to my parents that Roy had people assisting him with such gestures, but why shatter the enchanting illusion? I knew that Roy had handpicked these gifts, bearing in mind the intricate details. Over the years, the needlepoint picture my father painstakingly completed adorned their home, bringing joy until my parents' passing. Subsequently, it found a new home in the library room of my Godmother, Waltraud, where it continued to radiate its warmth long after. This gift, bestowed by Roy's kind heart, became a cherished emblem of enduring happiness.

  It occurred to me that perhaps the greatest beneficiaries of this visit were not just my parents, who had the privilege of meeting the real Roy Scherer, the person behind the movie star façade that so few truly knew, but also Roy himself. He could shed the armor of stardom for those precious moments and be unguarded and unrestrained. In this extraordinary encounter, they found a profound mutual enjoyment in each other's company.

  "Who would've thought?" was the echoing sentiment in my mind. It reaffirmed that we all share the universal human desire to love and be loved for our genuine selves. It didn't matter whether my parents—a loving German couple retired in Hawaii or a renowned Movie Star yearned to break free from the trappings of fame. In a sense, Roy had become family to us, and we to him, forging an unbreakable bond across the divides of circumstance.

Chapter 10: Father's Day

As the 17th of June drew closer, a familiar ring interrupted my thoughts—Rock's voice filled the air, carrying that unique blend of warmth and urgency that was unmistakably his. "Hey, Gunther, you got Father's Day coming up. Got any grand plans for your old man?"

I chuckled in response, resigned to the geographical barrier that separated Hawaii and Long Beach. "Well, Rock, I sent him a card, and I will call him. But you know how it goes—the distance doesn't make for the grandest celebrations." With a playful glint in my eye, I ventured a whimsical notion: "Maybe I should take you out for brunch as a gift by your long-lost son!" Rock's hearty laughter echoed through the phone as he encouraged my absurd idea to become a reality.

"Why stop at just one son? How about we up the ante and go for two?" I suggested mischievously, savoring the intrigue of my proposal. Rock's curiosity got the better of him, and he asked, "Two sons, huh? Who's the lucky second one?"

With a cheeky grin and a touch of drama, I revealed my trump card, "Oh, just a close friend of mine who drifts in and out of Costa Mesa. We had plans to catch up while he's in town —thought it might add a little extra flair to the Father's Day brunch." My confidence grew as I described my friend, his charm, his physique, and our shared escapades on the sandy shores of West Street Beach—a spot affectionately known as the gay beach to insiders or One Thousand Steps Beach for the uninitiated.

Pushed Out of the Closet Without A Parachute

Rock's laughter reverberated on the other end of the line. "Hmm, two sons, sound interesting? Well, I guess that's one way to spice up Father's Day!" he exclaimed with an amused tone. Our conversation was nostalgic as he mentioned his wife Phyllis and their time in Newport Beach.

Rock recalled, "Back then, Laguna Canyon was a different world—a narrow, two-lane road, lined with those towering eucalyptus trees that formed a natural tunnel. It led to where they put on the Pageant of the Masters," he reminisced.

Although I was merely a young child back then, I could still recall the scene he vividly described. The memory of my mom shedding tears when they removed those towering eucalyptus trees to widen the Laguna Canyon Road remained etched in my mind. She lamented the loss of a unique drive that no longer existed. However, the captivating magic of "Living Pictures" being brought to life, transforming ordinary individuals into replicas of artistic masterpieces, continued to thrive each year.

Engaging in our conversation, I eagerly added, "You were referring to Pageant of the Masters, the 'Living Pictures,' right? The ones where they recreate famous artworks using real people, costumes, makeup, and a touch of enchantment?" My inquiry was infused with a genuine sense of wonder.

Rock responded with an affirmative nod, accompanied by a wistful sigh. "Indeed, that's exactly it—Festival of Arts and Pageant of the Masters. It's quite a spectacle, Gunther. If you ever get the chance, you should experience it. It's like stepping into an entirely different realm."

With enthusiasm, I chimed in, "Oh, I've seen it once before as well. Perhaps we could go together to witness it again?"

"Sounds like a wonderful plan," he replied. Rock's voice resonated with the bittersweet echoes of days gone by. "You know, back then, I used to make that drive down to the main beach, and let me tell you, it was like the irresistible call of a siren for the gay crowd. The Hollywood limelight caught wind of it in the 1940s, and it wasn't just me; other stars would flock to those shores, too. And as the years waltzed through the 1970s, 1980s, and well into the 2000s, Laguna Beach truly became a haven for the gay community."

With a tinge of reverence, Rock painted an exquisite panorama of Laguna Beach's glory days—the famed Boom Boom Room with its whimsical goldfish "bar aquarium" built right into the bar.

"Oh, how I remember the vibrant summers at Main Beach, alive with the energy of gay men, the soul-stirring melodies of Rudy serenading from the Little Shrimp, and the sense of togetherness found at Woody's after a sun-soaked escapade."

"You see," Rock continued, "the art scene was thriving, and many gay folks found their niche here. Unsurprisingly, Laguna claims to have one of the oldest gay bars in the western United States."

As Rock's words hung in the air, it was as if the echoes of the past merged seamlessly with the present, intertwining in the intricate fabric of history—a mosaic of experiences that had shaped lives and paved the path for progress. Terrence McNally once said, "Art changes people and people change the world." In the tale of Laguna Beach, the artistry of life, love, and identity was woven into the very soul of the town, casting a resilient light that continues to shine.

Returning to the narrative, it's worth noting that Rock was unfamiliar with the emergence of the new beach hangout, West Street. This secluded spot offered a respite from the prying gazes like Main Street Beach, where there would be those who would occasionally pass by, shouting "faggot" and other derogatory remarks and even tossing objects—a stark reminder of the less tolerant times.

However, as often happens, the city has undergone a significant transformation, though not necessarily for the better. The tide of mainstream influence has transformed it into a row of opulent mansions, making it nearly impossible for anyone who isn't a millionaire or billionaire to secure a residence in the area.

But that is another story for another book that someone should write someday. Who knows, maybe I'll be compelled to!

Our conversation meandered through the memories, much like a winding river. Ah, these shared moments, a treasure trove of experiences uncovered. These things in life bind us together and build bridges between the aspirations of my youth and the seasoned wisdom that Rock's life had accumulated.

I informed Rock that I would reach out to my friend Chris, checking if he'd be game for this escapade, and provide him with all the essential details—the when, where, and what-to-wear aspects. As the pieces fell, I realized I hadn't settled on a venue yet. My thoughts raced, exploring the options within the vicinity. Among the array of possibilities, one stood out: Maxwells, a restaurant nestled at the base of the pier in Huntington Beach—the very beach where, at the tender age of 16, I embarked on my lifeguarding journey, a chapter interwoven into my past.

Rock assured me he had connections at Maxwell's and suggested he handle the reservations. Knowing his fame and recognition could secure us a prime table, shielded from autograph seekers and the kind of impolite individuals who often lacked proper etiquette when approaching a celebrity, I was inclined to leave this task in his capable hands. However, I made it clear that regardless of his connections, I—or instead, we, Chris and I—were taking him out to brunch, end of discussion. There was no room for argument, and I insisted on footing the bill. After all, what son lets their father pay for the Father's Day meal? LOL

As we exchanged farewells, a smile lingered on my lips. Our bond felt even more potent, and the prospect of this unconventional Father's Day brunch held the promise of a truly memorable escapade. The excitement of sharing this news with Chris was unmistakable; I looked forward to delightfully surprising him. His curiosity about my friendship with Rock had already been piqued, and introducing him to Rock felt like the perfect opportunity. After all, Rock had graciously opened the doors to his Hollywood connections for me, and now it was my turn to introduce my circle of friends to his world.

Pushed Out of the Closet Without A Parachute

I connected with my friend Chris, sharing the delightful plan of celebrating Father's Day with Rock. With a hearty chuckle, Chris wholeheartedly embraced the concept, ready to dive into the festivities. I informed Chris that I had already briefed Rock about his profession and our shared connection through our volleyball escapades at West Street Beach.

Chris and I were affectionately known as regulars at West Street Beach, the shoreline I had mentioned to Rock earlier. Our shared passion extended to high-level beach volleyball, a sport we enjoyed numerous times. Chris, a tanned and blond-haired Adonis, effortlessly captured the attention of everyone on the beach. While competing against our adversaries, laughter became our constant companion, and in each other's company, the world around us seemed to fade away.

Despite the curiosity of onlookers and the potential judgments of passersby, our bond remained steadfast. We were two friends united by a shared joy, impervious to the opinions of others. Like Rock and me, our connection was purely platonic, devoid of romantic undertones. The reasons for this lack of romantic entanglement elude me now, shrouded in the haze of time. Perhaps Chris was already involved with someone else, or circumstances never aligned in that direction. Regardless, what endured was a friendship unburdened by romantic expectations, a bond that grew stronger without amorous complications.

Pushed Out of the Closet Without A Parachute

In the past few years, Chris had immersed himself in the culture, collecting Mexican art and intricately handcrafted treasures, which he later unveiled at the bustling Orange County Swap Meet. At a glance, one might doubt the feasibility of such an endeavor, but appearances often deceive. This venture had unbelievably flourished into a remarkably prosperous enterprise for Chris, which I first-handedly experienced. I assisted Chris and spent a day with him at the Swap Meet, witnessing the enchanting dance of commerce and creativity.

Through the years, our friendship had strengthened, fortified by shared experiences and prized memories. Eager to introduce Rock to Chris, I knew that Chris's discretion and intellect would perfectly match our gathering. While Chris's demeanor might not mirror the eccentricities of my friend Philip, whose animated gestures could be mistaken for an epileptic fit, or Rock's friend Dean, capable of engineering kitchen mishaps that defied belief, Chris possessed a quiet charm that promised a delightful day ahead. He was the kind of person who could seamlessly blend into any group, his amiability bridging gaps effortlessly.

As the much-anticipated 17th day of July was upon us, I orchestrated our ensemble to convene first at my abode in the Portofino. This strategic maneuver ensured a harmonious arrival at Maxwell's all-nestled cozily within the confines of a single automobile. Awaiting the rendezvous in the parking lot, Chris and I exchanged glances brimming with eagerness, and before you knew it, there he was—Rock Hudson, driving right up to us in his new Mercedes, a lustrous ode to luxury, joining us with a flourish.

As his door opened, I stepped forward, boldly making my grand introduction with a comical flair. "Ahoy, Roy!" I proclaimed with a wink, a devilish twinkle echoing the resonance of his familiar name. "Let me present to you the one and only Mr. Chris Bittle, and Chris, this, of course, is Mr. Rock Hudson, but I also call him Roy Sherer. But as of today, we can call him Dad!" The air practically hummed with the warmth of connection as their eyes met, his genuine smile a testament to the friendship that was instantaneously sparked.

Chris, ever curious, inquired, "And which alias would resonate with you more, sir?" With a contemplative pause, Rock responded with a testament to the complex interplay of identity and fame, "Well, my dear friends, 'Rock' is a name I've carried across the tides of time. Yet, 'Roy Sherer'—that's my truth, my essence. In the comfort of friendship's embrace, Roy feels like home, unless, of course, the curtain of public life is drawn."

With the official protocols exchanged and the heartwarming formality of their meeting drawn to a close, we showered Rock—or should I say Roy—with heartfelt Father's Day greetings, a duet of goodwill, and genuine warmth. I couldn't resist a final touch of humor, adding, "Today, Rock, your newfound sons have gathered in the name of togetherness, ready to celebrate and create new memories on this auspicious occasion!"

Pushed Out of the Closet Without A Parachute

By then, I had recognized Roy's penchant for playful antics, which I affectionately labeled as "goofing off"—a delightful dance of silliness and joy. Chris seamlessly melded into this spirited atmosphere, and together, we reveled in a splendid Father's Day brunch, our harmonious gathering scarcely disrupted.

Yet, as the universe would have it, one individual often feels compelled to interject. On this occasion, a visitor approached our table, recognition dawning on his face as he uttered, "Aren't you Rock Hudson?" However, a unique twist followed when he added, "Oh, and these must be your two sons."

Our response resounded in perfect synchrony, "YES, we are." As the curious stranger snapped a photograph and withdrew, our laughter erupted—a shared joy, the punchline known only to us.

That day remained with me, vivid and unforgetable, each thread of its significance woven intricately into my heart. Little did I fathom that in just a fleeting span of a couple of years, I would bear witness to the departure of both these cherished souls. A bittersweet surge envelops me as I pen down these chronicles, an ache that transcends words. The realization dawns like a sad refrain—these remarkable individuals would be snatched away from my grasp. Both would find themselves trapped by the cruel grip of the AIDS virus, a relentless specter that stalked their lives with unforgiving resolve.

Revisiting these recollections is both a tribute and a heavy burden to bear. As the narrative unfolds, I'm reminded that life is woven with moments of beauty and pain, of connection and loss. The laughter we shared and the wisdom we exchanged, now crystallized within these pages, stand as a testament to the profound impact they had on me. It's a poignant reminder that in our shared human journey, we traverse paths intertwined with joy, sorrow, resilience, and vulnerability.

The passing of time has added depth to these tales, and their lessons resonate even more profoundly. They remind us to cling to every fleeting moment, to embrace the connections we forge, and to carry the light of those we've lost within us. As I recount these stories, my heart echoes with their presence, and I'm reminded that in their absence, their legacies live on—inspiring us to live our lives with authenticity, compassion, and the courage to face whatever challenges come our way.

The day that unfolded at Maxwell's was imbued with a sense of promise, as though we were on the cusp of an exciting new chapter. Little did I know that it would become a fleeting moment suspended in time, a snapshot of connection before the tides of fate swept us apart. In the days that followed, attempts to reunite our small band proved futile, and as the year wore on, the weight of absence grew heavier.

Guilt gnawed at me like a persistent ache. I survived unscathed by the virus that claimed so many lives. The question "Why me?" echoed like a haunting refrain. It was a sensation akin to witnessing the aftermath of wildfires that would engulf neighborhoods, sparing one house while consuming the rest—a capricious hand of fate, a seemingly arbitrary choice.

In the wake of this unprecedented era, I became an unwilling attendee at a relentless procession of funerals. Friends, former roommates, acquaintances—all swept away far too soon, their laughter and presence now echo in memory. The weight of loss was staggering, a bleak reminder of life's fragility.

And yet, even amid the shroud of grief, glimmers of light persist. Those fleeting moments of joy, those threads of connection, lend strength to the heart. As I navigate these remembrances, my purpose becomes straightforward: to capture life's enigmatic dance.

Life unfurls its mysteries in the most improbable ways, and events can unfold with an unpredictable, almost fantastical quality. It's a tale of resilience, the human spirit that persists even in darkness. It's a tribute to the fate that weaves through our lives, reminding us that despite the most profound challenges, there is still room for hope, growth, and the unpredictable beauty of the unknown.

After our delightful brunch at Maxwell's, we embarked on a leisurely tour along the iconic Huntington Beach Pier. As we walked, I regaled my companions with tales of the lifeguarding escapades I had embarked on during my younger years. The day couldn't have been more idyllic, with the sun casting a warm glow on the surroundings and a gentle breeze whispering secrets through the air. Surprisingly, our little trio blended seamlessly with the pier's bustling crowd, our presence shielded by the allure of the ocean horizon.

Pushed Out of the Closet Without A Parachute

Standing tall, each of us well over 6 feet, we seemed to tower over the passersby, evoking an air of otherworldly presence that invited curious glances.

Amid our casual saunter, Chris chimed in, sharing his captivating accounts of adventures in Mexico, a place that had captured his heart and creative spirit. Engrossed, Roy listened with bona fide interest, his familiarity with such tales resonating from his globe-trotting experiences. Our intimacy was authentic, a testament to the bond forged during this impromptu encounter.

Chris's revelations flowed like tributaries of an enthralling narrative, including an unexpected twist. He disclosed a new venture—a series of pop-up storefronts he aptly termed "liquidation sales," each tailored to the season's theme. His stories revealed that his ingenuity had paid off; the Halloween-themed liquidation sale had generated profits surpassing his entire earnings from the previous year.

Our stroll eventually concluded, and Roy, the wheel in his capable hands, navigated us back to the Portofino. The sun was inching toward the horizon, casting its golden hue across the landscape, a gentle reminder that evening was descending upon us. As the twilight hour approached, a thought occurred to me—what better way to conclude this day of connection and camaraderie than to witness the sun's final bow?

With the gentle lapping of the waves as our soundtrack, I proposed a plan: a bottle of wine was procured, and we made our way down to the beach. Nestled close to the Belmont Plaza Olympic pool, a cluster of park benches and tables awaited us. As we settled into our chosen seats, the canvas of the sky transformed before our eyes. The sun's descent was like a masterstroke of artistry, each color blending seamlessly into the next as the horizon swallowed its radiant form.

In the tranquil serenity of that moment, as the world seemed to hold its breath, I was struck by the reflective beauty surrounding us. It was a poignant reminder that, bound by life's complexities, it's often the simplest pleasures that etch the most unforgettable memories into our hearts: the laughter shared, the stories told, and the awe-inspiring sight of a sun bidding adieu.

My dear friend Chris graced the golden sands of West Street Beach with his infectious energy.

Chapter 11: 4th of July, Olympics, & The Ritz

Following Father's Day, Rock and I were swept into the abyss of individual pursuits, each engrossed in our separate worlds. The hectic pace of our lives left little room for connection, and a sense of concern loomed between us.

On the 4th of July, duty beckoned, and I reluctantly had to decline an invitation to Dean Dittman's undoubtedly riotous party. My work commitments overshadowed the promise of a splendid celebration, but a silver lining emerged. Phil and I managed to secure the morning shift off, and together, we hatched a plan to rendezvous at the beach. There, under the sun's gentle embrace, we would bask in leisure before our work duties came to claim us.

That night, the skies over Long Beach harbor were set to erupt in a breathtaking spectacle of fireworks. Our event venue offered an unparalleled vista that encompassed the grandeur of Long Beach Harbor, the regal Queen Mary, and the enchanting Shoreline Villagewith its steadfast lighthouse. It was a front-row seat to an extravaganza, an opportunity to witness the waterfront's vibrant celebrations without the burdensome crowds. What's more, we were getting paid for this privilege.

Our role was simple yet essential, overseeing a buffet-style soiree. Guests could choose to savor the spectacle from the comfort of our indoor space or venture onto the patio, closer to the grand display.

Pushed Out of the Closet Without A Parachute

Our responsibilities were clear—keep the chafing dishes brimming with delectable offerings, ensure refreshments flowed freely, and swiftly clear away the remnants of enjoyment, dirty dishes, and empty glasses. It wasn't the conventional 4th of July festivity but a convenient way of commemorating that year's occasion.

The 4th of July unfurled its magic seamlessly, and we wrapped up our responsibilities at an earlier than usual hour. The clock had yet to strike midnight, but with his irresistible Southern charm, Phil couldn't resist one of his trademark persuasion campaigns to lure me into joining him for a nightcap at the illustrious Silver Fox.

He leaned in, a glint of his usual mischief in his eyes, and urged, "Come on, Guntha, can't you feel it? There's an Alabama Slamma' waiting with your name on it at the fabulous Silver Fox."

With a knowing smile, I conceded, "Phil, perhaps you're right. However, we met Rock Hudson the last time you coaxed me into that establishment. Now, anything else would indeed pale in comparison. But all right, I'll indulge in one drink, with the caveat that you'll be the designated driver tonight. You see, my bike, unfortunately, decided to grace me with a flat tire. I was just about to ask you for a lift home, so it's a convenient win-win situation."

The next few weeks passed in the blink of an eye as the hotel revved up for the 1984 Summer Games, known worldwide as the Olympics. The opening ceremonies were poised to dazzle on July 28th, and the buzz was electric. NBC had set up camp in our hotel, orchestrating meetings and events in anticipation of the upcoming athletic pageant. But here's a delightful tidbit I had overlooked: preceding the 1984 Summer Olympics, a 10-week-long Los Angeles Olympic Arts Festival unfolded. It served as a worldwide stage, spotlighting dance and music troupes hailing from every nook and cranny of our planet. And regarding global connections, here's a gem: my godfather, Werner Helms, clinched the gold medal in Stamp Collecting that year. Yes, you heard me right, and this was his second since he also won the gold and the 1972 Olympics in Munich, Germany.

As for my Olympic aspirations, be it Olympic Arts Festival or playing water polo, well, let's just say I got as close to competing as I could get, but it just didn't quite materialize. Oh, I had my heart set on making it to the Olympics in either swimming or water polo, but it wasn't meant to be. I played with many of the players who made the 1980 and 84 water polo teams when I attended UCI on an athletic scholarship.

I even played for the renowned Hall of Fame Coach Ted Newland at UCI in 1975. Those who played for Coach Newland either loved him or hated him. Which camp did I fall into? Let's just say we didn't see eye-to-eye, and coming from High School as an All-American and my high schools most valuable water polo player didn't make a difference to Coach Newland.

It was a tumultuous time when I was discovering my sexuality, and living on my own had its challenges. But I did play water polo well, and I had my moments, like when I swiped the ball and scored the game-winning assist against USC in the playoffs. Although we, the Anteaters, ended up as bridesmaids in the NCAA that year, I finally received kudos from the great and mighty one.

The only Olympics I had a real shot for was in 1980, but the U.S. decided to boycott. Even before the boycott happened, I played a year at Golden West instead of another three years at UCI. Golden West was only a Junior College, but they were ranked number one or two almost every year in water polo for the past ten to twenty years. In 1978, we won again, becoming the CCCAA Men's Water Polo Champions.

I received my AA degree and a scholarship to play water polo for the University of Hawaii at Manoa. I even participated on the US International team in 1979, but my hopes for the Olympics faded. It wasn't even worth the effort because since the US boycotted the Olympics, and at the time, I didn't have the means to support four more years of training.

Eventually, I swapped my water polo cap for a surfboard and a lifeguard tower—who knew I was destined to compete in rough water swimming competitions where I took 2nd place in Honolulu's annual rough water swim? Next, I ventured into triathlons, discovering I excelled in the first two events but couldn't quite find my running legs. After a year of trying, I figured running wasn't my forte. It wasn't until years later that I stumbled upon outrigger canoeing as my journey into aquatic adventures and beachside glory continued to evolve.

However, before I leap far ahead in this narrative, let's return to the Olympics as July transitioned into August. While I recount my past, it's essential to revisit that transformative summer when Rock Hudson, the ever-evolving luminary of the acting world, was also undergoing significant changes, as I was. He reached out to me excitedly, sharing plans for his upcoming voyage to Paris alongside his trainer and close platonic friend, Ron. Their relationship was a testament to the enduring bond of friendship that had transcended boundaries.

A straight man, Ron had found a special place in Rock's life. Rock shared the details of this forthcoming European escapade, a venture orchestrated by his publicist. This publicity tour would take him on an extensive journey across the continent, from the storied streets of Rome to the vibrant alleys of Barcelona and even the enchanting lanes of London. In a way, I was jealous of a life of travel. Anything to give me a break from the daily monotony of double shifts!

However, his journey would lead him back to Paris, where a strategic encounter awaited —a meeting with none other than Esther

Shapiro, the illustrious creator and producer of Dynasty. It was surreal to recall that we had playfully mimicked scenes from Dynasty at the Silver Fox, and now, my friend Rock might be offered a role on the show. With eager anticipation, I envisioned my friends and me crafting uproarious parodies of the episodes he could soon be gracing with his presence.

Little did I realize that the stories I received were fragments of the truth, delivered through sporadic phone calls from Rock himself or the occasional intermediary like Dean. This peculiar dynamic would intensify over time, leaving me with a lingering sense that something was amiss.

Dean's behavior had taken a strange turn, and I couldn't shake the feeling that things were going on beneath the surface, things they weren't sharing with me. What I would discover nearly a year later exceeded even the wildest reaches of my imagination. But let me guide you step by step through the events unfolding as I attempted to decipher the truth behind various happenings—happening in which I was invariably off the mark. No pun intended, even though all the crumbs led to the infamous Marc Christian.

Once the opening ceremonies commenced, the hotel pulsed with activity as NBC established its Volleyball Olympic headquarters, and I found myself at the epicenter of the excitement. It surprised me that all the Fencing events also happened in Long Beach, particularly at the Long Beach Convention Center.

Pushed Out of the Closet Without A Parachute

Interestingly, some officials from the West German Team were occasionally present at the Hyatt Regency. Whether they were staying at the hotel or if they were NBC affiliates remained a bit of a mystery. Nevertheless, I was requested to assist with translation and directions. Luckily, the Convention Center was just a short walk away, its presence visible from the Hyatt. Despite my best intentions and even being offered a ticket to one of the matches, my busy schedule prevented me from attending. However, I managed to squeeze in a quick visit to the venue, if only to say I'd been there.

Suddenly, the hotel erupted in a turbulent trading frenzy. Olympic Pin Mania took us all by surprise at the hotel like a contagiously cheerful fever, and it seemed like everyone had caught the bug. Picture this: in the hotel's downstairs lobby, folks gathering in huddles, looking more like stock traders than vacationers, as they feverishly swapped pins like they were secret keys to the Olympic kingdom. Now, here's the kicker—even the hotel staff joined the pin party, wearing their pin-like badges of honor.

As for me, being NBC's right-hand person had its perks, which came in the form of handfuls of coveted NBC Olympic pins for various sports, including volleyball. I quickly realized these pins were like golden tickets in the Pinopoly board game that had suddenly taken over the hotel. Armed with my shiny NBC pins, I became the pin tycoon of the Games, wheeling and dealing with fellow guests. "Volleyball pins for a bit of Fencing flair? Sure thing! Want a dash of Swimming style in exchange for some Gymnastics pizzazz? You got it!" By the time the Games wrapped up, I was more bedecked in Olympic bling than a medal podium.

And the unexpected twist—I had so many perks; I had to become a pin philanthropist, spreading joy among fellow employees who missed out because my schedule was locked and loaded for those wild first two weeks of August. These shiny Olympic tokens were like my currency of fellowship, a unifying force in the bustling Olympic hub of our hotel.

Fencing, the art of dueling with finesse, had taken center stage from August 1st to August 11th, while Volleyball was already in full swing from July 29th, smashing volley after volley through to the second-to-last day of the Games on August 11th. The atmosphere was electric, especially with the U.S. Men's Team clinching the Gold and the U.S. Women's Team gracefully claiming the silver. Each day was a thrilling adventure, filled with meetings with these athletes, obtaining their signatures, trading pins, and lending a helping hand on behalf of the hotel. The vibrant spirit of the Games was alive and contagious.

The schedule was nothing short of chaotic in the bustle of Olympic events and the infectious excitement. With numerous events happening simultaneously, our days were an overflow of excitement. Yet NBC expressed their utmost satisfaction with our service, and the connection with everyone involved was simply delightful. Between the pin trading, autograph hunting, and ensuring that NBC was as content as a medal-winning Olympian, it felt like life was playing out like a fine-tuned athlete ready to compete.

I wished Rock was in town. It would have been nice to take him to one of the Volleyball Matches. But alas, he was gallivanting in Paris or some far-flung locale on his publicity tour. I could already imagine us sharing tales of our adventures once he returned. The truth was, with my hectic schedule, I started to miss his company and phone calls.

Our time together was abruptly cut short, leaving me with only Dean as my point of contact, aside from that one phone call we shared as Rock arrived in Paris. I'm glad I didn't have the time to dwell since my life was busier than the 405 and the 5 freeway at rush hour.

The days began to blend into one another like strokes on a painter's canvas. I was juggling so many back-to-back shifts that I unintentionally neglected paying my bills, leaving my roommate Pat to wonder if I still inhabited our shared space. My comings and goings became clandestine, slipping in late at night and departing before the first rays of dawn, leaving me with only a precious few hours of sleep.

With the ongoing work pandemonium, I suddenly realized I'd missed out on cherished moments with friends, particularly Phil. He stood on the precipice of profound life changes, and I was stunned to hear that he was bidding farewell to Long Beach. The news hit me like an unexpected panic attack; I hadn't even had the opportunity to bid him farewell. A colleague, with the zest for sharing neighborhood grapevine tidbits, ventured, "Phil had to make a return to Arkansas, Alabama, or somewhere in that vicinity, tending to an ailing relative."

I had been so preoccupied that I failed to notice what was happening with Phil. How could I have allowed work and the Olympics to overshadow my friendships? Rumors suggested that Phil might be securing an inheritance, but I knew he wasn't the type to engage in such matters. My thoughts were filled with nothing but good wishes for him, but his absence left a void, reminding us of the hurdles ahead for those who remained.

However, it was not all bad news. I received some exciting news from Dean: Rock indeed got the part in the series Dynasty and would return sometime in October, just in time to start shooting. But by the time I got this information, it was already late August, and my life was spiraling into total turmoil.

Once the Olympics had concluded, the hotel was returning to a more normal pace. However, the pendulum had started swinging to the opposite extreme. Some of my colleagues faced layoffs, while others struggled to secure enough hours to make ends meet. It was a stark reminder of the feast-or-famine nature of our industry, compelling me to take a proactive stance in my career.

A few coworkers suggested I apply at the new Ritz-Carlton in Laguna Beach, and I decided to follow their advice. I drove down for an interview and was hired on the spot. There was only one problem—the distance was too far for me to commute by bike, and fuel costs for

Pushed Out of the Closet Without A Parachute

La Bamba would be excessive. I found myself facing a significant problem.

I had a lengthy conversation with my roommate, Pat, explaining my predicament and the need to find a new place closer to the Ritz in Laguna Niguel. He expressed sadness at the prospect of my departure but fully understood my situation. Pat was considerate enough to grant me the time I needed so I wouldn't feel rushed into making a decision. However, I knew I had to act swiftly to secure a new living arrangement.

As luck would have it, I stumbled upon a room available for rent in Laguna Niguel, offered by an older gay man named Larry. I drove down to look, which was a perfect fit for me. Larry had ingeniously converted his condo from a one-bedroom loft into a two-bedroom space, with the loft bedroom featuring another bathroom. This would be the portion I would rent. I would also have full access to the shared kitchen. Furthermore, an outdoor deck was constructed above the garages, which was part of my designated area. I could envision placing an outdoor table and lounge chairs there, creating a cozy retreat that felt distinctly private from Larry's living space.

Larry was an artist who considered himself an abstract colorist. Equally interesting, he showcased his work at a gallery in Laguna Beach and gained some recognition within the artistic community. He was a kind person but appeared somewhat scattered, perhaps even overwhelmed. I couldn't quite focus on it until I moved in and witnessed him painting. It was an experience that needed to be seen to believe.

Larry's approach was akin to Jackson Pollock's, the famous abstract expressionist known for his unconventional painting technique. Like Pollock, Larry would splatter paint onto the canvas with profound emotional involvement. Each brush stroke was a passionate outpouring, resulting in a riot of colors, movement, and interplay of dark and light shades. By the way, Larry enjoyed my recounting of my "Pollock period" when I splattered paint on the bottom of the Long Beach Arena, which felt like a lifetime ago.

With a borrowed truck from a friend as my trusty steed, I executed a vanishing act from Long Beach, having given the Hyatt a mere three days' notice. It was a gesture that turned out to be unnecessary, as the hotel had become "deader than a doorknob." The management wished me well, and in one swift load, I was efficiently organized, packed, and gone. Pat was at work during my move, so I left him a heartfelt letter of gratitude, along with my final payment and my new address.

The bulk of my possessions consisted of my bed, complemented by two small bedside tables. I had constructed my shelving on the wall to display my trophies, trinkets, and framed photos proudly. Carefully, I removed them, patching up the wall as a parting gift for Patrick. He had kindly assured me not to fret about painting; he would handle that task himself using paint he had stashed away somewhere. My life was locked and loaded into my friend's truck, ready for relocation, reassignment, and the next adventure at my new home in Laguna Niguel.

With Phil's departure, no one else was left in Long Beach for me to bid farewell. The people from my college days had also drifted apart, each on their unique paths. It felt like the beginning of an entirely new chapter, yet I still had to get in direct contact with Rock. What would he think of my sudden move and the changes in my life? It was only the first week of September, and Rock wasn't expected back until the end of the first week of October. I had a lot on my plate, from getting acquainted with my new living space and job to building relationships with the people who would soon become my new family.

Transitioning to the Ritz was surprisingly smooth, given my prior experience with opening a new hotel. The similarities in their operations made the adjustment easier. As a banquet waiter, I was right in the midst of all the suspense, excitement, and intrigue that came with launching this luxurious establishment. The Ritz was fully booked from the get-go, and we had already held events that christened the brand-new ballrooms as we got the wheels turning.

Perched on the cliffs of Dana Point, nestled between South Laguna and Dana Point, the Ritz boasted a breathtaking oceanic backdrop, making it an idyllic location for weddings. However, this slice of paradise came at a hefty price, and it wasn't for the faint of heart. To reserve one of the smaller ballrooms for a wedding event back in 1984 could easily set you back 50K, yes, a whopping

$50,000—a sum that could serve as a nice down payment on a new home.

I fit seamlessly into the new luxury surroundings, performing at peak efficiency and settling into regular working hours. The Ritz Carlton was notably cautious about scheduling too much overtime, so I received a well-organized 8-hour shift schedule a week in advance, which minimized surprises.

One incredible perk at the Ritz was the employee café, where we could enjoy complimentary meals during breaks or before and after our shifts. It was a fantastic benefit, and the fancy locker rooms added to the experience. The hotel ensured my tuxedo collection was always pristine and ready for each shift. The staff at the Ritz handled everything, from fittings to necessary repairs, ensuring that everything ran as smoothly as a well-choreographed dance.

The initial euphoria of my new job was almost too good to be true, and as life often goes, perfection didn't last long. For unknown reasons, the hotel decided to terminate all senior management staff just a couple of months after their opening. Soon, the real reason materialized. It turned out they had brought in top-notch managers from various corners of the world to get the hotel up and running, as well as to train the staff until the operation ran like a well-oiled machine. But then, inexplicably, they let go of the managers who had done all the hard work, replacing them with their understudies, whom they could hire for a fraction of the cost—less than half of their predecessors' salaries. This decision was very unfair and primarily driven by budget considerations.

Unfortunately, the manager we had all come to respect and get along with was replaced by a man we were told to call Fahrrad. Ironically, Fahrrad means "generous," "selfless," "free," and "wise" in Arabic, a description that couldn't have been further from the truth in his case. Tyrant, mean-spirited, belligerent, arrogant, and deeply insecure would be far more accurate descriptions of his character.

He was particularly tough on the female waitresses or servers, as they were called correctly. They had to carry large trays loaded with heavy, oversized glasses. Fahrrad made us practice in an empty ballroom, akin to a drill instructor on speed. He barked orders while launching personal attacks on several of us. Given my size, strength, and experience, I was fine with the drills and was fortunate not to end up on his wrong side right away. But some of the girls weren't as lucky.

Then, when we thought it couldn't get worse, Fahrrad dropped a bombshell. Imagine this: we were being timed to bring in trays filled with 20 water glasses made of deep royal blue glass to represent the Ritz Carlton's image. However, no one realized the challenge posed by these peculiar glasses. They were top-heavy, and as one tray after another made its entrance, glasses tipped and crashed to the floor. Not a single server emerged unscathed. I was one of the lucky ones; I only lost one glass. I couldn't help but imagine how disastrous this could be at night when servers burst into a room, causing glasses to crash and shatter.

Fahrrad was furious and was determined to show us how it was done. Yeah, RIGHT! In the process, he lost half his tray while trying to lower it onto the stand. Turns out, he wasn't as mighty as his frail ego believed.

The glasses were eventually replaced with more balanced ones, but somehow, Fahrrad neglected considering the other items we had to carry. For instance, we were working at a beautiful wedding reception, and even celebrities like Cindy Williams, famous for her role as Shirley on the sitcom "Laverne and Shirley," were in attendance. It was a sit-down reception, which meant each course was brought in, cleared away, and readied for the next, all under the watchful eye of our infamous leader, Fahrrad. Everything went swimmingly until it was time to serve sorbet—the palate cleanser. These sorbets were served in top-heavy silver goblets that were simply dreadful. I mean, who in their right mind chooses such impractical items?

Anyhow, just like with the water trays, we waltzed into the room with trays full of sorbet glasses, and one by one, they came crashing down faster than a toddler's tower of building blocks. We tried wrapping towels around groups of glasses, but it was like trying to bath a cat— a valiant but ultimately futile effort.

I opened the door to enter the room, and there it was—a round scoop sorbet rolling across the floor like a croquet ball, being struck by an invisible mallet. It could have been a plot from a slapstick comedy if it weren't so hilariously absurd. The room erupted in laughter while Fahrrad entered full-fledged panic mode, screaming at everyone like he was auditioning for a role in a horror movie. Really? The problem wasn't with the servers; it was with the design. From that day on, I harbored a deep dislike for the man, and rightfully so.

Even with such an unlikable manager as Fahrrad, I continued my employment with the Ritz Carlton. The stability of a regular paycheck allowed me to take a significant financial step forward in buying my first brand-new vehicle. It was a shiny Toyota truck equipped with a handy camper shell on the back. This acquisition was partly due to my involvement in a new, unexpected side business that came about by pure chance.

My new roommate, Larry, had overheard me sharing stories of my past as an aerobics instructor. Intrigued, he mentioned that he had taken some classes at the Laguna Health Club and suggested I inquire about teaching there. So, I did just that. To my surprise, they were actively seeking well-trained instructors, especially when aerobics was still in its early stages. It didn't take long for me to become a regular part-time instructor at the club, perfectly complementing my steady work schedule at the Ritz.

Now, you might be scratching your head, wondering why on earth I needed a new truck with a shell on the back. Well, that's where life's unexpected plot twists and zany turns come into play. Fate led me through some truly wild and surprising transformations. Picture this: one fine day, a lovely older lady (older than me, so we're talking someone in their 50s) attended my aerobics class. After the class, this charming lady named Pauline approached me asking a rather intriguing question. She asked if I'd entertain the notion of giving private lessons at her place.

"Why, at your home?" I asked. She confessed to feeling a tad out of place among all the younger, fitter folks in my regular class. I told her I'd consider it if it could squeeze into my already-packed schedule.

Then came the clincher: she asked about my rates. I proudly shared my sweet deal at the Laguna Health Club, earning a base rate of $10 per class plus an extra dollar for each additional student. As a bit of a celebrity instructor, my classes were always packed, often with a waiting list. But Pauline had something else in mind. She dangled a tempting offer: "$25 per class, and if my coworker Lyn can join, I'll throw in an extra $10." I didn't need much convincing. I enthusiastically replied, "Where do you live? If we can work out a flexible schedule, I think we've got the perfect setup—a win-win for everyone involved!"

Pauline, Lyn, and I quickly formed a great bond, and I introduced them to a variety of workout routines. I even added mini trampolines to our sessions, where my trusty vehicle came into play. I needed a truck to transport all my fitness equipment, from rubber bands to lightweights, a boombox, and more, ensuring we had everything we needed to enhance our workouts. I also took up a new hobby as a home DJ, crafting my workout mixes.

I invested in a 4-track mixing board, which came in handy for making my aerobic tapes and arranging songs like "The Whale Song" that Rock had grown fond of. These changes were happening at lightning speed, and by October, my life had transformed into a whole new journey, setting the stage for a career that would span for the next 30-plus years. But I'm getting ahead of myself; there were plenty more unexpected twists in store.

It's fascinating how technology and life's twists seem to go hand in hand. Suddenly, I had my first-ever flip phone, feeling more connected than ever. With my new phone number and this much-needed mobile device, I could efficiently manage my burgeoning business as a private fitness instructor in my hand.

One of my first calls was to Rock to catch him up on all the life-altering changes I'd been through and to hear about his experiences. Mark Miller initially screened my messages, and it took some patience, but eventually, Rock returned my call. It was as if we had never missed a beat, and we had a lengthy conversation about the many changes in our lives.

Rock was about to dive into filming for Dynasty, and I couldn't have been happier for him. I did have to break the news that I wouldn't be able to attend his shows at the Silver Fox anymore. Still, I enthusiastically mentioned that the Boom Boom Room in Laguna

Beach hosted the same Dynasty Night event every Tuesday. I was looking forward to seeing him on their big screen.

Rock and I found ourselves busier than squirrels scrambling to gather enough nuts for the impending winter. Rock was deep into his Dynasty filming, and I was juggling my responsibilities at the Ritz Carlton alongside my growing aerobics business. Each personal training session with Pauline and Lyn extended into cherished moments of companionship, sometimes to drinks or dinner. What had started as a professional partnership swiftly evolved into a genuine friendship.

After several weeks, Pauline proposed a daring idea: why not embrace personal training as a full-time endeavor? It was a novel concept in those days. Luminaries like Body by Jake were renowned for sculpting Hollywood's elite. Celebrities such as Steven Spielberg and Harrison Ford were helped to get into better shape by fitness programs to prepare them for their daring cinematic adventures, including the Indiana Jones sagas.

Pauline's suggestion sparked a cascade of inspiration within me. "Hmm, Body by Gunther, offering personal attention to discerning businessmen and women right in the comfort of their own homes!"

The words reverberated in my mind like a harmonious symphony. "Personal Attention!" I exclaimed aloud as if announcing the birth of the arrival of a brand-new chapter of my life. I decided, then and there, that it would be the name of my new enterprise.

However, before embarking on this transformative journey, I had to navigate the legal requirements to establish my own business.

I delved into the offerings of a nearby community college, Saddleback College, conveniently located in close proximity to my new residence. While it was a junior college, it still held a treasure trove of certificates spanning diverse fields. Among these offerings, a course in business planning beckoned. This course promised to unravel the intricacies of birthing a business, guiding me through the labyrinth process of transforming my vision into a reality, all condensed into a comprehensive executive summary, aka, a Business Plan.

This document would serve as my calling card, briefly outlining my company's essence, articulating its raison d'être through a mission statement, and providing essential insights into the products or services I intended to offer. I recognized that employees would enter the equation further down the line once my burgeoning business demanded reinforcements. This was my roadmap, charting the course for structuring, operating, and nurturing my nascent enterprise. It echoed that age-old adage, "Failure to plan is planning to fail."

As everything fell into place and my roster of fitness clients grew, I gradually reduced my hours at the Ritz. However, Fahrrad, far from being cooperative, initially refused my request for fewer hours. He constantly loaded me with more trays and tasks, sending me into rooms to collect everyone else's trays besides mine. Despite my finesse in handling the workload, I reached my breaking point. While putting down the tenth tray in a row, my back gave way as if a switch had been flipped. I couldn't lift anything, let alone walk properly.

In typical Fahrrad fashion, he began yelling at me when I was immobilized. Fed up with his behavior, I went to human resources and requested medical assistance. My anger towards the hotel and Fahrrad led me to contemplate legal action, citing negligence and an unsafe working environment. My injury was genuine, and it eventually landed me in the hospital for a couple of days.

In their wisdom, the doctors prescribed a three-month hiatus from the working world and recommended that I enroll in specialized physical therapy. Now, there I was, a fitness trainer needing training! It was like a mechanic needing a tune-up. I reluctantly agreed, yearning to bounce back to peak form as soon as possible. Fortunately, the hotel's insurance came to the rescue, covering all my medical bills and even tossing in my regular salary during my "break." Ha ha...no pun intended!

Ironically, this unexpected pause gave me the perfect opportunity to complete my business plan. I put on my best suit, scheduled meetings with chambers of commerce all over Orange County, and enlightened them about my grand fitness empire dreams. As I handed out business cards like candy at a parade, the fruits of my labor started to ripen.

A remarkable stroke of luck miraculously followed. A Newport Beach Chamber of Commerce member, who also owned the Orange County Business Journal, saw something in me. She wanted my fitness expertise in more ways than one—training and writing a weekly article for her journal. As if that wasn't sweet enough, each piece came with a side of free advertising for my business, complete with my smiling face in a photo ad, logo, and phone number. Now, that's what I call a win-win deal!

Pushed Out of the Closet Without A Parachute

As I delved deeper into entrepreneurship, it felt like the Gods themselves were orchestrating a plan to help me cut the umbilical cord tying me to the Ritz Carlton and begin my full-time entrepreneurial journey. As fate would have it, something happened at the Ritz that gave me the perfect out clause.

After finishing my rehab and being given the green light to return to work, I was instructed to do specific stretches while working to alleviate the stress on my lower back. Plus, I wore a Velcro waistband for protection. I started my regular routine at work and was called into the large ballroom for a meet-and-greet meeting.

We were told that our next function would have as its guest speaker the famous football player, commentator, and inspirational speaker O.J. Simpson. How serendipitously life puts things together for us. Who would have known that years later, this famous American football player's 1995 murder trial would become one of the most famed criminal trials in American history?

The evening unfolded seamlessly, a flawlessly coordinated effort, with O.J.'s distinctive voice echoing through the hotel's corridors. I can still vividly picture the grand shrimp ice sculpture we had carefully wheeled back into the hallway, its pristine form now slowly succumbing to the gentle melt. We were given the green light to indulge in some shrimp as long as O.J. continued his captivating discourse within the confines of the room.

To our surprise, there were also half-empty bottles of Dom Pérignon. It would have gone to waste, but we were treated to some of our first sips of this exquisite beverage. It was a delightful surprise, especially since Fahrrad had been promoted to an office role, handling events elsewhere, and we had a more lenient manager overseeing the evening. However, what unfolded that night became a harrowing experience for me and one of our female servers.

The event was an enormous success for both the hosting group and the guest speaker, O.J., who graciously stuck around to sign autographs and take photos. Afterward, we were granted access to the ballroom to begin the post-event clean-up. This ballroom had balconies that provided breathtaking views of the Pacific Ocean, offering a stunning 180-degree panorama of the beautiful coastline. Before O.J.'s speech, some attendees had ventured outside to savor the view. Our staff had thoughtfully placed tray tables outside for guests to leave their empty appetizer plates and glasses.

As we tidied up and collected the trays, I stepped onto one of the balconies. It was already dark, but out of the corner of my eye, I noticed one of our servers sitting in a corner on the floor. She had her knees drawn up to her chest, was in tears, and trembling. I rushed over to her and quickly alerted another server, instructing him to fetch assistance immediately.

This young woman confided in me, sharing a disturbing encounter. She claimed that she had been assaulted by none other than O.J. Simpson. It's important to note that this incident occurred in 1984, more than a decade before the notorious Nicole Simpson episode. In a calm voice, she recounted her story. She had come outside to collect a tray, thinking she was alone. But lurking in the shadows was O.J., who allegedly made inappropriate advances toward her. When she rebuffed his advances, he started becoming aggressive, forcibly kissing and groping her. She resisted, but O.J. shoved her into the corner, causing her to fall as he stormed away.

The incident's aftermath brought us to the human resources office, but O.J. had already left the hotel by then. The office staff took written statements from the young woman and myself, mainly because I was the one who found her in distress. However, we soon realized that the odds were stacked against us. We were told, "It would become her word against O.J.'s, and we all know whose side they'd likely take." They insinuated that the young woman might have exaggerated the incident, suggesting no one was seriously harmed.

Can you believe it? In this era, the "Me Too" movement was still a distant concept and support for such cases was limited.

It was a classic example of the victim being treated as if they were the perpetrator, accused of trying to ruin someone's life. Yet, she was the one haunted by nightmares and suffered post-traumatic stress disorder for years to come. The traumatic incident drove her to quit her job, and I never saw her again. I did all I could to express empathy for her and highlighted the unfortunate reality of how such cases were often handled at the time. In some small way, I had hoped I helped her by being there to comfort her, believing her, and listening to her tell her story.

Pushed Out of the Closet Without A Parachute

About a week passed, and I found myself working a small breakfast meeting for the Mayor and City Council of Laguna Niguel. Handling the six or so members was quite a task, but I was determined to ensure things would run smoothly. The breakfast unfolded without a hitch, and once I had everything cleaned up, I retreated to one of the empty rooms where tables and chairs were stacked. It was my opportunity to perform the physical therapy stretches I'd been instructed to do whenever I had a moment between events. One particular stretch involved me laying on my back, pulling my knee to my chest, and pulling my leg over to the opposite side, sometimes accompanied by a satisfying crack from my back.

As I was mid-stretch, who should barge in but Fahrrad himself. He bellowed, "What the hell are you doing?"

Without missing a beat, I replied, "I'm just following the stretches recommended by my physical therapist. I've already tidied up the room and planned to head to the employee cafeteria."

He glared at me with a vicious look and declared, "No, you're not; you're going home. You claimed you were ready to return to work, but you're not. Grab your things and leave."

And leave I did, not the company, but the room, making a beeline for the human resources office to file a harassment complaint. I presented my case, explaining precisely what the doctor had instructed me to do. I clarified that I wasn't in pain and these were merely maintenance exercises. Guess what? I received another three months' paid vacation, but this time, the Ritz made it plain not to return.

The umbilical cord was finally severed, giving me a cushion to build up my clientele. I didn't bother fighting the decision because it wasn't worth the trouble. They were in the wrong, and I had every right to file a wrongful termination suit. However, they believed I wouldn't stick around much longer anyway. Sensing my disgust with the hotel.

As a side note, some of my co-workers who had become friends, informed me that Fahrrad was shortly later fired for reasons unknown to the general public. However, apparently, according to reliable sources, he had harassed so many other employees that he had become a potential lawsuit waiting to happen for the hotel. Karma eventually catches up. Doesn't it?

Chapter 12: Birthday and New Year

During Rock's Dynasty filming, Rock's birthday was a beacon of celebration on the horizon. I hadn't seen him since Father's Day, and our conversations had been reduced to phone chats. It was an amusing twist of fate that both Rock and my newfound confidante, Pauline, were ardent Scorpios, with their birthdays falling just a day apart—Rock's on November 17th, a Saturday, and Pauline's on Sunday the 18th. I tried to organize something on Friday, hoping that everyone could attend.

Unfortunately, Rock had already committed to birthday plans on Friday, the 16th, so I hatched a brilliant idea. Why not celebrate Rock's birthday and Pauline's birthdays together at the Royal Thai in Laguna Beach on Sunday? Rock, always game for a good time, agreed wholeheartedly. However, just when I thought the stars were aligning, he became a last-minute cancellation.

It turns out that Rock had stumbled upon a delightful tidbit—Dean had already planned a surprise bash for him on the 18th. Rock, in his ever-charming manner, instructed me to continue the festivities with Pauline, but after dinner, why not come up to Hollywood and join in the celebration at Dean's apartment? I was sure to be acquainted with everyone in attendance, and the prospect of reuniting in person after such a prolonged separation filled me with anticipation and joy akin to a long-awaited theatrical encore.

Pushed Out of the Closet Without A Parachute

Pauline's soirée at the Royal Thai Cuisine unfolded as a culinary symphony, a gastronomic masterpiece that delighted our senses. From the delectable Chicken Satay and the savory Pad Thai noodles to the succulent Hawaiian Shrimp and the aromatic Mussaman Curry, our table was graced with an array of dishes, each a palate-pleasing sensation. The abundance of flavors left me so satisfied that I felt compelled to embark on a leisurely post-dinner stroll, contemplating the impending journey to Hollywood.

I couldn't escape the reality that, regardless of traffic conditions, I was in for a four-hour drive tonight—two hours to get there and another two for the return trip. Fortunately, I had wisely taken a nap earlier in the day, as my hotel gig was over, and I was now in charge of my own destiny to accommodate an ever-expanding roster of personal training clients.

Upon arriving in West Hollywood, I presented the gift bag containing the Macallan Scotch Whisky I had carefully selected for Rock. I knew it would be a libation he'd savor, and I hoped it would provide enjoyment beyond this night of celebration.

The gathering was in full swing, marking Rock's second birthday soirée of the weekend. While others from his "A list" hosted a party at his home with a select roster of Hollywood luminaries, an underlying tension was linked to a particular guest. Rock alluded to "The Asshole" and "What's his name" still residing at his house, and it was no mystery that he referred to Marc Christian.

Pushed Out of the Closet Without A Parachute

The challenge of extricating this unwanted guest from his abode weighed heavily on Rock's mind. Dean's agent, Dick Lovell, suggested the possibility of securing Marc a film job in the hopes that employment might encourage him to depart voluntarily. Rock, however, expressed a desire to put the ordeal behind him and immerse himself in the festivities of the evening.

The party unfolded with the usual festive spirit, free from significant mishaps or "Brown Betty" incidents. Laughter and banter filled the air, with conversations revolving around the latest tidbits of Hollywood gossip and anecdotes about the enjoyable filming of Dynasty. I shared with Rock my journey into self-employment as a personal trainer and my budding career as a writer for the Orange County Business Journal, which, conveniently, offered free advertising in every article along with my contact details. My entrepreneurial pursuits were gaining momentum, and I was beginning to carve out my niche.

As the night wore on, there were the familiar sounds of laughter, camaraderie, and one heck of a fun party. The specifics remained a bit hazy, like trying to remember the punchline of a joke you heard in a crowded room—you know it was hilarious, but the details seem to have escaped me, like elusive socks in a dryer.

Despite all the gaiety, something about Rock caught my attention. His cheerful demeanor couldn't completely mask the subtle signs of change. He appeared to have shed some weight, and even when watching Dynasty, I couldn't help but notice a weariness and a slight gauntness in his appearance. Knowing that Rock had undergone quintuple bypass surgeries only heightened my apprehension. I wanted to make sure he was okay.

Rock asked me what I had been doing for fun, and I mentioned that I had recently taken up the demanding sport of outrigger canoe racing with a local team at Monarch Bay. It was grueling, but my companionship with my teammates made it worthwhile. At this point in my life, I was only out to my closest friends. The fact that I was gay was concealed from my clients and even my parents. But I couldn't shake the sneaking suspicion that my mother already knew. They say that mothers always have a way of knowing.

Though I could talk to Rock, it wasn't the place or time where I could ask him about his health seriously. During a brief moment with Dean alone in the kitchen, I did voice my concerns about Rock's well-being. I asked Dean if he had any insights into Rock's health, mentioning that he seemed to have lost significant weight.

Dean's response focused on Rock's desire to appear better on camera, suggesting that the adage about looking heavier on screen might have motivated him to shed some pounds. But the explanation didn't sit well with me as I found it hard to believe that Rock, who had recently undergone bypass surgery, would suddenly be so motivated to lose weight for appearance's sake. It just didn't add up, and my worries persisted.

As much as I wanted to broach the subject with Rock personally, I decided against it at his birthday party. After all, we hadn't seen each other in quite a while, and this was meant to be a joyous occasion. Instead, I made a silent commitment to cherish our time together and keep in touch more frequently to ensure he was in good health.

Feeling the weight of exhaustion tugging at me and fully aware that the party would likely continue into the early morning hours, I decided to make an Irish exit or at least a semi-Irish one. I reasoned it was better to slip away quietly, allowing Rock to relish in the celebration without disruption. I did express my gratitude to Dean for the invitation, assuring him that I appreciated it immensely. Dean, understanding my need to rest, assured me that Rock would understand, and with that, I left one of Dean's parties before midnight. As I embarked on my journey home, I couldn't help but feel like something was off with both Rock and Dean, or perhaps they were hiding something.

In the blink of an eye, Thanksgiving and Christmas were underway. During the festive season, Rock, Dean, and I all ventured in different directions to celebrate with our respective families and close friends. During this time, my bond with Pauline grew more substantial, and she played a pivotal role in jumpstarting my new career as a Certified Personal Trainer (CPT) through the industry-standard American Council on Exercise (ACE). To enhance my skills, I enrolled in continued education courses at Saddleback College, where I hoped to earn a certificate in sports kinesiology.

Pushed Out of the Closet Without A Parachute

Thanksgiving found me in Baja, California, where Pauline, Lyn, Pauline's gay roommate Randy, and a few other dear friends gathered. Pauline had recently acquired a charming place perched on the cliffs overlooking the beach, not far from Ensenada. I drove down alone to join everyone and have a fabulous time.

The following month, our paths converged again during the festive Christmas celebrations in Laguna Beach at Pauline's residence. This time, I wasn't navigating the event solo; I brought along a date to share in the merriment. Before anyone gets too excited, let me assure you it was a brief holiday romance, a product of a well-intentioned blind date set up by mutual friends. Long-term commitment wasn't on my radar back then, and the encounter evolved into a short but charming holiday tryst.

Rock and I engaged in only a few conversations during this time, but nothing out of the ordinary, although Rock's version of ordinary often danced on the precipice of drama. He assured me that things were progressing well, but there was still "The Asshole" firmly planted in his guest room. The enduring presence of this person baffled me, and I couldn't comprehend how he had such a grip on Rock.

In a moment of vulnerability, Rock confessed his fear of what Marc could unleash. He told me point-blank, "He could ruin me." He even dropped hints that Marc and his female companion might resort to tabloid tactics, threatening to expose his secrets of being gay in the National Enquirer if he attempted to evict him. I couldn't help but

Pushed Out of the Closet Without A Parachute

wonder if there were other transactions between Marc and Rock, perhaps involving hush money to maintain his silence.

Regardless of the drama with Marc, Rock's enthusiasm for Christmas was undeniable, and he expressed disappointment that we couldn't spend the holidays together. Like me, he was a festive soul, and this time of year held a special place in his heart. Nevertheless, he revealed that he and Dean were planning a gathering for January 2nd, a post-New Year's celebration, and they were eager to have me join. My calendar was remarkably free during this time, with most of my exercise clients away for the holiday season.

As the days of December passed, Rock's presence in my life seemed to wane, much like a comet gracefully fading on its celestial journey. The siren song of his work on the Dynasty series had him in its grip, and I couldn't begrudge him for it. Yet, a spark of anticipation ignited my spirit, knowing that a post-New Year's Eve soirée on January 2nd would soon bring us back together.

Intriguingly, I had come to perceive Rock's life as a splendid weave of meticulously spun tales, each told with subtle variations tailored to his diverse friendships and acquaintances. He seemed to possess a unique version of reality for every social sphere. Rock would share one set of facts with his close-knit friends and family, another rendition with those who, like me, were not privy to the inner sanctum of his castle, and yet another iteration for his work associates and fellow actors. His existence was an intricately choreographed ballet of compartmentalization, a dance that kept him in perpetual motion.

Little did I know at the time how accurate my suspicions were, but at that moment, I was trying to unravel the enigma surrounding Rock and his association with Marc Christian. The gay grapevine was buzzing with rumors, suggesting that Rock might be unwell. Even a casual viewer of Dynasty could recognize the subtle signs—the weight loss, the gauntness. I was determined to get the facts straight from the source and intended to broach the subject at some point at the party.

True to my tradition, I arrived at the party, but this time, I left my faithful guitar behind and brought a boom box with a tape I had recorded with some new arrangements to my songs. Rock was running late, as usual, and Dean, our gracious co-host, asked me to keep everyone entertained while he put together a spread of delectable appetizers and tantalizing snacks.

Over time, I became acquainted with many familiar faces in Dean's circle of friends and residents of his building, and they inquired if I was still involved with writing songs. I let them know I was able to record a couple of my songs. Over the past few months, I had meticulously prepared various renditions and even managed to lay down a recording of "The Whale Song."

When I approached Dean with a request to play it over his sound system, I stumbled upon Dean's attachment to a bygone era of technology. He seemed rooted in the '70s, when rotary phones, eight

Pushed Out of the Closet Without A Parachute

tracks, and Beta Max were gradually giving way to the new and exciting developments of cassettes and mobile flip phones, with even those evolving year by year.

However, I was in step with the ever-evolving music landscape, now on the cusp of the MIDI revolution. MIDI, a technical standard encompassing communication protocols, digital interfaces, and electrical connectors, acted as a conduit connecting an array of electronic musical instruments, computers, and audio devices. It pulsated with the rhythms of modern music, and I was eager to share it, even in a setting where time appeared to stand still.

Luckily, I had brought my trusty boom box, just in case, and it was the perfect addition to this occasion. Just as I was about to hit the play button, the door swung open, revealing the belated arrival of the man of the hour—Rock. He entered bearing gifts wrapped in festive paper for everyone, and his surprise at hearing my voice on a recording was palpable. He couldn't contain his curiosity, asking, "Who recorded this? It's exactly what we were discussing! It sounds wonderful."

With a proud smile, I replied, "I recorded it myself. I took a recording class at Saddleback College, and we put together a group album. Each of us contributed one song, and mine was 'The Whale Song.' I played all the instruments—my guitar, accordion, and recently acquired synthesizer. The ambient sounds were recorded at Dana Point Harbor, with seagulls providing the background chorus, and we even managed to capture the oldest boat I could find chugging out to sea with its fishing nets and day fishers.

Rock's praise resonated through the room, "Wow, Gunther, I must say you're quite the do-it-yourself kind of guy! Not just doing it yourself, but doing it well, all on your own."

I humorously interjected, "Well, it was me crafting the song, but we had some adept mixers in the studio, assisting with balance and harmonizing all the tracks seamlessly. It's a skill that takes time to master, but I'm absorbing it all like a sponge!"

With his signature charm, Rock quipped, "Well, bring that mighty sponge of yours right over here and soak up my grand Happy New Year's Hug!" Laughter bubbled throughout the room as we gathered around the living room table, eager to unwrap the party favors he'd thoughtfully prepared. They held mints and exquisite chocolates, simple yet sophisticated, a testament to Rock's penchant for the finer details.

Naturally, our curiosity about the latest Dynasty gossip ran rampant, and we were eager to glean insights into the forthcoming episodes. However, Rock remained resolutely tight-lipped, for he knew the perils of prematurely revealing the show's secrets. He enticed us, hinting that what lay ahead would be shocking. In his own words, he teased that he would be a pivotal part of one of those "must-see" episodes destined to be the talk of the town, much like the iconic lily pond showdown between Krystle and Alexis in "The Threat," filmed at a splendid Pasadena mansion which aired in 1983.

Pushed Out of the Closet Without A Parachute

As we hung on his every word, we couldn't fathom that Rock's episode would soon earn its place in television history, becoming not only Dynasty's most controversial episode but a seismic moment in the entire TV industry.

We could hardly contain our anticipation, eagerly awaiting the moment we could finally share the sensational events that Rock had alluded to. Little did we realize the turmoil that would soon engulf the Dynasty set and the entire world.

In February 1985, as Dynasty's Season 5 unfolded, we witnessed Rock Hudson in the role of Daniel Reece, the horse master and almost-lover of Krystle. Tragically, it would be Hudson's final performance. Reflecting on Dynasty's nine seasons, the series reached its pinnacle in 1984-1985 Season 5, becoming the number one show on TV.

All of us were clueless then, and I may have been the most naive of all. I chose to believe what both Rock and Dean told me despite a nagging feeling that there was more beneath the surface. Call it intuition, but there was the public persona, Rock Hudson, the celebrated actor, and then there was Roy, the sincere friend I had come to know. On that day, Rock seemed to wear his actor's mask more tightly than ever, concealing something profound inside.

The tension between these two identities was unmistakable. I hoped for honesty, but I knew it would have to happen away from the glitz and glamour of Hollywood parties, in a place where masks could be removed. We had grown close before, and I hoped we could again once the cameras stopped rolling. I had no idea at the time that the drama in Rock's life was about to climax, and our friendship would face its most monumental test.

For the remainder of the party, I closely watched Rock, trying to discern any signs of distress beneath his outward cheer. Later, as I chatted with Dean in his kitchen, a sense of déjà vu washed over me. Once again, I couldn't help but voice my concerns about Rock's health, but this time, it was with a more somber tone, expressing that circumstances seemed to be taking a turn for the worse.

Dean confided in me, sharing his suspicions that Rock might be battling anorexia. He recounted how Rock, who had once devoured meals with gusto, now barely ate, often remarking that the foods he once adored no longer appealed to him. It was a worrisome revelation, but we felt powerless to intervene. I knew Dean maintained a connection with Mark Miller and George Nader, longtime friends of Rock's who resided in Garner Valley near Palm Springs. Mark periodically assisted Rock with various matters and lived at Rock's castle for part of the week, maintaining a close connection with him. It seemed like a good idea to propose that Dean reach out to Mark so they could both offer their support to Rock discreetly and in a non-threatening way to understand the underlying cause of his weight loss.

As the party began to wind down, I seized a moment alone with Rock and decided to broach the subject gently. I asked him if everything was all right. Despite initial reservations, he confided in me, sharing his unexpected enjoyment of working on the show.

Pushed Out of the Closet Without A Parachute

According to Rock, the people he was collaborating with were exceptionally kind and professional, and they took excellent care of him. However, the situation at home with Marc Christian was causing him tremendous stress. Rock sighed, saying, "Marc may live at my house, but he means nothing to me. All I want is for him to leave."

I responded, "Rock, I've known you since March of 1984, and you've been talking about getting rid of Marc since we met. Perhaps it's time to consider seeking legal assistance to resolve this matter. It's taking a toll on your health."

Rock looked earnestly into my eyes, then changed the subject with a smile, saying, "Gunther, you don't know the half of it, but let's discuss something happier, like the wonderful arrangement of your song!"

Rock and I reconnected on a deeper level for the first time in several months, reminiscent of our initial meeting and time together in Hawaii. Rock shed the Hollywood persona and became Roy again, engaging in candid conversations, sharing jokes, and feeling like the genuine person I had grown to care for deeply. Although our affection was not romantic, it was a profound bond. I regarded Roy as a true friend, someone I could tease, playfully banter, and be brutally honest with. Ultimately, we both knew we wouldn't sugarcoat things for each other. That night, he confided in me, saying that apart from his longtime friend George Nader, my opinion was the only one that truly mattered to him. In his own words, "Because just like with George, I can have a no-shit conversation with you!"

Pushed Out of the Closet Without A Parachute

We delved into my decision to relocate to Laguna Niguel, and I couldn't wait to share some exciting news with Rock about my plans to purchase my own place. He was absolutely thrilled to see my passion for launching my Fitness Training Business and securing my own residence. Rock revealed that he had his own trainer himself and suggested we arrange a meeting soon. I gladly accepted his proposal.

Our conversation then shifted to my musical pursuits. I explained that I was gradually mastering the art of arranging music using electronic instruments and had even embarked on composing my first symphonic piece. Rock looked genuinely impressed and inquired, "How on earth do you find time for everything you do?"

I chuckled and replied, "Well, music has taken a backseat lately, but sometimes those creative urges hit, and I find myself writing music with my earphones on until the break of dawn." I also admitted that my musical aspirations had evolved into a more realistic and practical realization that music wasn't paying the bills while my personal training career was becoming increasingly lucrative.

Our one-on-one chat stretched for about two hours, and as the time came for me to head home, I suggested we set a date for our next meeting. Rock informed me that they would be filming his final episode on Dynasty, likely in the middle or toward the end of March. Once that was wrapped up, he promised to come over and visit my new place in Laguna Niguel. We planned to go out for dinner in Laguna and have a good old chat, just like old times!

Chapter 13: Rock's Last Visit

True to his word, Rock called me as soon as they announced his last episode was a wrap! He wouldn't reveal his character's fate in the series just yet, but soon that secret would be unveiled to the world. Nonetheless, he was temporarily jobless again and eager to reconnect with those he cared about.

I was keeping busy with my burgeoning business and looking for a place of my own. For the time being, I was still renting a room from Larry Christy, my quirky roommate who, upon hearing the news of Rock Hudson's impending visit, nearly went into cardiac arrest. Poor Larry!

Rock and Dean's arrival on a Saturday afternoon departed from our usual encounters, which typically occurred late into the night. This visit came on the heels of St. Patrick's Day, and as Larry, my dear roommate, answered the door, he appeared to be in a world of domestic activity. Larry had rearranged the furniture so many times it rivaled a game of musical chairs. He scrubbed the kitchen as though it were a crime scene and made more trips to the florist than a lovesick teenager preparing for prom night.

The result? The house was infused with the heady fragrance of Arabian Gardenias in full bloom. At the same time, the downstairs bathroom showcased an understated yet elegant arrangement of Sweet Peas that could rival the poshest powder rooms in town. Larry, with his obsessive commitment to cleanliness, was on the verge of an anxiety-induced coma. Playing the role of his unofficial therapist, I affectionately teased him, "Breathe, Larry, breathe! Remember, Rock's just a regular guy once you strip away the movie star aura. Inhale... exhale... It's just an afternoon with the Rich and Famous... the Lite version!"

Rock sauntered in as the door swung open, an armful of clothes and presents in tow. With a hint of fluster, Larry said, "Well, hello there, Mr. Rock Hudson! I'm Larry Christy, Gunther's roommate, and it's a delight to make your acquaintance."

Meanwhile, I continued to coach Larry with calming mantras, "Inhale... exhale... You've got this..." Descending the stairs to my cozy loft apartment, I couldn't resist channeling my inner Scarlet O'Hara from 'Gone with the Wind': "Rock, Rock... Rock if you go, where shall I go? What shall I do?"

Rock, playing along with a sinister grin, responded, "Frankly, Guntha, I don't give a damn!" Laughter filled the air, and poor Larry remained in a mild state of shock as I ushered Rock and Dean inside.

Rock began, "Well, Larry, what a splendid home you have here. These paintings are exquisite! Did you create all of these masterpieces?"

Larry, gradually regaining color in his cheeks, stammered out, "Oh, uh, yes, these paintings are mine, indeed. It's always a work in progress, trying to perfect them." He paused, caught in a conversation but not in a breath.

Pushed Out of the Closet Without A Parachute

Sensing Larry's need for rescue, I grinned, "And Larry, this dashing gentleman is Dean Dittman, the legendary party host of our late-night escapades." Larry extended a shaky hand to Dean, maneuvering in front of Rock with an air of royal deference. For a brief moment, I half-expected him to break into a courtly curtsey.

Rock's unexpected arrival had already sent Larry into a near-royal meltdown. Adding to the excitement was the handful of clothes, and the beautifully wrapped present Rock brought with him, which added an extra layer of intrigue to the afternoon.

"Remember when I mentioned months ago that I had a surprise for you, Gunther?" Rock asked with a sly grin.

I recalled the mysterious comment and responded. "Oh, that's right," I replied, "I was wondering what that surprise might be. So, what have we got here?"

Rock chuckled, revealing, "These are clothes I had in storage from the McMillan and Wife show. Given my larger stature, no one else at the studio could fit into them. But you, Gunther, you're the perfect fit. Try on this coat."

I slipped into the handsome camel-haired coat, which, with a few minor adjustments, would highlight my physique. "These clothes are top-notch!" I exclaimed. As I removed the coat, I noticed a tag inside one of the pockets, indicating it had been crafted by Rock Hudson's personal tailor from Cotroneo costumes in Hollywood. "Are you certain you don't want to keep these?" I asked.

Pushed Out of the Closet Without A Parachute

Rock's response was resolute: "I have a treasure trove of clothes from six seasons of McMillan, most of which I wore only once. I'd rather see them put to good use than collect dust in storage."

Rock's thoughtful surprises didn't stop at the closet-sized clothing stash from McMillan and Wife; he presented me with a large, wrapped gift that had been a long time coming. "This is a very belated housewarming or house-moving gift, Gunther," he explained. As I tore away the paper, I unveiled a substantial tin filled with an assortment of popcorn flavors, nuts, and treats capable of satisfying even the most insatiable snack cravings for the next month or so.

Grateful, I said, "You're always so considerate and kind, Rock, a quality that seems to have fallen by the wayside these days."

Still processing the surreal moment, Larry hesitated to chime in, so I nudged him, saying, "Larry, maybe we should offer Rock and Dean a seat, and I'll fetch some refreshments." Rock placed his order, opting for a sprite, and Dean followed suit, desiring the same. As we settled in, I couldn't help but ask Rock, "So, how does it feel to be free from the daily grind of being on the set of Dynasty?"

As Rock began to regale us with anecdotes about his work alongside the lovely Linda Evans and the show's dynamics, he couldn't help but sing praises of her professionalism and the sense of belonging he felt within their tight-knit television family. "John Forsythe," he revealed, "was the true patriarch of the family, and he had to approve all the scenes. But Joan Collins, well, she kept the show alive by playing such a fantastic 'bitch'."

Pushed Out of the Closet Without A Parachute

At the same time as these Hollywood tales, one comment caught my attention like a flashing neon sign. "I was exhausted," Rock confessed, "doing all those takes. I ended up resting in my trailer whenever I got the chance." I let the words hang in the air for a moment. I didn't want to broach the subject in front of Larry, but I couldn't ignore that Rock looked frail and worn. The change since I last saw him was concerning.

After a brief chat, Larry excused himself, mentioning a dinner engagement with friends. With Larry gone, I suggested to Rock and Dean that we could make dinner reservations somewhere to continue our conversation. However, Rock declined, expressing that the rigorous work schedule left him somewhat weak. He also mentioned experiencing slight nausea, so he was sticking to Sprite. I suggested, "How about I bring out a platter of crackers and cheese that I've prepared? We can relax and talk in more detail now that Larry's gone."

Dean and Rock liked the idea and stayed about an hour. At one point when Rock excused himself to visit the restroom, I took the opportunity to ask Dean about Rock's deterioration.

In a hushed tone, I leaned in closer to Dean to interrogate, "Dean, seriously, what's happening with Rock? He looks so frail, and you can tell he's lost even more weight."

Dean could sense my deep concern but seemed at a loss for words. He finally admitted, "Gunther, he's just not eating anymore, not even his favorite foods. I've tried to get him to see a doctor, but all he ever says is, 'Screw the doctors, what do they know, anyway?'"

Pushed Out of the Closet Without A Parachute

I was stunned, and my immediate reaction was, "Dean, this situation can't continue. It's painfully obvious that Rock is not well. He might be putting on a brave face, but we both know this isn't the Rock we recognize. He's usually the life of the party, spreading laughter and energy. But now, it's like his light is dimming. We need to take action. What can we do to help him?"

As Rock emerged from the bathroom, he shared his delight at our reunion and complimented my new place. He also extended his warm regards to my parents, fondly recalling our time together in Hawaii and their genuine kindness. However, he added, "I'm afraid Dean and I should begin our journey back to West Hollywood. I'm not feeling completely myself and need some time to recharge."

As Rock and Dean prepared to leave, I extended an invitation to an upcoming event, perfectly coinciding with the first anniversary of our Hawaiian adventure. I described the event, scheduled for the week after Easter, in a charming village near the San Juan Capistrano train station. It was a birthday celebration for my friend Pauline's son Chris, who was about to turn 40.

I mentioned some of the exciting activities planned, including a hayride, sing-along, and a mariachi band, knowing Rock's fondness for the latter. Rock eagerly accepted the invitation, turning to Dean, who also agreed. I assured them I would provide all the details once everything was arranged.

As I stood there, watching their car disappear into the distance, an overwhelming sense of foreboding gripped me. It was as if the universe was whispering for me to reach out and help Rock. Regret gnawed at my insides, knowing that this might have been my final opportunity to extend a helping hand to him, insist that he seek aid, and convey that we, his friends, cared more deeply than he could ever fathom.

Yet, fear immobilized me, the dread that any word from me might shroud what little control Rock still possessed over his fate. Nevertheless, I could perceive the starlight in his eyes fading. The obscurity of the unknown surrounded me. I sensed the weight of unspoken words as if fate was weaving a tragic inevitability beyond our control. I felt powerless, but my hope persisted.

In just a few weeks, as the time neared to finalize the numbers for purchasing food for our San Juan Capistrano party and hayride, I received an unexpected call from Rock. The call was from somewhere else; he told me he was in the desert, specifically Palm Springs. His voice was disoriented, and he lamented that hardly anyone reached out to him anymore. I tried to explain, "I don't call as much because Mark Miller usually screens your calls, which discourages many people."

Rock responded with a sigh, "I know, Gunther. I'm just frustrated with Marc Christian and needed to get away."

I probed gently, "What happened now? Is there something new?"

Rock's reply revealed a series of troubling discoveries: "I found out that Marc was getting paid for sex. I should have never gotten involved with him, especially since he exposed himself to me while I was having a massage at the Sports Connection in Hollywood."

I was taken aback and inquired, "Is that how you two met?"

Rock explained, "Well, as I mentioned, I was having a massage at the Sports Connection, but the door was slightly open. Marc kept on walking by with just a towel on, going from the sauna to the showers, and then he let the towel fall off, knowing I could see him. He did this repeatedly, coming on to me. I should have realized he had ulterior motives. While I was still Israel, he confessed that he needed money, so he started engaging in paid sexual encounters. This occurring in my home while I was gone"

This revelation left me speechless. I wondered about the timing of this unsettling disclosure during Rock's stay in Palm Springs and the impact it had on him and those around him.

Inquiring further, I asked Rock with a degree of frankness, "When you left for Israel to shoot the movie Ambassador, you mentioned you allowed Marc to stay at your place because he was crashing on his girlfriend Liberty's couch, right?"

Rock's voice carried a tinge of regret as he confessed, "That turned out to be the biggest mistake of my life. Things started fine upon my return, but as I began to inquire about his comings and goings—prompted by reports from my butler, James, and Mark Miller that other men were frequenting my home—I was horrified.

Pushed Out of the Closet Without A Parachute

I paused for a moment, carefully considering the situation, before posing a question, "Rock, when you confronted him, and he threatened to go to the tabloids and expose your sexuality, effectively ruining your reputation, couldn't you have considered an alternative? I mean, maybe offering him a substantial sum in exchange for his departure. Plus, get a legally binding document prohibiting him from disclosing anything, similar to non-compete clauses in business agreements. I'm not a lawyer, but perhaps that could have resolved the situation without such turmoil. Maybe you should talk to someone who deals in this type of blackmail and extortion."

As I was sharing these thoughts with Rock, I couldn't help but play devil's advocate in my mind. I wondered about the reliability of the information Rock was receiving, considering it was largely hearsay, except for Marc's alleged confession about accepting money for sex. But questions nagged at me: Why would Marc be having sex for money? After all, he stayed at Rock's home rent-free, without any financial burdens. The details seemed somewhat hazy. Frustratingly, I lacked answers for Rock, so I decided to steer the conversation back to the upcoming Hayride event scheduled for the following week.

As the date of the San Juan Capistrano birthday event drew nearer, I conversed with Dean. He mentioned that Rock was still in Palm Springs but assured me that, to the best of his knowledge, Rock intended to come. Pauline and her son Chris were genuinely excited about the prospect of his attendance, though they understood that Rock might have more pressing matters to attend to. I shared their excitement but also harbored concerns about Rock's eating disorder and his struggle to regain lost weight. Mostly, I hoped he would show up, allowing us the opportunity for a heart-to-heart discussion about relieving the stress in his living situation. Chris was a lawyer and might be the perfect person for Rock to consult regarding his situation.

On the day of the Hayride, I contacted Rock, leaving a message on his answering machine, but my phone never chimed with a callback. Instead, it was Dean who connected with me, noting their anticipated arrival at my place around 7 p.m. before heading over to the party, which was a mere stone's throw away.

Dean arrived as the clock neared 7:20, yet Rock was conspicuously absent. I couldn't help but voice my concerns to Dean, 'Is Rock all right? He never returned my call, and after our last meeting and how he appeared, I can't help but worry.' Dean reassured me that Rock genuinely desired to join the festivities but wasn't up to it. He then shared further insights from Rock's recent visit.

With empathy and sadness, Dean unveiled a poignant moment from our last encounter. "Remember when Rock excused himself to the restroom, and we shared our conversation?"

I nodded, the memory vivid in my mind.

Dean continued, his tone heavy with regret. "Well," he began, "Rock became quite ill there. He was consumed by embarrassment, so he rushed to leave."

My heart sank at the revelation, and I shook my head empathetically. "There's no need for shame," I offered softly, my voice carrying a note of compassion. "Had I known, I could have provided some relief with medicine. But I can't help but feel that Rock's ailment runs deeper than we suspect."

I finally voiced a question lingering in my mind with a heavy sigh. "Dean, have you heard the whispers about Marc Christian having AIDS and the fear that he might have transmitted it to Rock?" The room seemed to hold its breath, awaiting Dean's response to this ominous question.

Dean mentioned that he had heard rumors through various channels, as he wasn't directly involved in the filming of Dynasty, unlike Rock. "You wouldn't believe the things I've heard since Rock started filming Dynasty," he began. "There were even people speculating on the set that Rock might have AIDS, but honestly, I initially thought it was due to anorexia. Now, it's becoming clear that he can't keep anything down. I'm unsure if it's a physical issue or if something else is weighing heavily on him like the stress caused by Marc and his threats to expose Rock to the National Enquirer."

Dean's words conveyed genuine concern for our friend Rock, and I could sense the weight of the situation bearing down on him. It seemed like the best course of action for the evening was to put our worries about Rock aside and enjoy ourselves temporarily. Dean agreed, and we hopped into my new truck, heading over to the party with our best party faces on, determined to have a good time and make the most of the evening.

Pushed Out of the Closet Without A Parachute

Dean possessed an innate charm that could effortlessly steal the spotlight when Rock wasn't around. He had a knack for regaling people with humorous anecdotes, and he often shared stories about his stage experiences, such as playing Daddy Warbucks in the Regional Tour of "Annie" and his role in the movie "Bachelor Party." In addition to his theatrical ventures, Dean had been having a bustling 1985, making appearances on various TV shows like "Silver Spoons," "It's a Living," "T.J. Hooker," "Cheers," and even "Murder, She Wrote."

Despite his hectic schedule, Dean had managed to find time for our visit, and I was grateful for that. It seemed cathartic for him to be around me, as we spent much of our free time with Rock, forming a unique bond. It was as if we were holding onto the memories and the spirit of our times with Rock, keeping his infectious energy alive, even though he couldn't be here to enjoy the evening with us.

The hayride through the area by the San Juan Capistrano train station was nothing short of enchanting. I brought my trusty guitar along, and we belted out sing-along classics from "Puff the Magic Dragon" to those old Peter, Paul, and Mary tunes. Of course, some libations were in play, but I limited myself to one or two beers in my eternal role as the designated responsible adult. On the other hand, Dean was flirting with the harder stuff, and I couldn't help but worry about the impending vehicular acrobatics. So, I, in my infinite wisdom, offered up my bed as a noble sacrifice and decided I could make do with the couch if it meant keeping our dear Dean from vehicular shenanigans. But, lo and behold, Dean, instead of steering towards boozeville, made an unexpected U-turn towards sobriety central, fueled by coffee and a smattering of snacks. Not that this miraculous transformation scientifically cures intoxication, but it was Dean's magic trick of the evening.

As the festivities gradually subsided, we bid our farewells. Dean had made some fresh comrades in arms. Pauline and her roommate Randy, in particular, were smitten with Dean's antics. And, as for Pauline's son, Chris, the man of the hour, he couldn't have asked for a more spirited companion for his birthday bash. It indeed was a delightful soirée. Yet, amid the laughter and festivities, an absence lingered, an empty chair at the table. Oh, what a night it could have been if Rock had been there, his infectious spirit filling the air with even more magic.

The journey back to my house cast a somewhat melancholic hue over Dean and me. We couldn't help but yearn for Rock's presence throughout all the evening's revelry. Dean assured me he would regale Rock with every detail of the night's celebration and promised to visit him tomorrow to check up on him. I implored him to keep me in the loop throughout this ordeal since Rock, in his fragile state, felt too embarrassed to confront me directly. Thankfully, Rock had confided in Dean, a fellow traveler on the path of life, closer in age and geography.

Dean enveloped me in one of his trademark bear hugs, a gesture that always conveyed more warmth and solace than mere words ever could. His immense heart was evident in that embrace, and I knew he would keep me informed, bearing witness to whatever news might come our way.

"Dean, I implore you," looking into his eyes, "the moment you hear anything, whether it's a glimmer of hope or the weight of despair, reach out. We're in this together, and I'll drop everything to be there, okay?"

Dean nodded, his faith in a spiritual force evident as he spoke of helping Rock reconnect with his inner spirit. It was a perspective rooted in his steadfast belief in the Church of Scientology, a topic too profound for the post-party hours. So, I hugged Dean tightly once more and whispered, "You take care of our Rock... I think he needs us now more than ever." With that, Dean embarked on his journey back to West Hollywood, leaving me with the hope that he might be the Florence Nightingale Rock needed right now in his life.

Chapter 14: Losing All Hope

The following months were a trying ordeal for all of us. Dean and I struggled valiantly in our relentless pursuit of help for Rock. Dean served as the bridge between Rock and those residing in what was affectionately known as "the Castle," a moniker bestowed upon Rock's residence.

As time passed, Rock divulged that Rock's trusted secretary, Mark Miller, had now taken up residence there most of the week. Additionally, James, Rock's devoted butler, maintained a full-time presence. Astonishingly, it appeared that Marc Christian was still squatting on the property against Rock's repeated requests to vacate.

But there was yet another figure who had become an almost permanent fixture in Rock's abode: Ron Channel, his personal trainer. I briefly crossed paths with Ron at Dean's New Year's Eve gathering, and he came across as an amiable fellow. Sadly, our interaction was too fleeting to form a genuine impression. Nevertheless, as Dean conveyed, Ron had seamlessly slipped into the role of Rock's newfound confidant and closest companion.

At this juncture, my attempts to contact Rock had nearly dwindled to despair. Each call I made only connected me with an unfeeling answering machine unless James or Mark Miller picked up the phone. Reluctantly, I refrained from leaving any messages and would hang up if I failed to hear the sound of Rock's voice.

Pushed Out of the Closet Without A Parachute

My most promising avenue remained through Dean, who occasionally visited Rock's residence to engage in heartfelt discussions. Dean informed me that he had relayed the tales of our Hayride adventures to Rock, and it deeply saddened Rock that he couldn't join in the festivities. I requested a favor from Dean, asking him to implore Rock to call me whenever he found it feasible for a conversation.

In May, right around my birthday, Rock made what would become our final call. Little did I know it would be the last time I would engage in a meaningful conversation with my dear friend.

When Rock called me, he seemed to be in good spirits, and our conversation unfolded effortlessly, stretching out for hours. I couldn't resist asking Rock about his growing closeness with Ron. Rock promptly clarified that Ron was unequivocally straight, which Dean already revealed to me. Nevertheless, Rock disclosed that spending time with Ron provided a respite from dealing with "What's his name." That was how Rock mostly referred to Marc Christian unless he was employing more derogatory names like "The Asshole" or "That Prick."

In candid sharing, Rock disclosed that he had brought Ron along on his promotional tour to Paris and various parts of Europe. Dean was preoccupied with appearances on TV shows, and Mark Miller had declined the invitation, so Ron became his companion and confidant. Rock expressed a deep sense of fulfillment in witnessing Ron's awe and wonderment as he experienced places that Rock himself had taken for granted over the years. Through Ron's eyes, Rock found a renewed sense of magic in Europe from someone seeing it for the very first time.

Rock also shared that he had taken another excursion to Hawaii with Ron in February, lodging at the luxurious Mauna Kea. I couldn't help but wonder about the timing, considering he was filming Dynasty. Perhaps he had managed the trip just before the production commenced. Regardless, Rock mentioned that during the journey, all he did was bask in the sun and attain a state of complete relaxation.

I suggested that if he had informed me in advance, my parents would have been thrilled to make the journey to the other side of the island, even if it meant driving to Waimea to share lunch or brunch with him and Ron. Rock, however, expressed his reluctance to impose such a burden on them. He reassured me that he would have visited my parents if he had more time, but this trip was a brief weekend getaway.

Despite Rock's reluctance to discuss "What's his name?" my curiosity led me to inquire if there were any signs that he had heeded my advice about seeking legal counsel. He casually brushed off the notion, indicating that he cared little as long as he kept his distance and preferred to ignore the situation. He appeared to be entrenched in denial, leaving me no reason to belabor the point.

Rock seemed to be relishing his time, drawing close to Ron. Who was I to intrude upon his happiness? I felt a mild sense of being brushed aside, that is, until Rock brought up how much he missed my singing and inquired if I had composed any new songs. I eagerly shared with him that I had delved deep into electronic music arrangement and had set up a four-track in-home studio. This marvel allowed me to manipulate regular cassette tapes into four-track compositions, affording me an array of creative possibilities.

I couldn't hold back from mentioning that even the Beatles had recorded their groundbreaking album, Sgt. Pepper on four-track equipment. This record is often hailed as one of the most influential in music history, a true game-changer for pop music. Consequently, I had been diligently at work in my home studio, crafting new songs and ping-ponging tracks. I was also eager to share some of my latest creations with him.

Rock made a heartfelt request, asking that I assemble a tape for him to be delivered by Dean. The idea struck me as a brilliant one, an opportunity for Dean and me to infuse this gift with our messages to Rock, a touching tribute from our hearts. I couldn't shake the feeling that perhaps Rock was either unable or unwilling to travel back down to Laguna, perhaps due to his deteriorating health. Regardless, I eagerly embraced creating the tape, eager to contribute to his comfort.

As our conversation ended, Rock expressed his need for rest and promised to reach out once he had received the tape to share his thoughts. We exchanged our goodbyes, oblivious that this would be the last time our voices would connect in conversation. The haunting truth still lingers that I failed to perceive the gravity of his illness and the fleeting nature of the moments we had left. It remains a painful memory, etched into my soul, a constant reminder of what could have been.

Subsequently, I contacted Dean to convey my conversation with Rock and his request for a special tape filled with some of my new songs. In his ever-supportive manner, Dean saw it as a brilliant idea to lift Rock's spirits and proposed that we create this heartfelt gift during the upcoming weekend.

I hesitated, explaining that I had a few clients to train on Saturday morning, but the rest of the weekend was wide open. We settled on a date, and as Saturday approached, I found myself grappling with an unexpected bout of laryngitis, of all things. It was as if my voice had staged a sudden rebellion, likely due to the vigorous aerobics classes I had taught that week, where I had inadvertently strained my vocal cords. My voice had transformed into a croaky, pitiful rendition of its former self, challenging even simple conversations. I sounded like a wounded frog—ribbit and all!

I had optimistically hoped that my voice would have recovered, thanks to a regimen of warm water with lemon and honey. Alas, I still sounded like a wounded frog. Nevertheless, we soldiered on, making the tape. Dean, always one to lighten the mood, cracked a few jokes about my current vocal predicament. Despite my hoarse croaks, we found humor in the situation, and Dean suggested that we create another tape later when my voice was back to its harmonious self. After all, a froggy serenade might not have been the most soothing choice for Rock's listening pleasure, but he would probably understand and find the humor in our attempt!

A couple of weeks passed in anxious anticipation, yet I heard nothing from Rock. My curiosity grew overwhelming, prompting me to dial Dean's number to confirm whether he had been able to deliver the tape to Rock. Dean relayed that he hadn't encountered Rock at home, but James had kindly allowed him access to the house. Dean had left the tape on Rock's nightstand, reasonably confident that Rock would discover it eventually. Dean had also made Mark Miller and James aware of our heartfelt gift.

However, an unforeseen element crept into our contemplation: the inscrutable Marc Christian. Had he tampered with the tape, we wondered? With a tinge of worry, I implored Dean to reach out to Rock and determine whether he had listened to or even looked at the tape. The uncertainty of the situation loomed like a shadow over our well-intentioned gesture.

Another couple of weeks passed, marked by an unsettling silence. Then, on a Monday evening, July 15, 1985, as I tuned in to the Nightly News, my world seemed to collapse around me. The broadcast featured a shockingly emaciated Rock Hudson, standing alongside the beloved actress Doris Day at a news conference. They were promoting her new TV cable show, "Doris Day's Best Friends," which included footage of Hudson visiting Day's ranch in Carmel, California, a few days prior. It was a jarring sight, and although neither the show nor the newscast explicitly mentioned AIDS, the devastating reality hung heavy in the air. I had seen friends who had succumbed to the disease, and Rock's frail appearance echoed their tragic decline. Rock was wasting away into oblivion before our very eyes.

Shortly after the news report, my phone rang, and it was my mom on the line. She had witnessed the broadcast and was utterly taken aback by Rock's condition. She informed me that my dad had read in a German newspaper called the Zeitung that there were suspicions Rock had AIDS, although my dad didn't fully comprehend what that entailed. I reassured my mom that I hadn't seen Rock in some time but knew someone with more recent information—I promised to call Dean to gather the latest details.

As my parents and I grappled with the shock of what we had witnessed, my understanding with the ravages of this disease filled me with dread. The looming fear that Rock could be nearing the end of his life weighed heavily on my heart.

The next call came from Dean, and it was evident from the moment he spoke that he was overwhelmed with emotion. His voice quivering as he described the heartbreaking sight of Rock's deteriorating condition, I asked Dean, my voice filled with concern, "When was the last time you actually saw Rock?"

Dean, sounding somewhat disoriented, responded, "The last time I visited his house was to deliver the tape we made during the first week of June. We have had a few phone conversations since then, but the last time I locked eyes with Rock was sometime in May. He dropped by for a drink, and we spent the entire night engaged in deep discussions, tackling the world's problems head-on. You know how we get when we're together."

I asked for more details, such as, "How did Rock appear during that encounter?"

Dean mused, "He seemed much as he did when he graced your doorstep in April. Yes, he was slender, but my God, it was nowhere near the haunting image we witnessed on the television screen. And cameras tend to add a few pounds to a person."

We both fell into a momentary silence, grappling with the enormity of the situation. I concluded our conversation with a plea, urging Dean to gather any information and contact me immediately. It was abundantly clear that Rock desperately needed medical assistance if he hadn't sought it out already. The urgency of the situation weighed heavily on our hearts.

A day later, Dean called me to tell me that he and Mark Miller had successfully persuaded Rock to seek a new doctor. Dean credited Doris with being the driving force behind this decision, stating, "It was Doris who managed to convince him to pursue better medical care." I couldn't help but exclaim, "Wow, who would have thought it would be his old friend Doris Day who would lead him to do the right thing?

So, who is this new doctor, and where is he located?" I inquired, eager for more details.

Dean's response, however, raised suspicion. He informed me, "Rock is seeing a specialist in Geneva who specializes in treating anorexia."

Something about this still didn't quite add up, and I began to sense that Dean might not be entirely forthcoming with the truth. Rumors had been circulating widely, all pointing to the possibility that Rock was battling AIDS. I couldn't help but wonder why Dean seemed so intent on covering it up. The only conclusion I could draw was that Rock himself was either too proud or too scared to admit he had AIDS, perhaps choosing to camouflage it as a different ailment, even if it meant taking that secret to his grave about being gay and having the dreaded gay disease.

Only ten days later, my suspicions were tragically validated. It wasn't the outcome I had hoped for, and an overwhelming foreboding gripped me. Rock found himself in Paris, not Geneva, and the news that rocked the world was that he was being discharged from the American Hospital in Paris due to a diagnosis of Acquired Immune Deficiency Syndrome, or AIDS. However, what truly rattled me was the revelation that he had been diagnosed over a year ago in the United States. My mind raced with questions. How long had Dean been aware of this? It became painfully evident that he had lied about the Geneva specialist, and I couldn't contain my anger.

Realizing that certain friends were privy to certain truths while others were fed falsehoods left me feeling adrift and uncertain. I grappled with a gnawing uncertainty about what Rock had known and when he had known it. Did he carry the weight of his diagnosis with him during his time in Hawaii with my parents? The disconcerting web of secrecy and half-truths had taken root, and I felt an unrelenting need to unravel the tangled threads of this enigma and discover the truth.

I called Dean, but there was no answer, so I left an urgent message, my voice trembling with a mixture of anguish and frustration. "Dean, this is Gunther, and you need to call me as soon as you get this message. You have a lot of explaining to do. I entrusted you and Rock with my friendship, and is this how you repay me? The news of Rock having AIDS crushed me, but beneath it all, I had an inkling that this was a truth concealed for far too long. So, please, call me, and let's untangle this web of secrets. I demand to know the whole truth, and right now."

I found myself pondering what my parents might be thinking. Were they wondering if Rock had AIDS during his visit with them? My understanding of HIV and AIDS exceeded that of most people at the time because I had already witnessed the devastating toll it had taken on several friends in Long Beach. It was undeniably frightening, but one thing I was not afraid of was contracting AIDS through casual contact.

It was widely understood that the primary mode of transmission was unprotected sexual activity. There was no concrete evidence to suggest that saliva and kissing posed a significant risk, despite media sensationalism attempting to portray it as such. Of

Pushed Out of the Closet Without A Parachute

course, the risk was different if there were open sores or cuts in the mouth, but a simple, affectionate kiss on the lips should not have incited panic.

Yet, the world seemed to be in an uproar over the kiss exchanged between Rock Hudson and Linda Evans on the set of Dynasty. However, Linda didn't share the same level of distress as those exploiting fear to impose stringent regulations on movie sets, going to great lengths to appear overly cautious.

Rock's illness brought Hollywood face to face with its vulnerability and triggered a reaction that sowed new seeds of concern within the industry. Some speculated that it might prompt a reconsideration of how sexual content was depicted in movies, while others feared the potential rise of discrimination against gay actors.

Adding to the mounting sense of alarm, the Screen Actors Guild had recently classified open-mouthed kissing as a potential health hazard, requiring actors to be informed in advance if they would be performing such scenes. The industry was undeniably grappling with a complex and evolving set of challenges in the wake of Rock's illness.

The following day, I received a call from Dean, who sounded deeply remorseful about not sharing the truth earlier. He confided that Rock had explicitly asked him to keep it a Secret, and only a select few individuals were aware of his diagnosis. Dean revealed that Rock had discovered his condition in June 1984 when he had gone to investigate a red spot on his neck.

Pushed Out of the Closet Without A Parachute

Coincidentally, Rock had been reviewing a picture he received from President Reagan following his invitation to the White House for a dinner hosted by President Reagan and First Lady Nancy Reagan on May 15th. The photograph depicted the three of them together, and while reviewing the photo Rock noticed a dark red spot on his neck. Rock had initially contemplated having the spot removed by a plastic surgeon and sought consultation from a dermatologist in Beverly Hills. During the dermatologist's examination, a biopsy was performed, and the results surprisingly revealed the presence of Kaposi's sarcoma, a disease associated with AIDS patients. It was during this doctor's visit that Rock received the devastating news of his AIDS diagnosis.

A couple of days later, Dean received the jarring revelation. Rock arrived early at a dinner party he was hosting and casually tossed a pack of condoms onto the table. Attempting to lighten the mood, Dean cracked a joke, asking him if he had decided to pursue relations with women again. Rock's response shattered any semblance of fun. He replied somberly, "No, I went to have the spot on my neck checked, and they found out I have AIDS. The doctor told me if I have sex, I must wear a condom. I've never worn one of these damn things in my life!"

Dean later recounted that Rock appeared utterly distraught, a side of him he had never witnessed before. At that moment, he implored him to summon his inner strength, reassuring him that they would confront this formidable adversary together.

Pushed Out of the Closet Without A Parachute

In Dean's words, "I took it upon myself to consult a physician regarding Rock's attendance at our parties and dinners and whether there was a risk of contracting AIDS through shared items like glasses. The physician's response provided some reassurance—explaining that the virus perishes upon exposure to oxygen. He also told me not to live in fear, and we were advised to exercise caution when it came to potential exposure to blood or other bodily fluids." The drama of that moment hung heavy in the air, casting a somber shadow over Dean's once carefree gatherings.

Dean continued, "Gunther, there's no need for you to dwell on whether Rock had AIDS during his visit in April at your parents' house. While it's a possibility, it's important to understand that casual dining and contact wouldn't be a cause for concern. Medical experts aren't precisely sure how long the virus can remain latent in the body before manifesting outwardly.

The doctors do know that after Rock's multiple bypass surgery, he was frail and had shed weight, so pinpointing the exact moment of infection or its source is challenging. Marc Christian has undergone testing, and thus far, he reports being healthy. But here's the twist: Rock never disclosed his condition to Marc. Much like you, Marc discovered the news through recent reports, and, to put it mildly, he is furious!"

I confided in Dean, saying, "I can only imagine how furious Marc must be, and I wouldn't blame him one bit. I know Rock desired to get Marc out of the house, and according to Rock, they had ceased their intimate relations before I even met both of you at the Silver Fox in March of 1984. It's fortunate for Marc because if things had been different, he might have contracted AIDS as well."

Dean nodded in agreement and, once more, extended a heartfelt apology. I assured Dean that I forgave him and understood the difficult position he had been placed in. However, I made it abundantly clear that from this point onward, I insisted on being privy to the unvarnished truth, no matter how challenging it might be. Dean agreed, and I understood his character, recognizing that he might continue to lie unless compelled otherwise.

There were just a few lingering questions that nagged at me, such as whether Dean had indeed delivered the music tape we had created to Rock and whether he had honestly conveyed the details of the hayride. One pressing question remained: Why did Rock and my phone conversations abruptly cease?

Dean reassured me that he delivered the tape to Rock, although he couldn't confirm whether Rock had listened to it. This occurred just before Rock's health began its steep decline, and he continued to evade the medical attention that was so crucial at this stage. Additionally, Dean clarified that Rock harbored no ill feelings toward me. Instead, he had gradually ceased communication with most of his friends, seemingly cocooning himself within memories of days long past, with those who had been part of his life many years ago.

Dean explained it to me this way. "It was as though his short-term memories were being supplanted by the enduring ones as if

Pushed Out of the Closet Without A Parachute

recent events failed to imprint on his memory." Dean likened this phenomenon to what he had witnessed in an ailing relative afflicted by dementia—an inability to forge new memories, rendering recent events unrecorded and thus unrecalled. We were bearing witness to Rock's capacity to remember distant past events more vividly than those in the immediate past, a subtle yet undeniable shift.

To add insult to injury, Marc Christian embarked on a relentless pursuit, threatening to sue Rock for the grievance of not disclosing his AIDS diagnosis. As if this weren't enough, Tom Clark, Rock's former spouse, resurfaced, attempting to assert control and insisting that the real Mrs. Hudson had returned.

Upon Rock's return to the United States, he was admitted to the hallowed halls of UCLA Medical Center on July 30th. The hospital corridors were now graced by legendary stars of yesteryear, with whom Rock had once shared the limelight, luminaries like Elizabeth Taylor and Carol Burnett. What was once a place of healing had transformed into a poignant stage for Rock's farewell performance, a passionate goodbye to his fellow actors and old friends.

Merely months prior, Rock had decided to exclude Tom Clark from his will, a definitive step toward severing ties. Now, the situation had taken an inconceivable turn, with Tom behaving as if everything were back to its erstwhile normalcy. Yet, Rock's primary desire was to rid himself of Marc Christian and extricate him from his life and his abode. Concerned voices around Rock emphasized the importance of ensuring that Marc had access to proper healthcare, given that Rock had withheld the truth about his condition.

In response to this concern, they had arranged for Marc to be flown to Paris to consult with the same doctor who had treated Rock. On August 7th, the medical verdict arrived Marc tested negative for the AIDS virus and bore no antibodies to it. Subsequently, when Marc returned home, Mark Miller relayed Rock's explicit request for him to vacate the premises and find a new place to reside. Marc, however, demanded to hear this directive from Rock's own lips.

Mark Miller took him to UCLA, where Rock delivered the message, urging Marc to leave. Initially, Marc concurred, indicating he required time to secure new accommodations. However, as time passed, his disposition underwent a stark transformation, revealing the true nature of Marc Christian's character.

The entire spectacle unfolded like a chaotic circus, with each act more bewildering than the last. I found myself recoiling, wanting no part in the mayhem. While the desire to bid Rock a personal farewell tugged at my heartstrings, it became increasingly evident that his visit to my house in late March had been meticulously orchestrated for precisely that purpose—a farewell.

This revelation cast a painful light on his conspicuous absence from the hayride in April. By then, his health had embarked on a relentless descent, and Rock's intention was crystal clear. He wanted me to preserve the memories of him in robust health, not confined to a sterile hospital bed, locked in a relentless battle against a debilitating

Pushed Out of the Closet Without A Parachute

illness. In his wisdom, there was no need for me to make an appearance, potentially arousing suspicion amid the curious eyes of others. It was his way of gifting me one last enduring memory, a bittersweet token of the Roy I cherished.

Mark Miller remained blissfully ignorant of my true identity, entangled in the elaborate web of Rock's compartmentalized friendships. This careful division allowed Rock to guard his worlds, meticulously keeping them separate, like distinct acts in an complex play. In the labyrinth of our altered shared memories, I cherished my connection with the Roy Scherer side of him above all else. That was the person I laughed with, whose mischievous spirit had brightened countless evenings, whose warmth had wrapped around me like a familiar embrace.

But now, Rock was staging his swan song, a final heart-wrenching performance for those who had only glimpsed the charismatic superstar adorning billboards and magazine covers. This was his farewell, his curtain call, the last act of a lifetime spent entwined with Hollywood's dazzling facade, not revealing the genuine person concealed behind the mask of stardom.

I asked Dean whether he intended to visit Rock in the hospital. Dean's response resonated with my own tumultuous thoughts—he would only go if Rock extended a personal invitation. We both clung to the conviction that Rock, in these trying times, was, in many ways, playing a role for the ever-watchful public, slipping into the familiar persona that the world so ardently desired to see.

Pushed Out of the Closet Without A Parachute

In the realm of Dynasty, on the silver screen or under the blinding spotlights of the theater, Rock would dutifully perform his craft, a master of his art. But when the curtains fell, and the cameras ceased their ceaseless gaze, he'd retreat to Dean's haven, where he would ceremoniously shed the skin of the actor to reveal the honest Roy—the friend who was a delight to be around, possessed of a playful charm, a touch of mischief, and an infectious zest for life. It was that genuine friend we both yearned for, aching for his return like a refrain in a sad song.

But as the days dwindled, like a candle's feeble flame on the verge of flickering out, we harbored the haunting apprehension that this facet of his life might never reemerge, that Roy's side of had irrevocably transformed. The looming specter of his impending demise, only a month or so away, cast a somber shadow over our hearts, a shadow we couldn't escape, a shadow that would forever remind us of the inevitable loss of the Rock we once knew.

On October 2nd, the inevitable unfolded, and Rock, our beloved Roy, departed from this earthly realm. I shall refrain from delving into the sordid details, for they are widely chronicled in other tomes. Living through those moments was arduous enough, and distance became a shield of necessity.

My fervent hope was to attend Rock's memorial service. With a heartfelt appeal, I implored Dean, who associated with the individuals frequently present at the Castle, such as Mark Miller, Tom

Clark, George Nader, and Marc Christian, to convey my earnest desire to pay my proper respects.

Yet, in the unpredictable narrative of life, I could not have foreseen that Tom Clark, Rock's former boyfriend, and the famed Elizabeth Taylor herself would preside over this poignant gathering. The unexpected arrival of my maiden telegram, bearing the personal signature of Elizabeth Taylor, left me astonished and deeply moved. Like Rock, it felt like a relic from a bygone era, a touching testament to a connection that transcended time.

Pushed Out of the Closet Without A Parachute

Chapter 15: The Memorial

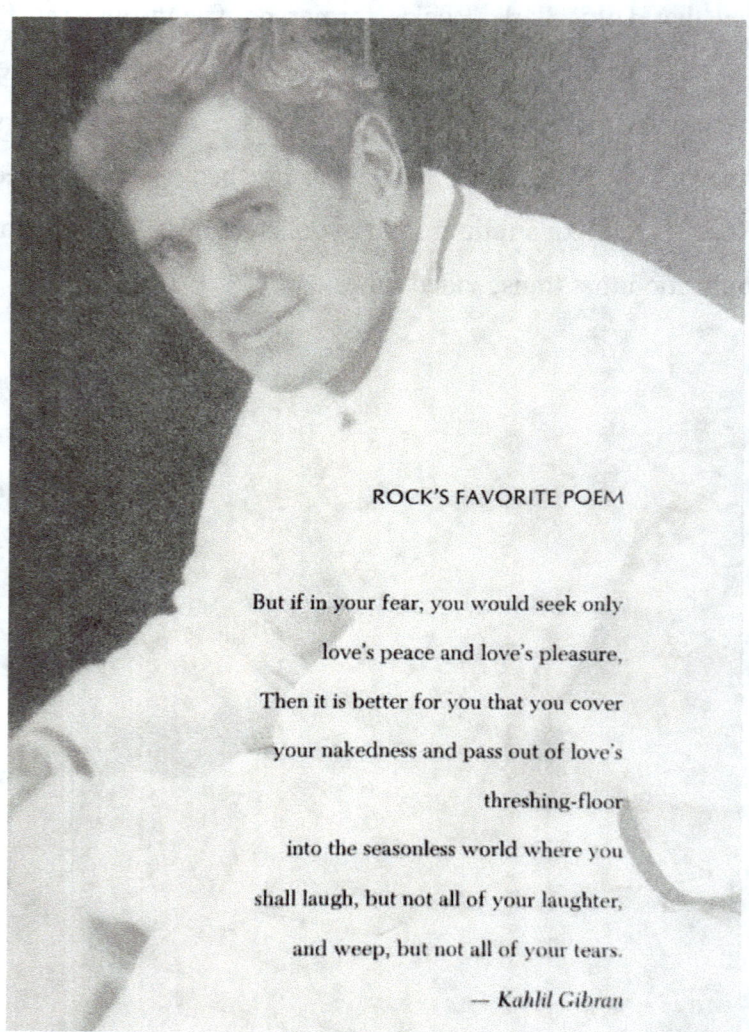

ROCK'S FAVORITE POEM

But if in your fear, you would seek only
love's peace and love's pleasure,
Then it is better for you that you cover
your nakedness and pass out of love's
threshing-floor
into the seasonless world where you
shall laugh, but not all of your laughter,
and weep, but not all of your tears.
— *Kahlil Gibran*

Pushed Out of the Closet Without A Parachute

This program was handed out to all Rock's Memorial Service attendees.

Within an ethereal realm of chaos and mourning, where the echoes of remembrance intertwined with passionate memories, it was time to bid farewell to a star whose radiant presence illuminated the silver screen and touched the hearts of millions. Rock Hudson, a name that reverberates with the power of stardom, would now find its place among the whispers of legacy. Like an ever-glowing beacon, his charisma and talent captivated audiences, etching an indelible mark on the annals of Hollywood history.

However, as we gathered to pay tribute, the air grew thick with shock and disbelief. The memorial service unfurled before us like a macabre tapestry of horror and bizarre spectacle. We found ourselves trapped in the haze of media frenzy, which created an unsettling, suffocating atmosphere. It was as if we stood beneath the relentless gaze of a scrutinizing world, trapped in this dungeon of drama and pageantry.

Our intentions were simple—to pay our respects, to mourn a man who held different meanings for different hearts. Yet, cameras swarmed like vultures, relentlessly seeking the perfect lead story, and we, mere mourners, were left to navigate the labyrinthine corridors of remembrance.

In the company of Dean Dittman, I embarked on an emotional journey to Rock's former estate, known as the "Castle" in Coldwater Canyon. We were on our way to pay our final tribute to our good friend, well aware that a friend like Rock can never be replaced. As we traversed the iconic streets of Beverly Hills, unspoken sorrow filled the air.

Before reaching our ultimate destination, we stopped briefly at the Church of Scientology, which held significance for many in the Hollywood community. While the institution has its share of controversy, Dean searched for solace within its walls, hoping for comfort and guidance in the confusion of grief. In a show of solidarity, I accompanied Dean during his visit, offering my presence as a gesture

Pushed Out of the Closet Without A Parachute

of support. Together, we navigate the intricate web of loss, drawing strength from our shared journey and cherished memories.

As we approached the gates of Rock's house, the scene resembled something out of a Hollywood crime scene. Helicopters buzzed overhead, their deafening noise forcing us to shout. A crowd of supporters and fanatics, some with signs condemning Rock to hell, filled the air with anger and spat at the cars that entered. Others advocated for gay pride and activism. Why had these people turned this memorial service into a battleground?

The memorial service for Rock unfolded in the midst of relentless pandemonium on that eventful October 21st. While police and private security guards tried to maintain order, allowing only invited guests, the neighboring streets became a bustling forum of curiosity. Even a neighbor of Hudson's "offered reporters temporary squatting rights for $300 a person," granting them the coveted privilege of witnessing the proceedings.

Against this backdrop of commercialized voyeurism, more helicopters hovered above Hudson's residence, its video cameraman trying to capture every frame of this morbid spectacle. Not to be outdone, a daring photographer disguised in camouflage dared to scale the canyon walls, only to be swiftly escorted off the property. Thus, within this chaotic tableau, the memory of Rock Hudson's farewell became indelibly entwined with the commercialization, crazies, and lawlessness that surrounded his final moments.

Pushed Out of the Closet Without A Parachute

Some of the notable figures in attendance were Carol Burnett, Elizabeth Taylor, Ricardo Montalban, Angie Dickinson, Susan Saint James, Esther Williams, Tab Hunter, Ross Hunter, and Robert Wagner, to name a few of the approximately 150 guests invited.

The entire memorial event felt surreal. I had hoped to converse with Carol Burnett, particularly given Rock's admiration for her. However, it seemed she had departed right after the official service. I sat a few chairs away from her in the tent set up on Rock's Estate, but you couldn't help but be overwhelmed by the constant noise of helicopters that drowned out the occasion's solemnity. The frustration and sadness were evident on Carol's face, a mix of grief and anger toward the press and those relentlessly pursuing a story.

Others in attendance seemed to be making obligatory appearances, while some were genuinely there to pay tribute to Rock. As for me, I struggled to come to terms with Rock's absence, having already experienced the loss of numerous friends in my young life. Incredible men were being cut down in their prime, their funerals etched in my memory. It was a painful reality, and from that point on, I decided to reserve my presence at memorial services only for those who held a special place in my heart, such as Rock.

As Rock had requested, a joyous celebration unfolded following the memorial service. Elizabeth Taylor and Rock's former lover Tom Clark had meticulously organized a party to share Hudson's favorite entertainment—Mexican food and mariachis. Miss Taylor allowed guests to honor Rock's memory by turning his desire for a lively gathering into a reality.

Although I had wanted to thank Miss Taylor personally for the invitation, she always appeared occupied and already in conversation with people. During a moment of unexpected luck, I found myself standing by one of the space heaters outside, trying to ward off the October chill. To my surprise, Elizabeth Taylor turned around simultaneously, her eyes meeting mine as we both acknowledged the intense heat emanating from the heater.

A chuckle escaped our lips as we shared a moment of humor while trying to navigate the sad occasion. Introducing myself, I expressed my heartfelt gratitude for what she and Tom Clark had orchestrated in honor of Rock. Miss Taylor offered a warm smile and spoke of the profound loss that everyone there felt. We agreed that Rock would be sorely missed, and I thanked her again for the thoughtful celebration. With a nod of understanding, she conveyed her desire to make sure the guests enjoyed the party, emphasizing Rock's desire for a memorable soiree.

The mariachi party enveloped us in a vibrant embrace as the night unfurled like a symphony of music, laughter, and shared memories. It was a testament to the enduring spirit of Rock Hudson, a celebration that transcended the boundaries of sorrow and embraced the joy of his life. Amidst the cheerful conversations and festivities, I was drawn into unforgettable encounters that would forever leave an imprint on my heart. I couldn't help but feel a sense of gratitude for the chance encounter and the opportunity to honor Rock's legacy in the company of Hollywood luminaries.

While I may not recall every conversation that graced that lively evening, a few etched themselves into my memory, adding a touch of magic to the gathering. Out of the blue, as if summoned by fate, Ricardo Montalbán, radiating undeniable charm, approached Dean and me. Curiosity danced in his eyes as he asked Dean Dittman whether I held a role in producing or directing. Seeing an opportunity for playful banter, Dean decided to engage in some teasing, spinning a tale of my visionary pursuits as a producer embarking on a new film venture, still casting certain significant parts. Ricardo's eyes flickered with intrigue as he handed his card to Dean, a silent plea for a glowing recommendation.

We laughed at how Rock would have relished Dean's innocent prank. Rock always enjoyed keeping people guessing and teasing them at parties, especially after a drink or two. We bid farewell to Ricardo and ventured forth, seeking conversations with other guests.

Remarkably, we bumped into the company of two incredible women, who I thoroughly enjoyed meeting. First, Susan Saint James, Rock's co-star in the beloved series McMillan & Wife, graced our conversation with tales of laughter on the set. As I spoke to her about my connection with Rock, I couldn't help but mention that Rock had graciously gifted me a collection of clothes he had worn during the show. It was as if those garments, once an integral part of Rock's on-screen persona, had found a new home with me, a towering figure like

Pushed Out of the Closet Without A Parachute

Rock. Luckily, his wardrobe fit me like a glove, even though his tailor meticulously crafted each piece perfectly to fit Rock.

Susan shared amusing stories that occurred on set and expressed how much fun it was to star alongside Rock. We both found it funny that he kept many of the clothes from the show. However, few people working in the movie industry could tower as tall as Rock and fit in his wardrobe. The unique connection I now shared with those clothing items served as a tangible reminder of our friendship. Among the pieces, the handsome Camel Hair jacket remains a cherished keepsake, while the cashmere sweaters and other items, over time, gracefully deteriorated. The fondness Susan had for Rock was evident, and I knew from Rock himself that he also held Susan in high regard.

Second, like an enchanting mirage, I found myself in the presence of Esther Williams. The delightful company quickly eclipsed a momentary lapse in recognition. She proved to be larger than life, both in stature and spirit, she entertained me with stories that spanned a lifetime. With a naughty twinkle in her eyes, she playfully offered a choice between the countless personas she had embodied throughout her eventful life, offering either a toned-down version or the devilish side. In her own words, she quipped, "Which Esther Williams do you want to hear about?"

Eagerly, I requested a glimpse of the devilish side, and as laughter cascaded between us, time seemed to stand still. For almost an hour, I shared in the pleasure of her tales, her enthusiasm filling the air, and I marveled at the privilege of being in the presence of such an extraordinary woman.

Dean and I remained engaged in conversation with fellow guests, but there was an air of anticipation as he leaned closer and whispered, "Gunther, I want to show you something."

I couldn't help but wonder what he had in store. He led me through a discreet back door of the house, and we embarked on a journey into the heart of Rock's renowned residence. Despite having known Rock since early 1984, I had never set foot in his home. Finally, Dean was offering me an exclusive guided tour of the secret sanctuary that was Rock's legendary abode.

The house appeared as I envisioned—masculine and steeped in a somewhat dated Spanish motif. It was clear that a distinctly manly presence had once inhabited these walls. Unfinished wooden beams adorned the cozy Spanish furniture, and a sizable wood-burning fireplace was a testament to the home's character. As Dean guided me through the house, we came upon the guest room, aptly named the Tijuana Room, painted in vibrant red hues reminiscent of a Mexican whorehouse. Dean's description elicited a chuckle from me.

Continuing our tour, we entered the master bedroom suite, where Dean paused, instructing me to hold on for a moment. With deliberate care, he approached the nightstand and opened its drawer, revealing a piece of our shared history—the tape we had recorded for Rock. Dean confessed that to this day, he remained uncertain if Rock had ever had the chance to listen to it. Filled with a sense of protectiveness, I requested the tape from Dean, determined to ensure its privacy, containing personalized messages meant exclusively for Rock's ears.

As I inspected the drawer's contents, I discovered syringes and other medical paraphernalia—a stark reminder of the battle Rock had waged during his final days. Among these were a few photographs capturing moments of our time together in Hawaii, which I swiftly retrieved. Overwhelmed by melancholy, I turned to Dean and suggested we return outside.

As we strolled back outside, it was evident that the press and media vehicles had departed, and the frenzy of media attention had subsided. Though some guests continued to enjoy their drinks, and the distant strains of mariachi music lingered in the air, the atmosphere had noticeably calmed.

Dean and I agreed to explore the gathering more, deciding to part ways temporarily with a plan to reconvene in about an hour. With that understanding, we ventured off in separate directions, each absorbed in our private reflections and interactions with fellow mourners.

In the company of a small group, I spotted someone I had been longing to talk to for a long time, Mr. Marc Christian. Throughout my extensive time with Rock, I had never had the chance to cross paths with Marc in person, only hearing about him through Rock and Dean's stories. Seizing the opportunity while Dean conversed with the captivating Angie Dickenson, I approached Marc, eager to introduce myself. However, I had been warned and decided to proceed with caution.

Meeting Marc face-to-face, I could perceive a subtle flicker of surprise, perhaps even astonishment, dancing in his eyes. It was evident that he, too, was grappling with uncertainty regarding my identity. To bridge this gap, I recounted my enduring friendship with Rock, a bond cultivated since early 1984. I shared intimate moments and tales that encapsulated the essence of our connection. The stories flowed, like the one about Rock's spontaneous trip with me to Hawaii, where we reveled in the company of my parents.

I unveiled photographs I had removed from the nightstand, capturing the candid laughter both Rock and I had shared, as well as a particularly unique one where we playfully lifted my mother like a swing. Marc's demeanor became increasingly inquisitive, his curious manner caused me to sense that he hadn't seen the pictures before. It was only when I casually informed him about the brunch at the Hilo Hawaiian Hotel that I realized he had not glimpsed these snapshots. It seemed I was the first to divulge the details of my adventures with Rock, and Marc's astonished bewilderment spoke volumes.

His inquiries intensified, probing into the timeline of events, the nature of my connection with Rock, and my very identity. Just then, Dean caught sight of our interaction, viewing it with suspicion, as he had already dubbed Marc "the enemy." Their eyes met, exchanging unspoken tension. Realizing the need for discretion, Marc proposed a future meeting where he could unveil his side of the story. "I believe you should hear it directly from me," he asserted.

Intrigued yet vigilant, I accepted his proposition, bidding him goodnight. As I started to walk away, Marc grabbed my hand and placed his phone number in it. A lingering suspicion arose as he squeezed my hand; beneath the surface, our conversation held a personal undercurrent yet to be revealed.

Setting aside the nagging question, I rejoined Dean and the captivating Angie Dickinson, ready to immerse myself once more in the alluring ambiance of the evening. Yet, the query about Marc's intentions lingered, keeping me guessing about his true intentions. His gaze hinted at an attraction that went beyond the boundaries of our seemingly innocent conversation.

Up until this point, all I had were secondhand accounts about Marc. Now, meeting him personally, I couldn't deny his striking handsomeness, which had drawn Rock to him. I had already discovered Dean's willingness to relay whatever Rock instructed him to say, leaving me with a need to hear both sides of the story. However, in the recesses of my mind, I harbored the belief that I probably would never hear from Marc again now that Rock had passed away. But I couldn't have been more wrong as destiny had other plans, as I would soon discover.

Dean and I had completed our rounds at the party, conversing with those open to talking. Among the illustrious attendees I had hoped to meet, the one who stood out as missing was Carol Burnett.

It was a shame that I never got the opportunity to speak to her, as it appeared she had departed right after the service, perhaps avoiding the initial unrest of the event. Given the initial frenzy, I couldn't fault her for the decision.

Our next step was to bid farewell to Elizabeth Taylor and Tom Clark, expressing our gratitude for the invitation and their efforts in organizing the event that allowed those in attendance to pay their respects. Although Dean and I hadn't taken the stage to share our own stories, more than a dozen others did. Their anecdotes painted a vivid picture of Rock, mostly humorous tales that captured the essence of who he was.

A valet summoned the limo driver, who had arranged to take us back to Dean's apartment. As we navigated the winding roads of Coldwater Canyon, making our way through Beverly Hills and back to West Hollywood, I reflected on the evening's events. "I suppose that's all left of this ordeal," I remarked to Dean, "and now we can try to regain some semblance of normalcy."

Dean, however, appeared less optimistic. "I'm afraid the ordeal has only just begun," he cautioned, "and I would advise caution when it comes to Mr. Christian."

I considered Marc's possible actions. "I doubt I'll ever hear from him again," I mused. "Do you think he'll attempt something like suing the estate?"

Dean nodded thoughtfully. "I wouldn't put it past him," he replied. "He's told me before that such a course of action was on his mind, particularly if he felt he wasn't included 'properly' in Rock's will."

As the limo proceeded onto Dean's street, I turned to him, expressing my heartfelt sentiments. "Dean," I began, "I hope we can remain friends, and you know I consider you my friend. Just because Rock is no longer with us doesn't mean our friendship also has to end."

Our arrival at Dean's apartment punctuated our conversation, and I knew it was also time for me to head home. "I need to return because I have an early client tomorrow," I explained. "But we should plan a get-together soon, whether you come down to Laguna or I head up to West Hollywood."

Dean nodded; his voice filled with appreciation. "You've been a good friend and a kind soul," he said warmly. "Both Rock and I admired and loved you for your honesty and, of course, your incredible musical talent. I hope your business continues to thrive. Please keep in touch. Drive safely and give me a call soon."

We shared a heartfelt hug, our eyes misty from the emotional day. It had been a taxing experience, and we both felt worn at the edges.

Chapter 16: Deception and Betrayal

Right after the memorial service for Rock, I received a call from Marc Christian, and initially, I was hesitant about meeting up with him. However, I felt the need to get to know him better and talk on the phone before meeting again face-to-face. As October unfolded, we engaged in lengthy late-night conversations, delving deep into our shared perspectives on Rock and the peculiar way he maintained discrete social circles in his life. I often referred to it as compartmentalizing certain groups in his life.

During those nocturnal calls, it became apparent that Marc and I held similar views about Rock's practice of presenting different narratives to different friends, almost like a game. The reasons behind this behavior remained perplexing, but it seemed like a barrier, preventing people from forming intensely close bonds with him. This intriguing revelation left me pondering Rock's character's complexities and the enigma he had become in his final years.

As Marc began to share his side of the story, I couldn't help but find it intriguing and thought-provoking. His narrative shed new light on the complex web of deceit that Rock had woven around his health condition, particularly the falsehoods he perpetuated regarding his AIDS diagnosis for over a year before it was made public.

My first question was about how they had met, and I wanted to compare Marc's version with what Rock had told me. Marc recounted their meeting at a political event, specifically a fundraiser for Gore Vidal. In contrast, Rock's humorous account had painted a picture of their first encounter at the Sports Connection in West Hollywood, which he jokingly referred to as the "Sports Erection." According to Rock, he had been in the middle of a massage when Marc passed by the room, dropped his towel, and exposed himself. Rock further explained that he had been looking for a walking companion after his bypass surgery and thought Marc's interest in health and fitness made him a suitable candidate.

The disparity between these two stories left me with more questions than answers, and I couldn't help but wonder about the true nature of their initial meeting. However, Rock attending a political event didn't sound like the Rock I knew.

I confronted Marc with the information Rock had shared with me, inquiring about the claim that Marc had engaged in sex for money while Rock was in Israel shooting the Ambassador. I asked Marc, "Is there any truth to that?"

Marc barked right back, "Absolutely not! After he returned from Israel, everything was great for a while, but then things changed, and he didn't want to go out to dinner, a movie, or anything with me anymore. It upset me, so I went to dinner with my friends. Rock's reaction was far from pleasant; he started saying nasty things about me."

The conflicting accounts of their relationship confused me even more as the truth behind these differing narratives continued to elude me. Who could I trust when both sides seemed to have reasonable explanations?

After a few more phone calls, I made up my mind and decided to invite Marc over to my place in Laguna Niguel. I needed to see his eyes to gauge whether there was any hint of deceit hidden within them. After a couple of weeks and several phone conversations, I extended the invitation for dinner on Friday night, November 16th. I decided to prepare an Italian meal, and ironically, our meeting date would fall one day before what would have been Rock's 60th birthday on the 17th. Had he still been alive.

I chose a night when Larry had plans to dine out, providing us the opportunity for a private conversation. Marc, like me, had a penchant for healthy eating, and we found common ground in our shared commitment to a nutritious lifestyle. He revealed his regular gym workouts and dedication to a health-conscious diet. Yet, much like Rock, he harbored one unhealthy vice—smoking. Despite this, I felt it was time to put aside the negative judgments formed by others and find out for myself who Marc truly was. It was a path to closure, a chance to uncover the real character behind the conflicting narratives.

I ensured Marc that every dish I prepared was organic, including turkey meatballs and whole-grain spaghetti. Marc brought a bottle of Chianti, and as we enjoyed our dinner, we delved into a candid conversation. During our talk, I glimpsed a sincere side of

Pushed Out of the Closet Without A Parachute

Marc, who felt he had been wronged by a group of individuals seemingly in control of Rock's life.

According to Marc, Mark Miller harbored intense hatred towards him. He seemed determined to exert total control over Rock's finances, treating him like a child who needed to ask for an allowance. Marc's own words, "Rock and I were a couple, and when he invited me to live with him, he assured me that he intended to take care of me. However, it turned out that the people I believed were working for Rock were trying to manipulate him and make decisions on his behalf."

Marc continued with heated passion: "These decisions, unfortunately, significantly impacted my life. They portrayed me as the villain, and those working in the house began fabricating rumors to drive a wedge between us. Mark and his partner George believed that I was solely after Rock's wealth. They had already formed this opinion long before getting to know me. Despite all my efforts to prove otherwise, their minds remained firmly set."

I noticed the pain in Marc's eyes, and I couldn't help but empathize with him. I shared my experiences, explaining that I had attempted to contact Rock multiple times at "The Castle," the house you resided in. I confessed that I refrained from leaving a message unless Rock was personally available to answer the call because I needed more faith it would ever reach him.

Mark Miller and Rock's butler James seemed to act as gatekeepers, determining who had access to Rock and who did not. I experienced significant frustration, and it was difficult for me to fathom what it must have been like for Marc to endure this on a daily basis while living with Rock.

Marc's body language and sincerity seemed to make a convincing argument, but why did Rock want him out of the house so badly? I had to find out and ask one more critical question. "Did you tell Rock you would go to the National Enquirer if he asked you to leave the house?"

Marc said, "First, he never asked me to leave the house. It was Mark Miller who made numerous attempts to get me out and consistently treated me in a hostile manner. Rock and I never fought, but I could sense him drifting away. This was because Mark, his new trainer friend Ron, and even the butler James were all against me. But let's not talk about Rock anymore… I want to know about you and if you're seeing anyone."

I sensed Marc was not only changing the subject, but he was shifting the mood dramatically. His hand on my leg and the intensity in his eyes held a fiery desire as he asked me if I was seeing someone. I confessed, "For almost a year, I've been single and afraid of getting involved sexually after witnessing many of my former friends succumb to AIDS and tragically pass away. I've attended too many somber funerals in the past year, and it has deeply affected my romantic desires."

Marc sensed my hesitation and gently asked if he could hug me. I hesitantly accepted, saying it would be greatly appreciated. But

Pushed Out of the Closet Without A Parachute

little did I know, after sharing a bottle of wine and feeling vulnerable, one thing would lead to another, and we would find ourselves in the passionate embrace of intimacy in my bedroom.

Before we ventured into any sexual intimacy, I made it a point to inquire with Marc about his HIV status, ensuring that he was 100% certain of being HIV-negative and recently screened. I emphasized my firm stance on practicing safe sex and reiterated my unwavering commitment to using condoms under any circumstance.

With absolute assurance, Marc replied, "I'm probably the safest person on the planet." He disclosed that he had undergone testing in Paris, where no signs of the virus were detected, and then again, he had been recently retested at UCLA at the behest of those managing Rock's Estate.

Nevertheless, I firmly asserted, "Regardless, I'm going to wear a condom." In reality, I had been celibate for the past year, channeling my energy into volunteer work with various AIDS organizations. I was also undergoing training to become an AIDS Support Buddy for the AIDS Service Foundation (ASF) in Orange County, which was in its inaugural year.

The evening grew more intimate, yet I couldn't help but notice that Marc's physique didn't quite match the image he had painted. Not to be too judgmental, but he appeared less toned and more out of shape than his earlier claims had suggested. Because of my fitness training, I can discern the difference between someone who merely talks about religiously hitting the gym and someone like me who commits to a rigorous fitness regimen without fail.

Beyond instructing my fitness clients on what to do, I actively engage in the exercises alongside them. I always start our sessions with stretching routines, often leading them through vigorous aerobics or boot camp-style circuit training. I repeat this routine five to six times daily, in addition to my strength training, which has kept me in excellent form. Nonetheless, I remain open to continuous self-improvement.

But, the absence of intimacy in my life for such an extended period had left me a tad overeager. Coupled with the novelty of using a condom, the entire experience fell somewhat short of expectations. However, lying beside someone and engaging in conversation proved to be profoundly therapeutic. I had hoped for Marc to spend the night, anticipating a cozy morning together.

Unfortunately, our reverie was interrupted when my roommate Larry returned home in the wee hours of the morning. Marc promptly started dressing, quipping, "I'd better head home. I didn't expect to spend the night, but perhaps next time." His parting words left me wondering if this might evolve into something more. The ensuing events were entirely unforeseen, and I hadn't anticipated anything beyond a potential friendship.

The following morning, I awoke and prepared a protein shake and some organic cereal. Larry emerged from his room, immediately firing off questions. "So, how did things go with Marc?" he inquired.

"I heard him leave your room late last night, so I assume something happened upstairs?"

I retorted, "Oh, come on now. How about you explain your early morning return?" Larry chuckled and replied, "If only I were that lucky... I wish!"

I sighed, "Well, my dry spell is officially over. Yes, Marc and I shared a pas de deux last night, but to be honest, there were no fireworks. We might give it another shot, but I still feel like I need to get to know him better. It feels like peeling the layers off an onion with Marc, and trust me, he seems to have many layers to peel."

"Oh my," Larry quipped, "Does that mean he was chubbier than you had hoped?"

I answered with a sly look, "No comment."

Larry chuckled as he got ready for a day of painting and artistic expression. It was a lazy Sunday, and my plans involved heading to the beach, some beach volleyball, and, hopefully, nothing that even remotely resembled work or responsibility.

Later in the evening, Marc called. He wanted to thank me for dinner and, in his playful tone, "all the rest." We delved deeper into the situation with Rock's Estate, and Marc expressed his frustration, particularly with Mark Miller and Tom Clark, who seemed to be making extravagant claims about being Mrs. Hudson.

Curiosity got the better of me, and I asked, "Why are you still there, then? Is Tom Clark the executor of Rock's Estate, or is it Mark Miller?"

Pushed Out of the Closet Without A Parachute

Marc clarified, "No, it's neither of them. The executor and trustee of the trust is Wallace Sheft from New York, bearing the impressive title of 'New York City accounting executive.' He holds full power to 'hold, manage, and distribute Rock Hudson's Estate according to the terms and conditions provided in the trust agreement.' This was established years ago... And who's probably not included in it? Yours truly!"

Marc sounded quite upset, and I didn't want to push his buttons, but I couldn't help but wonder, "Do you think the Estate should go to you?" Throughout the evening at dinner, Marc had insisted that his affection for Rock was for the man, not his wealth or what he could gain. However, the lines between his words and actions were becoming somewhat blurred.

I shifted gears and proposed meeting again, perhaps for a dinner outing. Marc mentioned his busy schedule but liked the idea of a future date. I left it up to him, thinking that if he were genuinely interested, he would take the initiative and give me a call to arrange something. To my surprise, I received another call from him later that week, suggesting we meet the following Saturday. I accepted, and he said he'd drive down to Laguna Niguel once more, and from there, we'd see where the evening took us.

On that Saturday, I had a few clients to see in the morning, leaving my schedule reasonably open for the rest of the day. Marc had initially mentioned he'd aim to arrive by five P.M., which would have given us plenty of time to decide on dinner plans or even catch the sunset at the beach. However, when Marc finally got there closer to six P.M. after a nearly two-hour drive, he seemed more inclined to relax and have a conversation than to rush to the beach.

Our conversation turned unexpectedly, feeling less like a casual chat and more like an interrogation. Marc was curious about what Rock and I had been up to for over a year and why he had never heard anything about me. It was as if he doubted my account, and I assured him I had spent many months seeing Rock regularly. We'd go out for dinner, or I'd join private parties at Dean's house to play the guitar. However, it felt like Marc wasn't buying any of it.

I proposed going out for dinner to Marc, but he reluctantly replied, "Not really. Maybe we can grab a pizza and eat it here?"

I agreed, saying, "Sure, but would you mind if we shared it with my roommate Larry? He's in his room, and I don't want him feeling left out." I had introduced Larry to Marc when he arrived, but Larry, being the introvert he was, excused himself and retreated to his room.

I explained to Marc that I had initially told Larry we'd go out to eat, assuring him he could have the place to himself. However, since our plans had changed, I felt it was only fair to ask if he'd like some pizza too. Marc appeared somewhat hesitant, but he ultimately agreed.

I knocked on Larry's bedroom door to inform him about "a change of plans." Larry, in his customary state of bemusement, acquiesced to the notion of partaking in a slice or two of pizza. "Fret not," I reassured Larry, "I shall procure two pizzas. What type would you prefer?"

Unsurprisingly, Larry's response echoed his usual sentiment: "Whatever you get is fine with me."

As the pizza arrived, Marc's inclination leaned toward enjoying our repast in the secluded confines of my upstairs patio. The residual glow of the setting sun painted a picturesque tableau against the sky, albeit not as exquisite as the beach vista I had envisioned. Still, it proved to be a tranquil setting for our meal. With a borrowed bottle of wine in tow, courtesy of Larry, I took my leave, assuring Larry that the lower level of the abode was his to command.

There, throughout the ambiance of the waning day, Marc and I savored our meal while he continued his probing inquiry into my connection with Rock. Little did I realize, throughout this relentless line of questioning, that Marc's true aim was not to unravel Rock's mysteries but to delve deeply into my own story.

After our meal, fueled by wine, Marc grabbed my hand and led me to my bedroom, where we reclined together. Strangely, neither of us shed our garments, yet we indulged in mutual intimate exploration that crescendoed into a shared moment of gratification—far from the melodrama of a cheap romance novel, yet undeniably peculiar. The evening unfolded with an air of oddity, reminiscent of the plotline of a lesser romantic twist. I was left with a sense of being used, devoid of any meaningful connection.

Pushed Out of the Closet Without A Parachute

As soon as Marc had satisfied his immediate cravings, he abruptly announced his need to depart, citing concerns about being locked out of his abode. It became evident that his thoughts were consumed by other matters, with no room for me in his mental landscape.

Over the following weeks, I attempted to contact Marc, but my calls went unanswered, and my messages remained ignored. It was clear that I was being ghosted, and the abrupt change in his behavior struck me as odd. He initially showed keen interest in me, only to abruptly cut off all communication. His change of feelings and disposition left me perplexed, feeling used, and turned off.

A few days later, while I was engrossed in my musical pursuits, working on mixing some of my songs, Larry's urgent cry for me to come downstairs jolted me into action. He insisted that I join him immediately. As I hurried downstairs, I saw Marc Christian on the television screen, flanked by his lawyer, Marvin Mitchelson. He was a renowned Hollywood divorce lawyer who had successfully introduced the concept of "palimony" settlements for unmarried partners, establishing himself as an expert in representing celebrities.

Unbelievable, Marc was suing the Rock Hudson Estate for a staggering fourteen million dollars. The truth struck me like a thunderbolt—I had been duped. Marc had never been interested in me; he had merely used our interactions to gather information for his lawsuit. I was consumed by anger at my naivety, berating myself for falling victim to Marc's manipulations when I should have known better. Dean tried to warn me, but my foolishness weighed heavily upon me.

I kept what transpired between Marc and me primarily to myself, but eventually, I felt the urge to dial Dean Dittman, fully aware that I was in for a hearty helping of "I told you so."

To my surprise, Dean displayed more understanding than I had anticipated. He pointed out that I had now experienced firsthand how manipulative Marc could be. It had been quite a while since Dean and I had engaged in a heartfelt conversation, so we seized the opportunity to catch up on life. I recounted how my business had taken off and how I was diligently training with a burgeoning workload.

But then Dean unloaded a bombshell that, had I been privy to earlier, would have had me steering clear of Marc with lightning speed. According to Dean, Marc had requested a visit, claiming he had pivotal news to disclose. Upon arrival, Marc unveiled his audacious plan to sue the Rock Hudson Estate. Dean, bewildered, inquired about the reason behind such an action.

Dean told me what Marc had told him: "My legal team is handling it." To make matters even more audacious, Marc offered Dean, "If you want a slice of the pie, all you have to do is back me up."

In simpler terms, he wanted Dean to assist him in crafting a web of deceit in exchange for a share of the substantial financial gain. Dean promptly escorted Marc out and bid him farewell while calling him a "whore."

Pushed Out of the Closet Without A Parachute

But what Dean revealed next was nothing short of shocking. "Gunther, a week after he visited my apartment, my home was firebombed... I lost everything. I refrained from reaching out because I've been grappling with a tumultuous disarray of emotions. All my possessions, my beloved pet cockatoo, and my cherished memories have been reduced to ashes."

I was in total shock as tears welled up in my eyes. As I contemplated Dean's tragic ordeal, I yearned to rush to his side and offer support, but he still needed to secure a new place to stay.

"Oh, Dean," I uttered with deep sympathy. "I had no idea. This is absolutely horrifying! Have they been able to determine if Marc was responsible?"

Dean responded with a heavy heart, "I tried to convince the authorities that Marc had a hand in this calamity. Rock feared what Marc might be capable of, and now, I fear for my own safety. Marc is a veritable monster!"

It all felt surreal like a scene plucked from a movie rather than an episode from real life. The notion of someone firebombing Dean's apartment left me flabbergasted. Who could harbor such malicious intent against him? And could Marc genuinely be capable of orchestrating such a heinous act? I realized that my only course of action was to steer clear of him and sever all ties. With that in mind, I promptly deleted and blocked his phone number to prevent any potential contact.

Pushed Out of the Closet Without A Parachute

In my quest for guidance, I contacted my good friend Pauline and her son Chris, the lawyer. During our next customary workout session, Pauline relayed Chris's advice, which was straightforward: avoid initiating contact with Marc and inform him of this decision if he attempted to reach out. As for the lawsuit looming over Marc, Chris recommended that I refrain from involvement unless I were subpoenaed to testify.

Months stretched into years as I anxiously awaited any news, but a deafening silence enveloped me. Maybe Marc had dropped the case, and they'd reached some settlement. My connection with Dean had faded, and I heard whispers of his declining health due to his diabetes. Little did I know the gravity of his downward spiraling situation; I would've rushed to his side had I known. Tragically, Dean passed away in January 1989, casting a shroud of sorrow over my world.

But what transpired afterward was even more tragic. On February 16, 1989, a jury awarded Marc Christian $21.75 million, citing the actor's egregious concealment of his AIDS diagnosis. The verdict infuriated me beyond words. What irritated me the most was the audacious claim that Marc had to remain celibate out of fear for his life. If his fear was genuine, why then had he recklessly endangered my life through our intimate encounter? Now, beyond a shadow of a doubt, Marc was nothing more than a manipulative pathological liar; this time, it was my firsthand experience and not hearsay!

Pushed Out of the Closet Without A Parachute

Dean Dittman's headshot profile he used for auditions.

Chapter 17: Without a Parachute

In mid-February of 1989, I was at a soirée in Laguna Niguel, a lively gay celebration marking a friend's birthday. Laughter and music filled the air, but a hush fell over the crowd as the television in one corner started broadcasting Marc Christian's appearance on a news program with his new lawyer, Harold Rhoden. He was there to share his side of the story, painting Rock Hudson as a deceitful figure who had kept the knowledge of his AIDS diagnosis hidden. As Marc's voice filled the room, he uttered these words that stirred a storm within me: "I fear for my life and cannot be intimate with anyone because I fear I might also come down with the disease, so I must remain celibate."

My anger surged like a wild river, and I couldn't contain myself in my righteous fury. I vented my frustration at the screen, my voice cutting through the room like a blade through silence: "You fucking liar! You had sex with me, you are a lying piece of shhh..." The realization of my outburst dawned on me as the gazes of those around me bore into my being.

"I must remain celibate... I must remain celibate... What a crock!" I exclaimed in frustration. Someone at the party I didn't know very well overheard and asked me if I had indeed had sex with Marc. I confirmed that I had.

The next question was probing, "How long ago did you have sex with Marc Christian?"

I replied, "A month after Rock's memorial service, we had sex on November 16th, or technically in the early morning of the 17th, which I know exactly because it would have been Rock's 60th birthday if he was still alive. Then we had sex again on the 15th of December."

This person pointed out, "So, you had sex after Marc was found to have no sign of the virus, yet he had already claimed he could no longer have sex, and yet he had sex with you." I nodded and added, "He actually told me, 'I am the safest person on the planet to have sex with.' In short, he would say one thing to entice people into bed with him and the exact opposite to create the illusion that he was so terrified of having sex that he had to remain celibate to win a multi-million-dollar lawsuit!"

The person at the party, who just happened to be a good friend of Mark Miller and George Nader, asked me if I would be willing to make a statement and sign a written deposition as the smoking gun to get a new trial.

I told him, "I'm not going to drag myself into this circus unless I can do it anonymously with a gag order or something that won't hurt my reputation and chances of losing clients. I'm a self-employed personal fitness trainer."

I also let him know that Paul Cohen had initially contacted me about any testimony I could give at the beginning of the trial. But all I had to offer was hearsay information, so I gave him Richard Lovell's number, whom I believed had more information than me and might be able and willing to testify.

As far as the sex I had with Marc. It was after the memorial, and I had no idea that Marc was claiming he could never have sex again. I had no comprehension he was suing because of the mental fear it caused him, which I now know to be absurd. He had sex with me, and if I were playing his game, I could sue him for precisely the same thing he was suing Rock's Estate for.

This is where the can of worms truly opened, and I found myself reluctantly pulled into the Rock Hudson Estate trial. It all commenced with a sworn deposition, during which I had received a verbal promise that my identity would remain shielded from the prying eyes of the press. However, to my shock and dismay, the very next day, my name was splashed across newspapers worldwide! "Holy shit!"

In a panicked frenzy, my first instinct was to reach out to my parents, with whom I had not officially shared my true self, even though I had a sneaking suspicion that my mom already knew I was gay.

When I finally made the call, my mom informed me that their phone had become a relentless, ringing beast, with Hawaiian newspapers on the line, demanding to know about Rock's visit and his AIDS diagnosis, probing into every corner of their lives.

I urgently implored my mom, "Please, don't answer the phone and entertain any questions for a while. This frenzy will eventually subside. For the next few days, unplug the phone, and if you need to reach out to me, plug it back in."

Then, my mom had a question for me. She remembered the memorial and what I had told her about it, but she didn't remember me mentioning Marc Christian, and she said, "You're not like that, Marc Christian."

I was taken aback and asked her to clarify. I wasn't sure if she meant it as a question.

She responded, "He's a weirdo. You're not like that? Right?" I couldn't help but ask her to define "weirdo," to which she replied, "You know what I'm talking about."

With honesty in my voice, I admitted, "Yes, Mom, your son is a weirdo."

She quickly reassured me, saying, "Oh, I don't mean it that way. You know I love you. It's your decision, but you must be careful these days."

I assured her, "I am, Mom. I'm extremely cautious. I tried not to get involved, but Roy was like family to us, and I couldn't stand that this man was taking advantage of him and now me. I had to take a stand, and everything will be all right. I just wanted you to know the true me, why I did this, and that I'm fine."

My mom sighed in relief, hearing the words she needed to hear. She knew I was only trying to do the right thing, and at least I had her support.

Pushed Out of the Closet Without A Parachute

The following weeks were nothing short of overwhelming for me. I underwent another recorded interview with an investigator who meticulously analyzed my interactions with Rock and Marc. Fortunately, I had scribbled down most of these events on my calendar, and that calendar was also submitted as evidence. This recorded interview, conducted over the phone, spanned about an hour and delved into various aspects of my story, covering everything I've recounted.

However, one crucial aspect was missing: I hadn't witnessed anything incriminating Marc regarding Rock's alleged threats. Rock had told me about these threats, and I only first met Marc at Rock's memorial service.

Then, I had to submit to not one but two lie detector tests. I forgot why two, but we had them done by two different operators who asked the same questions. I passed them both. But Marc Christian took a lie detector test by someone favorable to his lawyer and passed, too. So much for lie detector tests. I found out they are as good as the person who gives them.

Then came the onslaught from Marc Christian's legal team, as expected. They had a plethora of unkind things to say about me. But my track record was impeccable. I was an All-American swimmer, water polo player, decorated lifeguard, holder of two degrees from different colleges, glowing commendations, and stellar recommendations. I had received athletic scholarships as well as academic scholarships throughout my life. Nonetheless, it was their duty to tarnish my reputation.

Christian's new attorney, Harold Rhoden, went so far as to suggest that I was envious of the size of Marc's verdict. Ridiculous, as I had no interest in monetary gains. Then, he insulted me further by stating, "It's a wonder that the poor fellow didn't wind up in a padded cell." They concocted stories, claiming that I was interested in Rock Hudson's finances because he had supposedly reneged on a promise to give me $10,000. They even alleged that I resented Marc because he declined to go on a date with me.

And to top it off, they dared to suggest that I said, "If it hadn't been for you, I would have been Rock Hudson's lover." All these claims were pure hogwash, with no evidence to support them. I was not the one driven by financial motives; that was Marc Christian's pursuit.

Speaking to the press was an exercise of free speech, and I could do little to prevent it. But then came the threats, insidious and unsettling. At the outrigger canoeing club, where I dedicated myself to practice three times a week, someone unashamedly posted a letter on the club's notice board, accusing me of carrying AIDS and threatening to infect the entire team.

My outrigger club took me aside, and with my outing now public, they asked with a mix of concern and suspicion if there was any truth to this malicious letter. It was evident that fear and angst filled their minds, and they sought the truth from my lips.

I took a deep breath, knowing I was treading a path I never anticipated. I explained the intricate web of the ongoing court battle, describing how this despicable act was just one of the spiteful tactics against me. To quell their fears, I bared my medical records, presenting my HIV-negative test results as an indisputable shield against these sinister claims.

Although the team allowed me to continue, the air had changed, poisoned by suspicion and hesitation. I felt eyes upon me, scrutinizing my every move with newfound wariness. It was a stark reminder of the peril that often befalls those who dare to stand up for what is right. This somber lesson reveals why many shy away from such battles, choosing to evade the harsh, unrelenting blowback that can assail the brave.

The ordeal took an even darker turn as my good friend Pauline was returning home from work one day. Out of the shadows emerged one of Harold Rhoden's investigators, brazenly approaching her with an insidious claim: "Do you know that your personal trainer has AIDS?" Pauline recounted how she had fearlessly told them to "F" off, told them they were "FN" liars, and told them to vacate her property immediately before she called the police.

Realizing they were stooping to these deceitful tactics—I knew I had to act. I took the painful step of contacting each of my clients, exposing the lies being spread about me and urging them to ignore these venomous falsehoods. Despite my earnest efforts to assure my clients that these were false attacks on my integrity, one client decided to distance themselves from me and no longer have me train them.

It was heartbreaking to lose a client who, despite believing in my innocence, felt overwhelmed by the implication of rumors and decided to seek another trainer. This is precisely why I tried not to get involved in the first place, but in life, there comes a time when you have to stand up for what is right and what you believe in. This was my moment to shed light on the deceit and lies that Marc was using for monetary gain.

My livelihood was under siege, and there seemed to be no depths to which these pernicious forces wouldn't sink. I began to glimpse the extent of their brutality, but the question remained: who was orchestrating this campaign against me?

I couldn't shake the chilling thought of Marc showing up at Dean's house just a week before it was firebombed, and now, he and his team were attempting to tarnish my reputation. They were infiltrating my neighborhood, reaching out to my clients with false and damaging information to harm me and discourage me from coming forward. It was becoming increasingly clear that I needed to explore legal avenues, perhaps even suing Mr. Christian and, at the very least, securing a restraining order to shield myself and my clients from his menacing presence.

The contrast between my life in 1985 and where I stood in 1989 couldn't have been starker. Four years earlier, I was a budding entrepreneur, striving to carve out a niche as a personal trainer and still renting a room from Larry Christy. However, by 1989, significant changes had unfolded. I had managed to purchase my very own condo on the golf course.

It was nestled in the West Nine area of Laguna Niguel, right in the city's heart. It was conveniently close to Laguna Beach, West Street Beach, and the luxurious Ritz-Carlton. I had established a robust fitness presence in the community and had reached a point where I no longer needed to advertise actively; word of mouth and referrals from my satisfied clients kept me consistently busy, sometimes even more than I had initially anticipated.

In addition, my engagement in community activities flourished, driven by my commitment to give back and create a positive imprint on the place I now proudly call home. Many clients transformed into an extended family, and alongside my outrigging teammates, who had come to accept my true self, my life blossomed into profound fulfillment.

I had previously shared my role as an AIDS Support Buddy, a position that closely connected me with individuals battling AIDS diagnoses. My primary responsibility was to offer a compassionate ear and provide support whenever required.

In addition to my endeavors with the AIDS Service Foundation, I also volunteered for Laguna Shanti. I organized their AIDS gift basket drive during the festive Holiday Season, orchestrating the assembly of more than 300 gift baskets. Drawing on the generosity of my clients and friends, we joined forces for wrapping and delivery. Through the collective effort, we garnered over twenty thousand dollars from the vibrant Laguna Beach community, fostering a small yet determined army to stand by my side in support of this vital cause.

I mention these activities not to seek recognition but to underscore that I was never someone seeking personal gain, as depicted by Marc Christian and his lawyers. I was once told by a wise woman, my 94-year-old neighbor at the West Nine, Virginia Cordner, that there are two kinds of people in the world: "Those who give and those who take." I found greater fulfillment in giving than receiving, and I can unequivocally state that Marc's treatment of Rock Hudson, Dean Dittman, and myself was the complete opposite.

Between 1985 and 1989, I grappled with an array of heart-wrenching tragedies. Each passing year brought more sorrow into my life. I bid farewell to my roommate, Pat Zega, with whom I shared a home at the Portofino in Belmont Shores. The loss of my dear friend, Chris Bittle, hit me hard. Chris had accompanied me as we treated Rock Hudson to a memorable Father's Day brunch at Maxwells in Huntington Beach.

Another painful goodbye was to Bryan Beavers, one of my first roommates in Long Beach. Bryan held a significant place in my life; he served as one of the organists at the Crystal Cathedral Church and played piano at my senior recital at Long Beach State. I lived with him for a short period while transitioning from northern California to the Long Beach area.

Pushed Out of the Closet Without A Parachute

These individuals weren't just acquaintances; they were close friends who had enriched my life in countless ways. Sadly, AIDS claimed their lives, as well as many others I knew, some more casually than others. It was a devastating period for the gay community as a whole, and witnessing what Marc was doing was disrespecting not only me but Rock Hudson's memory. It filled me with profound disgust and sorrow.

Navigating the treacherous path of the trial, especially with the Rock Hudson Estate's lawyer, Robert Park Mills, felt like tiptoeing through a snake pit. Each step brought the risk of encountering venomous fangs, and every twist and turn in this case seemed to reveal a new viper lurking in the shadows. However, I did manage to make some correct decisions along the way.

Robert Mills was enthusiastic about me taking the daily talk show circuit, a path resembling what Marc Christian was relentlessly pursuing. However, I had already lost one client due to the shadowy maneuvers of either Marc Christian's lawyer, his investigators, or perhaps even Marc Christian himself. I refused, much to the dismay of Robert Mills and his investigator, Paul Cohen. They attempted to sell me the idea, promising fame and the possibility of writing a lucrative book that could make millions. "No, thank you," I firmly responded, "I'd rather forge my fortune through other means and not tarnish my fitness business, Personal Attention for the fleeting allure of fifteen minutes of fame. I was already in the midst of my fifteen minutes of infamy."

Pushed Out of the Closet Without A Parachute

In early April 1989, I had an unexpected encounter with Marc in Laguna Beach, right at the Boom Boom Room, a gay bar with a small dancing area. I occasionally went there to watch Rock on Tuesday Dynasty nights. His icy glares conveyed more than just disdain; they carried a sinister message.

Another message was delivered through one of Marc's henchmen, who loitered around him like a menacing specter. The veiled threat was chilling and ominous: "If you jeopardize Marc's settlement, he will unravel your life... Oh and have a nice day!" It left me shaken to my core, contemplating whether my condo could be the next target for arson, much like Dean Dittman's had been.

Questions raced through my mind. Could these Marc Christina associates be the same individuals responsible for the heinous fire-bombing? To what extent would Marc Christina go to keep the millions the jury had awarded him? The encounter left me in turmoil, prompting me to contact Pauline and her son. I felt things were spiraling out of control, and a conversation with Chris was now urgent.

Chris remained remarkably composed as he outlined my do's and don'ts. "First," he advised, "do not entertain talk show invitations or interviews. Steer clear of the press and media. I understand your desire to share your side of the story, but they have a knack for twisting things and presenting a completely different narrative. Second, under no circumstances should you communicate with Marc

Christian. If you spot him in Laguna, immediately turn around and leave, be it a restaurant, disco, bar, or any place else."

I hesitated briefly and confessed, "I've already done a small interview with the Advocate, a gay magazine. I believe they will handle it fairly."

Chris said, "We'll see, but in my experience, these folks are all about making a sensational splash. From now on, it's best to maintain silence, even with your friends, because you never know who they might talk to, and they could use your friends to get to you... excluding the present company, of course. If you need to vent or talk, confide only in my mom or me—no one else."

I received an early copy of the May 1989 issue of the Advocate, and I was taken aback by Michael Szymanski's article "Out of the Bedroom Closet." This was precisely what Chris had warned me about—how they sensationalize stories to make them more marketable or palatable, twisting your words into something entirely different.

Two sections of the article particularly enraged me. I thought, "Come on, Advocate!" They quoted me as saying, "Sex with Marc Christian wasn't all that great," and "He laid back on my bed and threw his legs up in the air. I was a little surprised. I put on a condom; we didn't really discuss it. Then I screwed him."

Though the words didn't originate with me, I understood their potential to trigger Marc and possibly lead him to initiate legal action against me. What I had said was, "Marc told me he was probably the safest person on the planet, but that didn't matter—I was still going to use a condom. We did discuss it briefly, and one thing led to another, and we had sex. When asked who did what, I replied that I wore the condom; you can figure out the rest. How dare they fabricate quotes! I'll never trust the Advocate again."

Another misrepresentation, though not in quotes, left me equally frustrated. They insinuated that "If they wanted me on television, I had a price: $30,000." I hadn't phrased it that way. What I had conveyed was my refusal to appear on daytime TV shows, interviews, or late-night segments. I explained, "If I go on those shows, it might negatively affect my Fitness Business, potentially costing me anywhere from $30,000 in clientele business." I couldn't fathom why they felt the need to portray me as someone trying to exploit this tragedy for personal gain. This experience left me thoroughly furious, and from that point on, I resolved to heed Chris's advice and never grant another interview.

At least they did get one part correct. They captured the quote, "I went through life with one foot in the closet, and now I've been pushed out of the closet without a parachute." I added, "I just know I won't be returning to the closet now." Oh, and also the part, "It was a mistake to get involved with Marc Christian." Despite the primarily favorable tone of the article, they couldn't resist sowing seeds of doubt in people's minds, all at my expense.

At almost the same time, on April 22, 1989, the judge's verdict was released. Ironically, Marc's lawyer said, "Superior Court Judge

Pushed Out of the Closet Without A Parachute

Bruce Geernaert's ruling Friday was accepted only because Christian cannot afford to seek a new trial. It's a drastic cut, and we're disappointed. I think it's going to be disappointing to the jurors."

They decided against having a new trial, which, in retrospect, was a blessing in disguise for me. I shuddered at the thought of becoming a sideshow act in that courtroom drama.

Shockwaves reverberated through the legal community when the jury unveiled its verdict, mainly due to the unexpectedly large cut in the award. Predictions circulated that the amount might undergo even more reductions in subsequent proceedings. The testimony I presented and my sworn deposition undeniably played a role the judge's ruling. I knew this would infuriate Marc Christian, emphasizing the need for heightened vigilance against any potential attacks on me or my business.

While it essentially boiled down to a "he said, he said" situation, Judge Geernaert deemed the jury's original award excessive. Consequently, he made significant adjustments, reducing punitive damages from $7.25 million to $500,000 and compensatory damages from $14.5 million to $5 million.

Mark Miller was responsible for the punitive award, while Miller and Hudson's estate shared the compensatory damages. Robert Mills, legal counsel for Hudson's estate, had urged the judge to lower the award to $1 million and expressed the estate's likelihood of appealing, as the damages were still regarded as excessively high. Andrew Banks, representing Miller, also welcomed the judge's decision as a 'great first step' but also hinted at potential plans for an appeal.

Following the judgment, I purposely didn't monitor the case's develpments if they didn't involve me personally. However, I learned that rather than pursuing an appeal, the parties involved eventually reached an out-of-court settlement.

Information I received from individuals connected to Mark Miller, particularly those who initially encouraged my involvement in the matter from Laguna Niguel, indicated that Marc Christian ultimately received a sum slightly exceeding 2 million dollars. This was still a substantial reward for what I perceived as dishonesty. It's worth noting that I refrained from reciprocating and taking legal action against him for jeopardizing my life.

However, it wasn't intimidation from Marc's associates that held me back. Instead, it was my unwavering commitment to my business that took precedence. The success I had painstakingly built was a testament to my dedication and relentless effort. Of course, I can't discount the friendly nudge from Pauline, who saw a spark in me that I hadn't even recognized within myself. I had crafted a thriving enterprise that garnered positive attention from the media, and Entrepreneur Magazine showcased me in their 1991 edition, featuring a compelling article about my business journey.

Remarkably, I was a trailblazer in Orange County, among the first to advertise and provide personal training services. While others soon followed suit, I played a role in introducing certification processes. Another critical point: I was part of the inaugural group of trainers to attain the coveted designation of CPT (Certified Personal Trainer), recognized by esteemed organizations such as the Aerobic and Fitness Association of America, American Council on Exercise, Saddleback College, International Dance-Exercise Association, and the American College of Sports Medicine. My journey had indeed left its mark on the fitness industry.

    I never crossed paths with Marc Christian again, and even though I had to endure unprecedented circumstances, I could finally embrace my true self openly. If someone inquired about my sexual orientation, I had no qualms about sharing that I was gay. I didn't impose my identity on others, but I didn't conceal it either. In 1989, I became more active in gay sports, taking my passion for athletics to a whole new level.

    My journey into the realm of gay sports commenced in 1988 when I delved into indoor volleyball. The genesis of this adventure traced back to the vibrant souls I encountered while engaging in beach volleyball at West Street Beach in Laguna. Our odyssey reached its zenith at the NAGVA Championships in Montreal, Canada. The tournament carried a poignant undertone as I felt the absence of Chris Bittle, my beach volleyball partner, contemplating how his spirited presence would have elevated the team he played a pivotal role in assembling years ago.

Pushed Out of the Closet Without A Parachute

Our Laguna Beach West Street volleyball team showcased our skills and passion at the prestigious NAGVA tournament in the vibrant city of Montreal, Canada.

Pushed Out of the Closet Without A Parachute

At the same time, I continued my commitment to outrigger canoe racing with my mainly straight team. However, I switched to the neighboring Dana Point Outrigger Club and even recruited a few gay athletes to join us. Remarkably, everyone was incredibly accepting and supportive.

Simultaneously, I immersed myself in sporting extravaganzas and charitable galas hosted by the vibrant gay community. Fundraising for AIDS became a personal mission, and the spirited arenas of gay rodeos beckoned me, crisscrossing the nation in pursuit of thrilling competitions.

In those days, the infectious craze of boot-scootin' swept through the gay community, and Floyd's in Long Beach emerged as my favored gay country club. There, Sunday Tea Dances unfolded into lively two-stepping and spirited line dancing, creating a tapestry of unforgettable moments.

During the off-season of canoeing, I delved into the world of gay water polo. I proudly represented Los Angeles at the March 1989 IGLA Championships, where we secured the first-place spot. I also earnestly attempted to form a gay water polo team in Orange County to participate in the Gay Games in New York in 1994. We didn't quite get enough members for a water polo team, but we still mustered enough participants to start a swim team instead—enter "Orange Juice Aquatics."

Pushed Out of the Closet Without A Parachute

Our Los Angeles Water Polo Team clinched the coveted 1st Place at the March 1989 IGLA Championships in picturesque Vancouver, Canada.

As a united team, we marched together in the March on Washington on April 26, 1993, with the Orange County contingent of over 300 gays and lesbians from behind the "Orange Curtain." We aimed to draw attention and underscore civil rights, wielding a sea of rainbow flags and tears of hope among the over 300,000 lesbian and gay marchers.

Our collective aspirations included overturning the ban on gays and lesbians in the military, securing more financing for the fight against AIDS, advocating for equal rights for the GLBT community, championing marriage equality, and fostering a profound sense of legitimacy in the pursuit of equal rights for all people.

A year later, in 1994, we enthusiastically participated in the Gay Games in New York. The opening ceremonies unfolded at Baker Field/Wien Stadium of Columbia University, and the closing ceremonies took place at Yankee Stadium. Harvey Fierstein and Julia Sweeney announced the athletic teams as they circled the field.

I proudly earned several swimming medals at the Gay Games IV while representing Orange Juice Aquatics, where I also engaged in water polo with the San Diego Team. Our collective efforts led to a commendable second-place finish, with my former team, Los Angeles, securing the top spot.

It was a truly magical and unforgettable moment in my life, made even more impressive by the celebrity presence, including Billie Jean King, Greg Louganis, Taylor Dane, Cyndi Lauper, and Patti LaBelle, who performed "Over the Rainbow," followed by a spectacular shower of fireworks!

Notably, ten world records were shattered in the master swimming events, and Team Orange County made a commendable showing. Gay Games IV boasted 11,000 athletes, making it the most prominent sporting gathering at the time, surpassing even the previous Olympic Games. The legendary Greg Louganis graced the event with his presence, thrilling spectators with exhibition dives and serving as the announcer for the diving events.

While my dedication to fitness training and athletics took the spotlight, my aspirations for a music career, though deeply cherished, gracefully transitioned into the realm of a beloved part-time hobby. I reconciled with this metamorphosis, warmly embracing the unfolding tapestry of life.

Sometimes, I ponder what alternate destinies might have unfolded had Rock Hudson not faced the scourge of illness or if a cure had emerged during his time with us. However, the profound impact of the AIDS crisis had reshaped the foundation of my outlook on life.

I recognized the value of my health and fitness, allowing me to embark on journeys to exotic locales while enjoying the comfort of two homes—one nestled in the idyllic mountains of Idyllwild and the other, my beloved condo on the West Nine, conveniently close to the beach.

I refused to take my blessings for granted, especially considering the profound loss that befell me. In the mid to late '80s, nearly all of my friends vanished from my life, victims of the cruel AIDS epidemic. Yet, I miraculously traversed a literal minefield of despair and devastation, emerging on the other side with my story to tell.

As I gazed toward the future, I brimmed with excitement and hope. One heartfelt desire remained—to find a life partner with whom to share the remainder of my journey. Spoiler alert: As I pen these final pages, I celebrated 26 years with my husband, Dan, a milestone that encapsulates a chapter in my life that began with the extraordinary Roy Scherer.

Roy, better known as Rock, introduced me to captivating individuals and unveiled a world of fascinating stories and experiences that have left an indelible mark on my soul. I hope he would be proud of my unshakable support during times when many chose to remain silent. His legacy extends beyond that of a movie star; he was a kind-hearted soul and a remarkable friend. In dedication to Rock Hudson and the cherished memory of our time together, I offer this book as a testament to his enduring presence. You will forever remain in our hearts.

Pushed Out of the Closet Without A Parachute

Navigating the vast expanse from Molokai to Oahu, cradled in the embrace of a meticulously carved Koa outrigger.

Pushed Out of the Closet Without A Parachute

*Basking in the glory of our triumphant second-place victory at the U.S. Championships,
we reveled in the spirit of achievement during our Outrigger crossing from Catalina Island.*

Pushed Out of the Closet Without A Parachute

The aquatic dreams I nurtured under the vibrant banner of "Orange Juice Aquatics." Our journey reached its zenith at the Gay Games in New York, where we dove into the waves of competition.

Pushed Out of the Closet Without A Parachute

Basking in the glory of our triumphant moment, the San Diego Gay Men's Water Polo team.
Joyously commemorates our well-deserved 2nd Place victory at the illustrious Gay Games IV 1994.

Pushed Out of the Closet Without A Parachute

Pushed Out of the Closet Without A Parachute

My volunteer work with Laguna Shanti and the Orange County AIDS Service Foundation

Pushed Out of the Closet Without A Parachute

Pushed Out of the Closet Without A Parachute

In the spirited days of 1991, I took center stage in the exhilarating Gay Rodeo Circuit, showcasing my prowess in chut dogging, better known as steer wrestling, and engaging in a medley of other thrilling events.

Epilogue

Following Rock Hudson's departure, the ripples of Marc Christian's tumultuous actions sent shockwaves through those caught in its relentless spiral of drama. Mockingly, Marc's life took an unexpected turn when he passed away in June 2009.

In my investigation, I discovered that Marc Christian MacGinnis owned a house on Knoll Drive in the Hollywood Hills. The house was purchased for $545,000 in April 1992, approximately eight months after the settlement of the lawsuit against Hudson's estate. After Marc's death, a realty website valued the house at over $1.2 million.

In a poignant twist, Brent Beckwith, Marc's partner of nine years, found himself drawn into the same vortex of greed that had characterized Marc's legal battles as he sought what he believed to be his rightful share of the estate. All of it!

This lamentable twist gave birth to a novel legal concept: Interfering with an "Expected Inheritance." A concept starkly contrasting the essence of Rock—his selflessness, compassion, and generosity that graced every fiber of his being.

Unfortunately, Marc Christian's lawsuit diverted Rock Hudson's intended charitable funds into unsought hands, casting a shadow upon his philanthropic aspirations. Along with the money that Marc received, his multiple lawyers ended up with millions as well, leaving nothing for Rock's intended benefactors.

Pushed Out of the Closet Without A Parachute

How ironic that my character was questioned as I dedicated myself to crafting a career and contributing to my community. At the same time, Marc Christian's saga persisted, tainting the lives of those he encountered. Amidst this disheartening narrative, it remains crucial not to lose sight of Rock Hudson's authentic legacy—a luminous tapestry woven with joy and laughter on the silver screen, leaving an indelible mark on the world.

I hope I have shed light on Rock's need to compartmentalize his life, skillfully juggling distinct personas for his iconic Rock Hudson image—distinctly separate from the Roy Sherer persona, portraying an approachable, affectionate individual.

Let us also remember Mark Griffin's profound words in "The Untold Truth of Rock Hudson," who noted, "Long before Rock arrived in Hollywood, he understood that if he wanted to be accepted, the very nature of who he was would have to be edited out of the frame." So, if we decide to retell this story, let's do it correctly with his spirit intact. There's far too much artificiality being served to viewers today.

My understanding of Rock as a genuine person, not a made-up icon, allowed me to see through the stereotyped persona Hollywood created for him. In the end, as Rock set off a firestorm of controversy and AIDS-related panic in Hollywood, remember it wasn't Rock who created the narrative of the all-American heterosexual male. Hollywood made him and groomed him through the studio politics of his day.

Pushed Out of the Closet Without A Parachute

Indeed, Rock Hudson, born Roy Scherer, was remarkable—a caring and kind-hearted person who genuinely strove to make everyone around him happy. It took me some time to understand why he had sectioned off certain aspects of his life, and I initially had misconceptions. His intention wasn't to hide his true self from different groups of people; instead, he aimed to please everyone.

In real life, there's an adage that perfectly encapsulates this sentiment. Attributed to John Lydgate, it goes: "You can please some of the people all of the time, you can please all of the people some of the time, but you can't please all of the people all of the time." In his wisdom, Rock Hudson found a way to navigate this truth and discovered the best approach to achieve just that.

I've given the reader a glimpse into my life story, weaving a narrative that brings a Hollywood Superstar to life through the lens of an outsider looking in rather than from the inside looking out. While we're familiar with the movies Rock Hudson made and the renowned actors he collaborated with, it's crucial to recognize that he was someone who originated from a small town in Illinois. He wasn't just an iconic figure but a genuine person who took the time to forge a friendship with me, leaving an everlasting impact on my life.

During that week in Hawaii, which he spent with my parents and me, Rock reconnected with his true self, Roy Sherer. During moments like these, I comprehended why he had such mixed feelings about the name Rock Hudson. To him, his Hollywood name represented a love-hate relationship. While it symbolized his masculinity and catapulted him to become one of his generation's most celebrated movie stars, it came at an exorbitant cost.

The alcohol and smoking that ravaged his liver would have eventually caught up with him, and AIDS merely hastened the inevitable. Like many other gay individuals, I was overjoyed to witness his ultimate decision to lay his entire life bare. In doing so, he thrust AIDS into the consciousness of middle America.

Before Rock's courageous act, the Reagan administration had responded sluggishly to the early stages of the "Gay Pandemic." It was Rock who made people aware of and prompted conversations about AIDS, which in turn paved the way for progress in finding a cure or at least medications to manage this deadly disease.

In closing, I want to extend my sincere apologies for the delay in sharing my story. Fear of litigation and the looming specter of Marc Christian's actions cast a long shadow over my decision to write this book. However, the passage of time and the recent documentary, 'Rock Hudson: All That Heaven Allowed,' offered an intimate portrait of Rock Hudson's enduring legacy and role in changing public perceptions of AIDS, rekindled my inspiration.

It reminded me of the importance of sharing the other side of Rock's story from the perspective of an ordinary person profoundly affected by the events surrounding a Hollywood legend. From someone who discovered the true Roy Sherer and how down-to-earth he was when away from Hollywood.

I hope that "Out of the Closet Without a Parachute" has not only unveiled the layers of the man behind the icon but has also shed light on the intricate story that led me to this point—a journey of self-discovery and transformation.

Thank you for being part of this remarkable odyssey. May the echoes of my shared moments resonate in your memory.

Gunther Allen

THE END

Pushed Out of the Closet Without A Parachute

"A friend is one to whom one may pour out the contents of one's heart,
Chaff and grain together,
knowing that gentle hands will take and sift it,
keep what is worth keeping, and with a breath of kindness, blow the rest away."

— Dinah Maria Craik

www.ingramcontent.com/pod-product-compliance
Lightning Source LLC
Chambersburg PA
CBHW050207130526
44590CB00043B/3037